THE COOK'S ATELIER

THE COOK'S ATELIER

RECIPES, TECHNIQUES, AND STORIES
FROM OUR FRENCH COOKING SCHOOL

Marjorie Taylor AND Kendall Smith Franchini

WITH ANNA WATSON CARL

PHOTOGRAPHY BY ANSON SMART

ABRAMS, NEW YORK

CONTENTS

THE RECIPES

THE STORY OF THE COOK'S ATELIER

In the heart of Beaune, just past the Place au Beurre, is a pretty little shop with slate-gray shutters and a vintage baker's bicycle filled with flowers parked beside the front door. Gleaming copper pots hang in the shop windows above iron tables displaying cook's tools—narrow wooden rolling pins, copper-handled whisks, vintage chef's knives and cleavers, and marble mortars and pestles. A handwritten quote by Julia Child graces the window: "People who love to eat are always the best people." The name of this place, stated simply on a patinaed copper sign, is "The Cook's Atelier."

Inside, sounds of old-time French jazz float through the air, and an aroma of baking madeleines wafts down from the kitchen above. Clanks of pots and pans and the rhythmic chop-chopping of knives on wooden cutting boards blend with the whir of grinding coffee beans and the hiss of the vintage Italian espresso machine. The rustic stone walls of the wine shop are hung with simple wrought-iron racks, displaying a carefully curated selection of small-production wines from France, Italy, and Germany. Everywhere is the evidence of a copper obsession: jam pots and fish poachers, tall stockpots, cake molds, and every shape and size of sauté pan and saucepot imaginable.

In the back of the shop, the light-filled atrium is full of more culinary treasures *à vendre* (for sale)—stacks of old and new wooden cutting boards, vintage madeleine tins, and a collection of creamy white ironstone soup tureens. Zinc pitchers filled with freshly cut flowers sit near a collection of restored mezzalunas and bone-handled French cheese knives. An old butcher's scale sits atop a farm table, surrounded by stacks of linen kitchen towels and preserving crocks full of wooden cook's tools like olive-wood spoons, spatulas, and citrus reamers. A small selection of well-sourced pantry items lines the wall: extra-virgin olive oil from the South of France, aged vinegars from Banyuls, vanilla beans from Madagascar, local Burgundian grainy mustard and honey, salted capers from Sicily, and a mix of spices. It's a shop for cooks, created by cooks.

A heavy wooden spiral staircase—original to the seventeenth-century building—leads up to the second-floor all-white kitchen. A neat row of vintage carbon steel chef's knives adorns one wall, and bright copper pots hang over a Lacanche range. The kitchen is bustling with a cooking class underway. Ten guests from around the world, decked in linen aprons, gather around the marble-topped prep table, busily making lunch from baskets of fresh ingredients just purchased at the market. Platters contain neat rows of scored duck breasts, ready to pan-sear. The students tightly pack caramelized red and golden plums into a heavy cast-iron skillet and cover them with a sheet of homemade *pâte feuilletée* (puff pastry). Chanterelles sizzle with garlic and shallots, and a pot of bright orange *potimarron* (winter squash) soup simmers on the back of the stove. A selection of farm cheeses sits on a vintage board, waiting to be served after the main course.

Once the cooking is done, aprons come off, and guests climb another staircase up to the third-floor dining room, where a wall of windows overlooks the atrium below. A zinc-topped table is set for lunch in simple French fashion. A gray armoire stands against the wall, displaying a collection of favorite antique treasures, thirty years in the making: shelves of crystal stemware, mismatched stacks of creamy white vintage café au lait bowls, a collection of *confiture* (jam) jars filled with flatware, and one-of-a-kind flea market finds, like French creamware, silver spoons, and tiny copper molds. Candles are lit and Champagne glasses are filled as guests toast one another in anticipation of the long French lunch.

HOW WE CAME TO LOVE FRANCE

People ask us all the time how two American women—a mother and daughter, nonetheless—ended up creating a French cooking school in Burgundy. It's a long story, but one we love telling, as it reminds us that, with enough determination and grit, anything is possible.

Our vision for this place started more than twenty years ago, when we were still living in Arizona. Kendall was always a Francophile, even as a little girl. We aren't entirely sure how that happened, considering we were both born and raised in Phoenix—which, in more ways than one, is a very long way away from Beaune. In high school, she studied French and had a very memorable teacher whose own experience in France resonated with her. After a trip to Paris for the first time with her high school class, the spark was officially ignited. She became intrigued with everything about

France—the language, the culture, and the food. On early morning walks together before work and school, our talks often centered around France and the idea of joie de vivre—the way French people take time to savor everything, be it a coffee, a meal, or a conversation. We tried to adopt this philosophy as best we could in our everyday lives, never imagining that we would ever actually live in France one day.

As the years went by, Kendall began spending more and more time in France. She studied French and art history at university, and took every opportunity to study abroad in college. After graduating, she returned to France to teach English in Nîmes. A year later, she moved to Paris and got an internship at Christie's auction house, working part-time on the side to pay the rent. She lived in a tiny 205-square-foot (19-square-meter) apartment— roughly the size of a laundry room. She stayed in Paris for several years, working and studying, and I visited her as often as I could.

Since it had always been just the two of us, it was hard to live an ocean apart. Her dad had passed away when she was a little girl, so I raised Kendall predominately as a single parent. I always encouraged her to follow her dreams, and I knew it was just a matter of time until she figured out a way to settle in France permanently.

A LOVE FOR FOOD AND WINE

I've always loved feeding people and gathering others around the table. Although I come from a large family, where big holiday gatherings were a normal part of growing up, the food prepared was never really the focus. I certainly didn't come from a long line of great cooks, and so I spent many years teaching myself. I've always been hugely inspired by the writings of Julia Child, M. F. K. Fisher, Elizabeth David, Madeleine Kamman, and Alice Waters, and essentially taught myself to cook following many of their recipes. I admired their passion and the way they described how to cook in detail, using the techniques required to prepare each recipe by hand. Of course, these women all happened to be Francophiles, and I'm sure it's not by accident that I've always felt connected to French food in the same way that Kendall has been drawn toward France. One of my very favorite cookbooks is *Chez Panisse Cooking* by Paul Bertolli and Alice Waters. I have a very well-worn copy that I continue to read to this day. I especially love the passage: "Good cooking is in the very best sense a craft, involving the heart, head, and hands simultaneously. . . . Teach your hands, above all, to remember that you are preparing food, not culinary artwork, that is to be savored and shared with others at your table. . . . This is cooking."

In my mid-twenties, I began apprenticing at a series of French-inspired restaurants in Phoenix because I wanted to learn the classic techniques of French cooking. I started at the ground level, learning my way around a commercial kitchen and developing my culinary skills. Eventually, having a knack for pastry, I got a lucky break and was hired in the pastry department of a small French restaurant where I worked for several years before becoming the pasty chef. But ultimately, being an entrepreneurial spirit, I began to think about creating a business of my own.

After years working in kitchens, in 1999, I opened Ruby Beet, a small restaurant and cooking school, with a fellow pastry chef. We renovated an old bungalow in Heritage Square, the historic part of downtown Phoenix, which was situated across the street from Pizzeria Bianco (run by James Beard Award–winning chef Chris Bianco). Herbs and edible landscaping filled the garden beds around the old house, and we planted a small kitchen garden just outside the back door. Our food was simple, seasonal, and locally sourced. We shopped at a farmers' market in the center of Phoenix, and bought organic produce from farmers such as Bob McClendon and Maya at the Farm at South Mountain. We made our own bread, pickled our own beets, and worked with a local butcher to source our meat. It certainly wasn't easy, but we tried to practice our farm-to-table philosophy even then. Dining at Ruby Beet was like having dinner at a friend's house. We would sit outside on the front porch at dusk, drinking wine and shelling peas, and the first twenty people or so who came got to join us for dinner. Kendall worked with us when she came home from college during summers and holiday breaks. When I look back on this time, I realize that it was the perfect training ground for The Cook's Atelier.

In 2006, when the time had come to move on from Ruby Beet, I chose to spend six months in Burgundy, working and studying with cookbook author Anne Willan of La Varenne at Château du Feÿ. This was such a pivotal experience in my life—getting to live and cook in France—and it gave me the opportunity to figure out what I wanted to do next. I loved living in Burgundy, shopping at the local markets, and especially, being in the same country as Kendall. At this point, while living in Paris, she began developing a keen interest in wine. After taking an introductory wine class at Le Cordon Bleu, Kendall took a part-time job at Legrand Filles et Fils, a little wine bar and wine shop in the second arrondissement, to learn more.

During this time, she visited me at La Varenne on the weekends, and I went up to Paris often to see her. On a whim, we visited a little town called

Beaune that summer and fell for its charms. The notion of moving to France permanently became more realistic. But before I could make that decision, I had to return home to figure out the logistics.

In September 2008, we knew it was time to take the leap. I arrived at Charles de Gaulle airport in Paris with nothing more than a suitcase, some of my favorite cookbooks, a few copper pans, and my giant dog, Lily, a 120-pound (54-kg) bloodhound.

I had just sold everything—the house I had bought in my early twenties, my car, and all my furniture—to move to Beaune. Kendall was already living there, pursuing viticulture and oenology studies at the CFPPA (Le Centre de Formation Professionnelle et de Promotion Agricole) wine school. During one of our frequent mother-daughter phone conversations, before I had completely made up my mind to make the big move, Kendall said, "Mom, you've been telling me my entire life that I can achieve anything, if I put my mind to it. Now it's your turn!" Encouraged by her, I made the decision that day to move. I took a leap of faith: I had no apartment, no job, and no safety net back home in case things didn't work out. I jumped, hoping the net would follow.

Beaune is a charming, medieval city with an authentic feel, just two and a half hours from Paris by high-speed train. Surrounded by idyllic farmland and endless vineyards, it attracts visitors from around the world every year to see the famed Côte d'Or wine route. Burgundy is renowned for its culinary heritage, evidenced by the fact that many of France's Michelin three-star chefs come from the Lyon area, just south of us. Burgundian cuisine, with its famed dishes like escargots bathed in garlicky butter and bœuf bourguignon, a hearty beef stew simmered in local red wine, can be quite rich, thanks to the abundance of excellent local meat, poultry, charcuterie, and cheeses. However, we are especially taken with the region's vegetables. Burgundian farmers, whether they are growing grapes or raising animals, have a similar, old-fashioned mentality. They keep their productions small and focus on quality, often using older farming methods, such as horse-plowing, to leave a gentler footprint on the land.

There's no better way to grasp Burgundy's abundant food culture than to visit the bustling Beaune market on a Wednesday or Saturday morning. Located in the Place des Halles, just around the corner from the beautifully

tiled roof of the Hospices de Beaune, the local market is one of the best in the region, if not France. Rain or shine, the square fills with white tents and tables overflowing with the season's bounty.

In the spring, you'll see delicate peas and fava beans, plump white asparagus and tiny Gariguette strawberries, and big bunches of pale pink peonies. Summer brings heirloom tomatoes in every possible shape, size, and color, sweet cantaloupes and rosy apricots, crisp haricots verts and buttery salad greens, and tall bouquets of gold-and-black sunflowers. In the cool months of autumn and winter, you'll find bright orange potimarrons and other winter squash, fingerling potatoes and hearty greens, golden chestnuts and a bounty of local, wild mushrooms. Inside the adjacent indoor market, cheese and charcuterie vendors set up shop, with purveyors of local duck and other poultry (including the famed *poulet* de Bresse) and meat, along with a few of our favorite local farmers.

This market is special because it's an actual living, breathing market, very much still frequented by locals. And they come out in droves—especially on Saturdays—pulling shopping carts on wheels, which they fill to the brim with fresh produce, *boules* of grainy bread, cheeses, pâté, and other provisions for the week. The market is a meeting place, where friends and neighbors exchange *bisous* (one kiss on each cheek as a greeting) and catch up over coffee or a glass of wine before or after their shopping. In the midst of this calm weekly shopping ritual, we fly through the market at high speed carrying overflowing baskets, with a trail of clients in tow, and the locals can't help but chuckle out loud at the crazy Americans. At first, they were curious: "Who are these people? How many people are they feeding?" With time, they came to appreciate the fact that we wanted to share the beauty of the market with others.

We love this place not only for the fantastic food and wine, but also for the tight-knit community, the slow rhythm of the seasons, and the close relationships we've been able to forge with the people who grow the food we cook. But most of all, we love Beaune because it's home.

THE EARLY DAYS ON RUE MAUFOUX

My first year in France, I had a long-stay visitor visa and wasn't legally allowed to work. Kendall was continuing her studies at the CFPPA and working at Kermit Lynch, an American wine merchant with an office in Beaune. Although I had a little money saved up from the sale of my house, we knew that it wouldn't last forever, so we had to figure out a game plan. We began to lay the groundwork for a business idea. Both of us being very detail oriented with a strong appreciation for aesthetics and remarkably similar tastes, it was a natural transition to becoming business partners.

Though we didn't yet know exactly how the business would look, we knew that we wanted to create a convivial gathering place where we could share our love of food and wine with other cooks from around the world. It was an idea years in the making that involved lots of brainstorming and countless glasses of wine. We started with no formal business plan, just a strong gut instinct to create a place that we would love, and hoped that others would, too. We envisioned taking guests to the market to purchase local produce, artisanal cheeses, meats, charcuterie, and freshly baked bread from our favorite producers. We dreamed of teaching hands-on cooking classes, using classic French techniques, followed by long, leisurely lunches around the table. In the evenings, we imagined hosting candlelit dinner parties with new and old friends. We had no idea exactly how this would come to be, or where we would find the space, but we were continually drawn to this idea. It took years of research, work, and study—independently and together—to figure out a way to take the things we love about the French lifestyle and to combine it all into a business. I remembered thinking to myself that all I needed was a kitchen and a stove.

The first year in Beaune, we started to meet and build relationships with local farmers and artisan food producers, and figured out how to set up a small business in France, which was certainly no easy task. We explored Burgundy, discovering small farms and wineries, and became regulars at the Beaune market. As fate would have it, Kendall married a Frenchman, Laurent Franchini, in 2009, and they settled as newlyweds in Beaune. As the good-natured guy that he is (and the newly designated "Frenchman" of the family), he helped us navigate the miles and miles of French red tape involved in setting up the business, and was also instrumental in helping us find our first location early on.

Later that same year, we happened to be walking down rue Maufoux (a quaint little street in the center of Beaune) and noticed a second-story apartment with big French windows thrown open to reveal painters inside, meaning there was a strong possibility it would soon be available for rent. We went inside to investigate. It was light-filled, with tall ceilings, ornate plaster moldings, and original hardwood floors. The place was about the size of a postage stamp, but I was smitten. It was adorable and, most important, available.

In spite of its potential, the place was a wreck and needed significant work. We decided to convert the front bedroom into a teaching kitchen, and use the original kitchen as a prep area, with a small sink for washing dishes and a tiny washing machine for linens. The living room became the dining room, and the smaller bedroom became a storage room (and bedroom for me).

Every night after work, Kendall and Laurent would come help me work on the apartment, renovating it completely on our own. On weekends, we would go to *brocantes* (flea markets) to find vintage furniture and French tableware.

The final touch to the apartment's renovation was the stove. As a cook, I had always had my heart set on a Lacanche. Founded in 1796 and hand-made in a village of the same name, each one of these stoves is custom-built to order. I contacted Jean Jacques Augagneur, the company's CEO, telling him that I was starting a cooking school in Beaune, and that I wanted to buy one. He invited us to come visit the showroom and met us personally. He even sketched out a compact range on paper that they could build to fit into our tiny kitchen. The last bit of my savings went for that stove.

Finally, it was time for a name. For months we wracked our brains. We felt strongly about our concept, and we wanted a name that was humble and inspiring, but not pretentious, and that would evoke the Franco-American connection. We decided on The Cook's Atelier, as our vision was to bring cooks of all levels together to share and learn in an approachable, convivial workshop setting.

We put together a very simple website and in less than four months, we had our first booking which was, hilariously, a party of ten Frenchmen. The small kitchen was inviting, with our newly installed Lacanche stove, well-worn copper pots, and a rustic farm table that we used for food prep. We hung shelves on the kitchen walls, displaying little family heirlooms like a porcelain figurine of Mary to remind me of my mom and her strength of character, and a well-used collection of cookbooks from inspiring cooks, like Julia Child's *Mastering the Art of French Cooking* and Madeleine Kamman's *The Making of a Cook*.

Our subsequent years teaching cooking classes in this tiny space were full of wonderful people and countless memories. We created a rhythm for our market classes and an ambiance that was truly magical. We never advertised, so most guests came by word of mouth, and we welcomed many repeat clients. People loved the classes, and afterward, often enjoyed the experience so much that they lingered well into the evening hours, drinking wine and enjoying the meal. We have watched total strangers become lifelong friends. And in our years on rue Maufoux, we knew that we had created something very special. We hit a sweet spot, just at the right time.

We like to say that it was the building that chose us.

After five successful years, we outgrew the small apartment on rue Maufoux. As much as we loved it, we knew it was time to expand, but didn't want to lose that unique ambiance we had worked so hard to create.

Encouraged by a good friend, we started looking for a larger space. We were beginning to visualize perhaps adding a cook's shop.

One day in January 2013, we had plans to visit a few spaces. The first two we saw required so much renovation or were so expensive, they weren't even in the realm of possibility. The last building we saw was a dress shop on rue de Lorraine. It had a certain old-world charm and stately exterior that we felt drawn to.

As we toured the building, we could visualize exactly how The Cook's Atelier could grow and evolve. The space was flooded with light, thanks to three floors of floor-to-ceiling windows overlooking a central atrium, with a large skylight. It was perfectly laid out: There was space for a separate dining room, a big second-floor room that would make a spacious teaching kitchen, and a ground-floor area perfect for a wine shop and culinary boutique. There was even a pretty little room for an office, just over the shop front. At the end of the visit, we took a look at the rear of the building. In very faded paint above the garage was the word "ATELIER." We took it as a sign, and that sealed the deal.

It was yet another big leap of faith for us, expanding from the comfort of our tiny apartment space to a full-blown shop and cooking school, as we had no safety net to sustain us if things didn't work out. As foreigners, we had learned that opening up a brick-and-mortar space is especially complicated. Failing was not an option, and we had to believe that the vision of The Cook's Atelier would carry us through. We didn't know exactly how we were going to pull it off, but it was too good an opportunity to pass up.

Having a culinary boutique and wine shop has allowed us to offer our guests access to all our favorite wines, cook's tools, and pantry provisions. From the beginning, we've taken joy not only in teaching others how to cook, but also in introducing them to the best growers and producers in the region. What we cook is only as good as the ingredients that we use, which is why we feel so fortunate to be in Burgundy. In addition to the regular market cooking classes and five-day workshops we continue to offer, we also host wine tastings and winemaker dinners featuring our favorite local winemakers. Our guests still tell us that the time they spend with us at The Cook's

Atelier is the highlight of their trip to France. They continue to linger at our table long after the long French lunch has concluded, enjoying wine and savoring the joie de vivre.

But at the end of the day, The Cook's Atelier has always been about family. In those early years on rue Maufoux, Kendall was either pregnant or carrying one of her children on her hip during every class. I remember her pouring wine with one hand and holding baby Luc or Manon with the other. We built the backbone of our business around a simple idea—good food and a life surrounded by the people we love. It truly has become a family affair.

Laurent officially joined the business as shopkeeper in 2013 when we purchased the new building, with the big responsibility of keeping everything straight. His vital role downstairs—both as a business manager and the friendly face who greets every person who comes into the shop—completes our team. He's the grounding force that keeps us calm when things get hectic. Despite the craziness of juggling a small family business in a foreign country and raising little ones, Luc and Manon, we know we are very fortunate and blessed to have become a part of the community and to be able to call this place home.

OUR COOKING PHILOSOPHY

Our goal at The Cook's Atelier is to help guests become more confident cooks. We welcome a wide variety of cooking levels, from total novices to restaurant chefs, in our Atelier kitchen. Our cooking philosophy is simple: It's all about using seasonal ingredients, mastering classic French techniques, and developing intuition in the kitchen. Rather than focusing strictly on classic Burgundian cuisine, our recipes are inspired by the bounty of the region, with seasonal vegetables and artisanal products always front and center.

QUALITY
INGREDIENTS
AND THE
IMPORTANCE OF
SEASONALITY

Your cooking will only be as good as the quality of ingredients you use. No matter how gifted you might be in technique, the end result will never be quite as good if you don't take the time to pay attention to the seasons, and to where you source your food. Living in Beaune, we are fortunate to be able to find our ingredients locally and quite affordably. France, for the most part, still puts a significant value on the pleasure of eating well and supporting small farmers and artisan producers. As the world gets more and more homogenized, we feel that traditions such as kitchen gardens, small farms, and charcuterie- and cheese-making, as well as artisanal baking, should be protected. We do our best to help support these crafts by shopping locally and sharing these traditions with our guests as well. We enjoy teaching our guests what to look for when buying artisanal products, and encourage them to support their own small, local food producers back home.

We are big believers that less is more when it comes to good cooking, and when you use best-quality ingredients, even the simplest dish will shine. Like the French, we shop for food more frequently and in smaller quantities, planning a menu around what's available. We have a knack for spotting authentic farmers at the market and enjoy engaging with them and learning about their stories. To us, a true artisan food producer is someone who is growing, harvesting, and producing food, rather than just selling it at the market. We gain immense satisfaction in knowing that we are supporting small farmers and eating clean food. It's important to strive to buy fresh produce in season—not only does it taste better, it's also healthier and generally more affordable. We share our philosophy of shopping locally and seasonally throughout the pages to follow, and we hope to inspire you to do the same wherever you live.

THE
IMPORTANCE
OF
TECHNIQUE

Having a strong grasp of classic cooking techniques and basic core principles—from how to hold a knife properly, to mastering classic sauces and stocks, to understanding how to properly sear, sauté, roast, braise, season, and so on—is the key to becoming a better cook. We always teach our students how to first make things by hand, instead of using a food processor or stand mixer, so they really get a feel for the process. Not that we are against machines, but there's no substitute for your hands in the kitchen. When making bread or pastry dough, for example, using your hands gives you a memory of exactly how the dough should feel, so the next time you make the recipe, you'll know when to add more flour or when to stop kneading. We created this book as an extension of our French cooking school, providing an approachable and beautiful Cooking School section, to give in-depth instruction on classic French cooking techniques and recipes we feel every cook should know (see pages 333–91). As you practice and begin to master the fundamentals of French cooking, your confidence as a cook will improve, empowering you to develop your own style of cooking.

HONING
YOUR
INTUITION

As you become a better cook, part of the journey is to let go of just following a recipe. We feel it's important for a good cook to begin with certain fundamental classic techniques and methods, and then, with some practice, start to hone in on their own intuition in the kitchen to make a recipe ultimately into their own. Cooking should be enjoyable, and in our minds, it's difficult to be a good cook if you don't take pleasure in the actual process—and in eating. As you gain more and more confidence, you will be able to adapt recipes, making adjustments here and there, depending on what's available in your region. We hope that you view our recipes not as rigid dicta, but as suggestive guides to help hone your cooking instincts.

GATHERING À LA FRANÇAISE

One of the things we love most about living in France is the unwavering rhythm of mealtimes and the time spent around the table. We relish the rituals—the sourcing of ingredients, the cooking and the preparation, and taking pride in setting a beautiful table. For us, it's about enjoying the meal, the company, and the conversation—and savoring the experience as a whole.

Like the French, we've adopted the tradition of eating each meal in courses. For family time, even a humble meal is eaten at a leisurely pace and never rushed. For our workshops and the long French lunches that follow, meals usually include a more elaborate presentation. We select dishes that complement each other so there is an overall sense of flow to the meal. From a simple family gathering to a large dinner party, this relaxed way of eating—savoring each course on its own—draws out the conversation and allows everyone to linger just a bit longer around the table.

We strive to create a beautiful ambiance, and so that means putting thought into the menu and using things we've collected over the years to create an inviting table. No matter if the meal is intended to be casual or formal, the intention of our gatherings is to create an experience and to have all of the elements work together to evoke a certain feeling.

Eating and gathering in this way reminds us to savor the things that matter most: family, friends, and good food. It's about taking time to pause in the midst of our busy lives, to put value and joy back into the act of eating. The seasonal menus and gatherings throughout the pages that follow are inspired by glimpses into life here in Burgundy, and the recipes that accompany them are an expression of how we like to cook, using the bounty of the region all year long. We hope to encourage you to seek out the beauty in your own area and to gather in your own way. We believe that a meaningful life, no matter where you live, is all in the details.

THE FRENCH CHEESE COURSE

A meal in France would not be complete without a cheese course: a welcome interlude between the main course and dessert. In France, a cheese course can be served in lieu of dessert, paired with a rustic country boule and perhaps with some fresh fruit. The French would never serve it before a meal, as they believe that the cheese course is a wonderful way to encourage guests to stay around the table a bit longer and is a perfect excuse for another bottle of wine.

The French take their cheese very seriously. The famous French gastronome Jean Anthelme Brillat-Savarin once wrote, "A dessert without cheese is like a beautiful woman who is missing an eye." And with hundreds of varieties to choose from, you could try a different cheese every day for a year and never repeat. Each region of France has its own specialties, and many have the AOC (Appellation d'Origine Contrôlée) or AOP (Appellation d'Origine Protégée) designation, which identifies the region or village of origin and traditional methods of production.

We are fortunate to have an incredible cheese shop in Beaune, Fromagerie Hess, and we often buy cheese there, or from our favorite producers at the market. We always serve a cheese course during the long French lunch after our cooking classes, featuring our favorite local varieties. We share our friend Yan's cheeses, especially his Tomme de Brebis (aged sheep's-milk cheese), Couronne Marguerite (ash-covered goat cheese), and La Gabarre (a soft, seasonal goat cheese from the Morvan). We buy Frédéric's Tomme de Chèvre (an aged, pressed goat cheese), as well as Colombier Fermier (a soft, round, local cow's-milk cheese), and Époisses, Burgundy's famous pungent, golden-colored cheese that's so creamy it can be eaten with a spoon. Other favorites include Saint Marcellin and Saint Félicien—creamy cow's-milk cheeses from the Rhône-Alpes. When preparing the cheese course, we like to include selections from Burgundy, as well as other regions of France. The finest cheeses are still unpasteurized. Not only does this add to the flavor profile, but it means that the cheese is living and, like wine, will evolve and mature with age. When visiting a specialty cheese shop, be sure to tell the cheesemonger the day you plan to serve your cheese course, so they can make the best selection for you, depending on the ripeness of each cheese. It's important to serve cheese at room temperature to properly enjoy its flavor and texture. Remove it from the refrigerator at least an hour before serving.

When preparing our cheese board, we make sure to include a variety of types (cow's, sheep's, and goat's milk), textures, colors, and *affinages* (ages). The cheese course is as much about presentation as it is taste, so you want to make sure the selection is visually appealing. As a rule, we like to serve odd numbers—usually five, seven, or nine cheeses at a time, depending on the number of guests. We present our cheese course in generous wedges or in whole rounds on vintage wooden boards, or sometimes under antique cheese domes, along with the appropriate cheese knife.

It's customary to select a slice of each cheese from the board. Remember to begin with the most mild cheese and work your way through, reserving the last bite for the strongest one. When serving, be sure to keep in mind the original shape of the cheese when slicing—for example, if cutting from a small round of goat cheese, cut a small wedge from the round and continue. If the cheese is already cut into a wedge, slice a thin whole slice from the side rather than cutting off the tip. The idea is to ensure that everyone is served the same proportion of cheese and rind. If someone begins by cutting off the tip or "nose" of the cheese, the final guest being served would be left with the just the rind.

Cheese can be stored separately in the vegetable drawer of your refrigerator for a few days loosely covered in cheese paper or parchment paper. Never store cheese in plastic wrap, as it prevents it from breathing.

The cheese course is a highlight of any French gathering, and it's one of the many pleasures of living in France that we have wholeheartedly embraced. We encourage you to bring this tradition to your table.

Driving through the Côte d'Or in any season is transforming. This famed thirty-six-mile (fifty-eight-km) stretch of vineyards, extending north to Marsannay and south to Santenay, produces some of the world's most coveted wines in an idyllic, pastoral setting. The narrow two-lane road snakes through a hilly patchwork of neatly pruned vineyards and medieval villages, divided by a network of low stone walls. The autumn vines, after harvest, glow in brilliant shades of gold and burnt sienna, earning the area the name the Golden Slope. Ancient stone crosses dot the landscape, marking the entrances to Grand Cru vineyards, and horses pulling plows slowly make their way up and down the sloping paths between the vines. There is no mistaking the beauty and mystery of this noble landscape and its rich sense of history.

It's impossible to understand Burgundy wine without an appreciation of *terroir*, the unique combination of soil quality, terrain, sun exposure, and, of course, the winemaker's touch. Two vineyards sitting side-by-side can have very different flavor profiles and price tags. The slope of the hill, the directness of the sunlight, the nutrients in the soil, an early frost or unusually hot summer—all of these factors affect the grapes, and thus the taste of the wine. Winemakers work their magic around the nuance of the terroir and the climate, always taking care to preserve the integrity of the soil and the vines. Much is left to nature—irrigation isn't allowed in Burgundy, and vines are planted very close together, forcing their roots to reach down deep into the earth to look for water and nutrients. Burgundian winemakers know a little secret: Vines, like people, benefit from a little struggle. Ultimately, the vines that suffer produce fewer grapes, but of a higher quality.

We always advise others to learn about Burgundy wines first by tasting. Wherever you live, find a knowledgeable local wine merchant who can recommend bottles within your budget for you to take home and try. When tasting, take note of the label—the winemaker, where it's from, the vintage (year)—and any particular nuances you enjoy. As you become more knowledgeable about the wines of Burgundy, you'll come to understand that there are certain vintages that are particularly noteworthy. However, all vintages are great; it's just a question of when you drink them, meaning that a modest vintage at maturity is a more satisfying experience than drinking a great vintage too young. Once you determine a particular winemaker you like, or a style that you prefer, you can begin to explore similar wines with the help of your local wine merchant. Keep in mind that learning about wine, like cooking, is a lifelong experience that should be enjoyable.

ENJOYING
WINE WITH
FOOD

In Burgundy, wine isn't saved just for a special occasion. In the same way that they appreciate good food, the French love good wine, and enjoy savoring a glass with their meals. Serving lunch or dinner without wine would be as unthinkable as skipping the meal altogether.

At The Cook's Atelier, we share the French passion for pairing wine with food. We love getting to know local winemakers, and hosting winemaker dinners in the shop. In the same way we source quality ingredients for our food, we are also passionate about selecting well-made wines to serve alongside. In our wine shop, we carry a carefully curated selection of small-production bottles that we love to drink, from France, Italy, and Germany. Of course, we have a soft spot for Burgundy, and have a unique selection from our favorite local producers.

The local wines are incredibly food-friendly. Some can be enjoyed fairly soon after bottling, but most benefit immensely from some time left in a cellar. Like cheese, wine is a living thing, and when left to age, its characteristics evolve and deepen.

When planning a menu, we like to pair each course with its own wine. We always start off with an amuse-bouche and a glass of chilled Champagne, as the bubbles are festive and awaken the palate for the meal to come. For the first course, if it's a salad, we will serve a crisp, mineral-driven white Burgundy. If there are a couple of dishes before the main course, we might serve a more recent white vintage first, followed by an older vintage.

For the main course, we like to serve a lighter red, often something a bit fruitier and younger. Despite being made mostly from Pinot Noir, red Burgundies have an incredibly diverse range of flavor profiles. Depending on the style of the winemaker and the vineyard's unique terroir, some wines taste more fruit-forward, with flavors of red currants, dark cherries, and raspberries, whereas others have earthy undertones, with scents of damp leaves, leather, mushrooms, and tobacco. Regardless, red Burgundy wines tend to be lighter in body, with a racy acidity and a smooth finish. As the meal draws to a close, we save the best wine for last. With the cheese course, we'll serve a heartier, more complex aged red wine.

HISTORICALLY SPEAKING

Burgundy has been a winemaking area since the Roman times, but it was the monks of Cîteaux who began cultivating the land and dividing it into vineyard plots around AD 1000. The monks understood, many centuries ago, the magic of terroir: They recognized that some pieces of land, based on the soil quality, terrain, and sun exposure, produced superior wines to neighboring plots. They kept detailed notes on their winemaking discoveries, and they began making stellar wines that were enjoyed by the likes of the Dukes of Burgundy. The church mostly controlled Burgundy's vineyards until the French Revolution, when the land was turned over to the people.

Thanks to its mineral-rich soil, dramatic climate swings, and varied terrain, Burgundy has a mosaic of hundreds of different appellations (approved wine-growing areas) that are different in style and taste.

In the world of wine, Burgundy is truly a region unto itself. Whereas Champagne and Bordeaux conjure images of sprawling wine estates with state-of-the-art tasting rooms, Burgundy feels much more agricultural and reserved. In Burgundy, winemakers are first and foremost farmers, and some of the best wine *domaines* (wineries) are still small, family-run operations. In days past, growers sold their grapes to larger *négociants* (merchants), who made and sold wine in bulk, but today, more and more growers bottle their own wines. Domaines in Burgundy tend to produce very small quantities of wine, often because they own many small parcels of land in several different areas, rather than one continuous vineyard. In fact, some vineyard plots may only have a few rows of vines.

It takes a lifetime to understand this complex region. We always recommend that people come visit Burgundy for themselves—to see how the vineyards are laid out, to meet the winemakers, and to enjoy the beauty of the region. There's nothing quite like sipping a wine just a few feet from where the grapes were grown.

Burgundy wines are made mostly from single grape varieties—predominantly Pinot Noir (red) and Chardonnay (white)—and it's worth noting that

these two varieties first originated in the region. Pinot Noir and Chardonnay are "noble" grapes, meaning that they don't have to be blended with another grape variety to make exceptional wines. Winemakers around the world try to replicate Burgundian-style Pinot Noir and Chardonnay, but they never taste quite the same. It's not just about the grape variety, but also about the terroir, the winemaking practices, and the winemaking style that are all unique to Burgundy.

The major wine-growing region stretches seventy-five miles (120 km) from Marsannay to the north, on the outskirts of Dijon, to Mâcon in the south, and comprises four wine-growing areas: Côte de Nuits, Côte de Beaune, Côte Chalonnaise, and Mâconnais. Additionally, Burgundy includes Chablis, which is situated north of the Côte d'Or as well as Beaujolais, to the south. Geographically and stylistically separate from the rest of Burgundy, Chablis is a cool-climate appellation known for its bright, mineral-driven Chardonnay, while Beaujolais is most known for its light, fruity red wines made from the Gamay grape.

The Côte de Nuits, famed for its velvety, age-worthy Pinot Noir, and the Côte de Beaune, prized for its complex, honey-colored Chardonnay, are considered the top wine-growing areas, and together comprise the Côte d'Or. This narrow thirty-six-mile (fifty-eight-km) route hosts some of the world's most expensive vineyard real estate, in villages like Gevrey-Chambertin, Morey-Saint Denis, Chambolle-Musigny, Vosne-Romanée, Aloxe-Corton, Puligny-Montrachet, and Chassagne-Montrachet.

Despite being overshadowed by its famous northern siblings, Côte Chalonnaise and Mâconnais are both interesting wine regions, where you can find plenty of unique Pinot Noir and Chardonnay, as well as a local, dry white grape variety, Aligoté.

Burgundy wines are classified into four major categories:

Regional wines This is the most basic level of wine, comprised of grapes grown anywhere in Burgundy and labeled "Bourgogne Rouge" (red wine) or "Bourgogne Blanc" (white wine). Sometimes they will be labeled by the grape variety, Pinot Noir or Chardonnay.

Village wines These wines are named after the village where the grapes were grown. They have a more distinct style and more complex structure than regional wines. On the label, you'll see the producer and the village name.

Premier Cru wines These wines represent vineyards, mostly in the Côte d'Or and a few in the Côte Chalonnaise and Chablis, which are prized for their unique microclimates and soil quality and are subject to stringent regulations on grape yields and sourcing. On the label, you'll see the name of the producer, the village, usually the vineyard, and the classification "1er Cru" (Premier Cru).

Grand Cru wines These are the finest wines in Burgundy, and only account for about 2 percent of the region's wine production. These superb wines represent the thirty-three most prized vineyards in Burgundy. Like Premier Cru wines, Grand Cru wines are subject to stringent regulations on grape yields and sourcing. On the label, you'll see the name of the producer, the vineyard, and the designation "Grand Cru."

Whether you're buying a Village wine or a Grand Cru, it's important to look at the producer's name, which is always listed on the bottle. Most winemakers in the region have a collection of appellations—Regional, Village, Premier Cru, and Grand Cru—so it's possible to find a great wine from a talented winemaker within your means. Understanding the winemaker's style, as well as where the grapes were grown, will tell you a great deal about the bottle before you've even tasted it. Though labels are a good starting point to understanding the facts about the wine, at the end of the day, it's all about the taste and the winemaker.

JEAN-NICOLAS MÉO | WINEMAKER

In a dimly lit wine cellar in the village of Vosne-Romanée, Jean-Nicolas Méo, one of Burgundy's top winemakers and the owner of the famed Domaine Méo-Camuzet, pours a small glass of 2014 Échezeaux Grand Cru and swirls it ceremoniously. He sticks his nose inside the glass, inhaling deeply, before taking a sip. "This is quite powerful," he declares. "It has nice structure, good tannins, and acidity. I feel that the wine is well knit together, but it needs some age." He takes another sip and says, "In another ten years, it will really have some finesse."

Jean-Nicolas invited us to join him one afternoon in his cellar for an early taste of several bottles from the 2014 vintage, and we jumped at the opportunity. In addition to the remarkable Échezeaux, we tasted several Premier Cru wines: an elegant Fixin Clos du Chapitre, a sturdier Vosne-Romanée, an easy-going Chambolle-Musigny "Les Cras," and a Clos de Vougeot, whose complexity shone through early on. Delicate and smooth, yet structured, his wines have a lively acidity that leaps out of the glass. Even at this young stage, his wines are absolutely delicious. "I like very approachable, soft wines," he explains. "I enjoy the sensual side of wine much more than the intellectual." Jean-Nicolas is a passionate winemaker currently making some of the best wines in Burgundy.

His family owns some of the most desirable real estate in the Côte d'Or: Domaine Méo-Camuzet has forty-three acres (seventeen and a half ha) of vineyards and bottles six incredible Grand Cru wines (Richebourg, Clos de Vougeot, Corton Clos Rognet, Corton La Vigne au Saint, Corton Les Perrières, and Échezeaux), ten Premier Cru wines (from Vosne-Romanée, Nuits-Saint-Georges, Chambolle-Musigny, and Fixin), plus some red village and regional wines, and a few whites.

Despite growing up in a family of *vignerons* (winemakers), Jean-Nicolas never planned to become a winemaker. In 1984, when he was twenty years old, living in Paris, and studying business, he received a surprising call from his father. "He asked me to move to Burgundy to run the family domaine," he recalls. His father, Jean Méo, a politician who served as a member of Charles de Gaulle's cabinet, had been living in Paris for years, and had leased out his family's land to *métayers* (sharecroppers). Many of these were reaching retirement age, and Jean was faced with the decision to either find new tenants or a family member willing to run the winery. "Neither of my sisters was interested," says Jean-Nicolas, "so that left me." Despite fond memories of childhood holidays spent with his grandparents in Vosne-Romanée, it was still a difficult decision to leave Paris. "Today, it seems evident that you don't let a domaine like this go, but back then, the life of a winemaker wasn't glamorous. I remember telling a friend that I was going to move to Burgundy, and he said, in all seriousness, 'Oh, you're going to become a peasant?' Things have changed quite a bit in the past thirty years."

Jean-Nicolas began studying oenology in Dijon and moved permanently to Vosne-Romanée with his wife, Nathalie, in 1989. Fortunately, he had a good team to help guide him. Christian Faurois and Henri Jayer, both former leaseholders, agreed to stay on and share their knowledge with Jean-Nicolas. Christian became the estate manager and Henri, already a legendary winemaker with forty years' experience, helped train him in winemaking. Henri was pivotal in introducing basic winemaking practices to Burgundy, like sorting the grapes and green harvesting, both of which reduce the grape yield, but create finer wines. "Sorting used to be very controversial," Jean-Nicolas explains. "In Henri's generation, quantity was valued over quality, as the grapes were sold to négociants to make bulk wine. Winemakers in his era were merely agricultural workers, doing backbreaking work by hand. Life was difficult, and money was scarce."

Things began to shift in the 1980s, as the winemakers' mentalities slowly began to change. Rather than making large quantities of mediocre wines, winery owners began bottling their own wines in small quantities and taking pride in creating a quality product. Jean-Nicolas worked hard to reinvent his family's winery, investing in new equipment, hiring additional labor, and building out the winery buildings. Under Henri and Christian's tutelage, he learned every step of the winemaking process, and within a few years, he was creating fine wines of his own that beautifully reflected the Côte d'Or's complex terroir. Today, Burgundy is at the pinnacle of the wine world—a fact that Jean-Nicolas does not take for granted, as he is part of the generation who ushered in this new era.

OUR KITCHEN POTAGER

Having direct access to a garden helps a cook stay in tune with the food she prepares. It doesn't have to be grand—it can be something as simple as a window box full of herbs or a small terrace with a few pots of lettuces and tomatoes. It's the idea of taking something that you've grown, harvesting it, and using it in a dish that you prepare to bring the experience of cooking full circle.

We have a small kitchen potager at Kendall and Laurent's house, just a few steps from their front door. We grow vegetables, lettuces, and herbs in small raised beds, including *roquette* (arugula), leeks, green beans, peas, fava beans, radishes, artichokes, squash, cucumbers, and even raspberries, all that we use in our cooking classes during the season. In the warmer months, their garden becomes an outdoor living room of sorts, and we often spend Sundays there, planting, weeding, or harvesting. We are big believers in composting, both for the sake of the soil and as a way to recycle leftover food. We keep old stone crocks on the kitchen counter to gather up scraps, like vegetable peels and eggshells, during the cooking classes, and transfer everything to a big bin that we take back to the garden to compost.

We enjoy spending time in the garden and feel it is very important for Kendall's children, Luc and Manon, to have an understanding of where their food comes from and to be participants in the process. It is a lesson that we are happy to cultivate.

COOK'S TOOLS | *BATTERIE DE CUISINE*

At The Cook's Atelier, we work with tools that are as beautiful as they are useful. We have no interest in collecting gadgets, but rather in curating a collection of practical, well-made classic French and European kitchen tools that we can one day pass on to our children and grandchildren.

Cleaver We use a cleaver when we need to cut through bone, when breaking down poultry, or for cutting individual lamb or pork chops from a rack, for example. A well-made cleaver is heavy and should have a very sharp carbon- or stainless-steel blade. Make sure to care for cleavers as you would any knife, with regular sharpening. Hand-wash and dry immediately.

Cotton and linen butcher's twine We use butcher's twine, in both white cotton and natural linen, for tying a roast, trussing a chicken, or making a bouquet garni. We find it to be visually beautiful and a very utilitarian item to have in the kitchen.

Cutting boards It's important to invest in at least one big, wooden cutting board, as this is something you will use every day. We use large Boos Blocks in our kitchen, made from renewable and sustainable hardwoods. They provide the perfect surface for chopping or preparing mise en place. Be sure to maintain its character by oiling it with a food-safe mineral oil and drying thoroughly after each use. Never leave a cutting board in water, or it can crack.

After chopping garlic or onions, or anything with a particularly strong smell, remove the odor from the board simply by sprinkling coarse salt on the board and using half a lemon to work the salt around it. Rinse and dry the board immediately. To disinfect a board after cutting raw meat, wash it with hot, soapy water and dry immediately, and then wipe with distilled white vinegar to remove any bacteria. We don't use any plastic cutting boards at The Cook's Atelier, as we feel wood is better for your knives. If properly cared for, a well-made cutting board can last a lifetime.

Distilled white vinegar We keep a glass bottle of distilled white vinegar by our kitchen sink, and use it for cleaning and disinfecting everything after each class: wooden cutting boards, countertops, knives, and salt and pepper mills. We also use it to disinfect the sink after rinsing out a chicken: We add a bit of baking soda and vinegar and scrub the sink well, and then rinse. It's an all-natural cleaning solution that is both food-safe and environmentally friendly; it also removes strong odors left over from garlic, onions, and shallots.

To clean with vinegar, wet a kitchen towel with warm water and add a little vinegar. Wring out the towel and use it to wipe down anything that you'd like to disinfect, from the inside of the refrigerator to counters to cutting boards. Rinse the towel and add a bit more vinegar after cleaning each area.

Dutch oven Every cook needs a large, enamel-coated cast-iron Dutch oven. We use ours for searing and braising meat for stews, such as bœuf bourguignon or coq au vin, as it's easy to transfer from the stovetop to the oven. An oval Dutch oven is a nice shape for roasting whole chickens.

Food mill We use an old-fashioned food mill—essentially, a sieve with a hand crank—to make homemade applesauce, canned tomato sauce, and pureed soups. It's also a wonderful tool to use when making a creamy potato puree.

French pastry tins We have a collection of new and vintage French pastry tins, like madeleine pans, brioche tins, and tart pans in various shapes and sizes. They are all made from French tin, which develops a lovely patina over time. Unlike nonstick pans, tin conducts heat evenly and creates a lightly crisp, golden brown crust.

Glass jars Our pantry is full of glass jars, perfectly lined up and filled with spices, salt, flour, sugar, vanilla beans, dried pasta, beans, and grains. We like to store dried goods neatly in jars, as it makes it easy to find what you're looking for. We use Weck and Le Parfait jars and vintage ones that are in good shape. Old glass confiture jars stand in our glass-front cabinet to store a mix of flatware.

Gratin dishes We collect a variety of gratin dishes in assorted shapes and sizes, and use them nearly every day for roasting vegetables or making savory gratins. We have some enamel-coated cast-iron gratin dishes, as well as the more traditional white French porcelain ones. We often serve the food in them directly from the oven to the table.

Jam funnel A jam funnel is helpful when transferring hot jam into canning jars. It has a wide mouth that helps protect from splashes and spills, and the neck is just the right size to fit into the jar. It also helps to ensure that the jars are not overfilled, by indicating the proper amount of headspace to leave at the top.

Kitchen shears A good pair of kitchen shears is required in the kitchen. They should be heavy and very sturdy. They can be used for basic tasks like cutting kitchen twine, or snipping greens off carrots, or for more heavy-duty tasks like breaking down poultry. Care for your shears as you do your knives: hand-wash and dry immediately. Wipe them down regularly with food-safe mineral oil and sharpen as needed.

Kitchen torchons We rarely use paper towels at The Cook's Atelier, except occasionally when drying poultry or meat, and instead use cotton or linen kitchen towels, called *torchons* in French, that can be washed and reused. We lay them out to soak up extra water from lettuce or blanched vegetables, and we use the linen ones for polishing wine glasses before a dinner party.

Kitchen tweezers This tool is convenient to have in the kitchen to remove pin feathers from poultry as well as fine fish bones.

Knives Good knives are essential. They are an investment, but with a little extra care, they will last a lifetime. A cook doesn't need a huge knife set—really only four distinct knives: a paring knife, an 8- or 10-inch (20- or 25-cm) chef's knife, a boning knife, and a serrated bread knife.

We use vintage carbon-steel Sabatier knives that we sourced from a third-generation knife maker in Thiers. With sturdy wooden handles and hand-forged carbon steel blades, these handmade knives are extremely sharp and, over time, they develop a beautiful patina.

It's important to use a honing steel before every use, as it straightens the edge and makes it extra sharp. If you're planning to do a lot of chopping in one day, be sure to use the steel occasionally during the process to keep the knife nice and sharp as you are cutting. Periodically, as the knives become dull with use, we suggest sharpening with a whetstone.

Finally, it's important to treat your knives with care. Never put them in the dishwasher: Instead, wash by hand and dry immediately to prevent rusting. We store ours on a large magnetic knife rack, as this helps protect the blade and tip from any damage. We also regularly oil the wooden handles with a food-safe mineral oil.

Mandoline We use a classic stainless-steel French mandoline with interchangeable blades to thinly slice potatoes for *gratin dauphinois*, vegetables like radishes, or fennel for salads. It's important to wash by hand and dry immediately—this will prevent the blade from becoming dull in the dishwasher. Use with care! We recommend always using the hand guard (and using the mandoline before your glass of wine) to prevent injury. If the blade becomes dull, have it professionally sharpened.

Marble slabs We are fortunate to have marble countertops in our kitchen, which is the ideal cool surface for rolling out tart crusts and pastry dough. We aren't overly picky about them, and don't mind a bit of age and patina. If you don't have marble countertops, we recommend keeping a marble slab in your kitchen or on your counter for rolling out pastry. This ensures that your dough stays cool, which will result in a more tender, flakier crust.

Mezzaluna A mezzaluna, which means "half-moon" in Italian, is a curved knife with wooden handles, one for each hand. The blade, made from carbon steel, is extremely sharp, and we use it to quickly chop a pile of herbs for pesto or escargots, using a quick back-and-forth rocking motion. We sell beautifully refurbished 150-year-old vintage mezzalunas at our culinary boutique, and we can barely keep them in stock. This is one of our favorite cooking tools.

Mortar and pestle We have several mortars and pestles, some marble and others ceramic. They are wonderful for making aïoli or for grinding spices by hand. We are always on the hunt at local flea markets for vintage mortars and pestles, and it's the treasure of the day when we find an old one. It's important to wash the mortar and pestle by hand with soap and water, and to dry them immediately, so the flavors of the spices or garlic don't soak into the material.

Parchment and cheesecloth We try to avoid disposable products whenever possible in our kitchen. We only use plastic wrap if it's absolutely necessary, say, to wrap tart dough. Instead, we opt for parchment, cheesecloth, and locally made linen covers. They are a wonderful, eco-friendly alternative to plastic wrap. We often use unbleached parchment for lining baking sheets and for creating a lid when poaching pears. We use cheesecloth for tying up a bouquet garni and for straining consommé.

Pepper mills Every cook needs at least one pepper mill to grind peppercorns. We keep several on hand, one for grinding black peppercorns, one for white, and one for a blend. Be sure to look for one that allows you to adjust the grind.

Pots and pans If you do a lot of cooking, we recommend investing in good-quality professional-grade pots and pans. We cook with copper, enamel-coated cast-iron, cast-iron, stainless-steel, and classic French black steel pans, all professional-grade and made in France. Good pots and pans are a lifetime investment—you'll use them daily, and they'll last forever, if you care for them properly. We recommend the following pots and pans for the serious cook: one large stockpot, one large sauté and braising pan, two round fry pans (small and medium), and two saucepots (medium and large).

We have a soft spot for copper cookware. Copper conducts heat very well and allows for even cooking.

We also enjoy cooking with cast iron, using it to sear meat or make a tarte tatin. If properly cared for and regularly seasoned, cast-iron pans will last for a lifetime. Never use detergent when washing a cast-iron skillet, and never let it soak. Wipe it out and scrub it with salt, then rinse and dry immediately. A new piece is always very porous, but the more you cook in it, the smoother it will get.

Scales A digital scale is a must for baking, because it provides much more accurate measurements than cups or spoons. Look for a scale that can measure both metric and imperial weights, for easy conversion of recipes.

Small tools There are several small tools that are essential for the French kitchen. We use our bench scraper as an extension of our hands when making bread or pastry dough. It's helpful for scraping up dough scraps, cutting butter for *pâte feuilletée* (puff pastry), and dividing up *pâte sucrée* (sweet dough) for *tartelettes*. A well-made wooden reamer is a must for juicing lemons. A sharp, classic French stainless-steel vegetable peeler makes quick work of peeling carrots, potatoes, apples, and pears, and even shaving radishes into thin slices for a salad. Quality wooden and horsehair brushes are incredibly useful—we recommend one for cleaning mushrooms, one for scrubbing vegetables, one for pastry, and one for breadmaking. Other favorite tools include a boxwood spoon for drizzling honey, and a boxwood pastry cutter for cutting fresh pasta and dough. And, of course, a favorite small tool at The Cook's Atelier is the classic sommelier corkscrew, or wine key opener. Every cook should enjoy a nice glass of Burgundy wine while preparing a meal.

Strainers We have an assortment of strainers in various sizes, some with finer mesh than others, and we use them daily. Smaller ones are perfect for dusting confectioners' sugar, medium ones for straining sauces and blanching vegetables, and a cone-shaped *chinois* for straining soups and stocks. When in doubt, strain. It's an easy way to remove any impurities and to refine a dish.

Truffle shaver A truffle shaver is a cook's tool specifically designed to slice truffles into thin, almost-transparent slices. Look for a stainless steel one with an adjustable blade.

Whisks We have an assortment of whisks in various sizes: larger ones for whipping cream or egg whites, and smaller ones for whisking a sauce or vinaigrette. We are especially fond of our copper-handled whisks.

Wooden spoons Every cook needs several long-handled wooden spoons in their collection, for everything from stirring soups and sauces to mixing *gougères* dough to jam-making.

There are certain high-quality provisions that we always keep on hand in our pantry. Along with regular staples such as lentils, dried legumes, capers, various vinegars, finishing oils, and homemade preserves, we are sure to have plenty of basic items on hand to create an impromptu meal.

Bouquet garni A bouquet garni is a bundle of fresh parsley, thyme, and a bay leaf, tied up with a piece of kitchen twine and dropped into a pot of soup or stock. Sometimes we tie up the herbs, along with some black peppercorns, in a piece of cheesecloth, as we do for our Pot-au-Feu (page 298). This infuses the soup or stock with extra flavor as it cooks, and is easily removed and discarded once the cooking is done.

Butter Butter is the ultimate French larder ingredient, and we use plenty of it. In France, you can still buy handmade regional butters from small creameries. We recommend using unsalted, high-quality European-style butter, due to its high fat content and full flavor.

Chocolate We use high-quality dark chocolate for baking. We buy 65 or 70 percent cacao chocolate from Pâtisserie Passion Millot, a little chocolate shop just down the street from The Cook's Atelier. This small family-run *pâtisserie* (pastry shop) hand-selects and roasts their own cocoa beans to make a variety of chocolates and French pastries. We buy it by the kilo and store it at room temperature in a cool, dark place.

Coffee When it comes to coffee, the Italians do it best. We source our coffee from Laboratorio di Torrefazione Giamaica Caffè in Verona, one of Italy's premier artisan coffee roasters. This is truly the best coffee we've ever tasted, and we are thrilled to offer it in our shop.

Duck fat We always keep a little jar of rendered duck fat on hand. It's an easy way to make any dish a bit more decadent, and there's no more delicious way to eat potatoes than sautéed in duck fat. When you render the fat from a duck breast (see pages 214–17), pour off the fat, strain it through some cheesecloth, and store it in a jar in the refrigerator for up to two months.

Eggs We buy pasture-raised eggs from our favorite producers at the market, as they are much fresher, and taste better, than store-bought ones. Farm-fresh eggs are more abundant in the spring and summer, as the chickens follow the natural rhythm of the seasons, and they don't lay as many eggs in the cooler months.

It is important to emphasize just how different pasture-raised eggs are from industrialized ones. Industrialized chickens are raised inside with limited access to the outdoors and are fed a grain-based diet. Pasture-raised chickens are allowed to roam freely on the land and benefit from a high-protein diet of insects, thus producing more flavorful eggs with bright orange yolks.

Just like produce, eggs in France are produced in a more natural way, and they are not always uniform in size. They can range from medium to large in the same carton, and it's up to the cook to determine which size egg to use, depending on the recipe. For our recipes, we generally use eggs that are medium to large in size, and adjust the number of eggs accordingly, if needed.

Wherever you live, it's important to buy pasture-raised eggs from local farmers if you can, as they are used in so many facets of cooking and baking.

Foie gras Foie gras is a very important part of France's culinary heritage and can be made from either goose or duck livers. We purchase *foie gras entier* (whole foie gras) and *terrine de foie gras* (pâté) from a local artisan producer who we know well, and enjoy it for special occasions.

Garlic We always use fresh garlic, never jarred or powdered. When you buy garlic, it should be firm, and the papery skin should be tight. Avoid garlic that's soft, dried out, or has a green sprout. When cooking with garlic, first peel it and separate the cloves. We cut the cloves in half and remove the inner germ, as this can sometimes add a bitter flavor. If the germ is green, this is an indication that it is an older head of garlic and the green germ definitely should be removed before chopping. To make a paste, pound the garlic in a mortar and pestle. We store whole garlic bulbs at room temperature in a stone crock for up to two months.

Herbs We prefer to cook with fresh herbs. We keep them on the counter in glass jars filled with cool water, much like freshly cut flowers. If we have an abundance of herbs in the summertime, we will dry them to use later in the winter months. To dry fresh herbs, such as parsley, chervil, thyme, basil, tarragon, or bay leaves, simply arrange the leaves in a single layer on a parchment paper–lined baking sheet and leave out until thoroughly dry. They can also be dried in an oven at a very low temperature. When completely dried, place the dried leaves in a tightly sealed glass jar. We use these herbs in our Flavored Sea Salts (page 67).

Honey We keep several varieties of local raw, organic honey in our pantry to use in recipes and when baking. Wherever you live, try and seek out locally produced raw honey, from your farmers' market or a specialty food shop. The bees will thank you.

Infused oils Making herb-infused oil is the perfect way to use up a surplus of fresh herbs in the summertime. We often make basil oil, though you can use any green, leafy herb, like parsley, chervil, thyme, rosemary, or dill. Keep in mind, when making herb oil with thyme or rosemary, the color of the finished oil will not be as vibrant, so we always include some fresh flat-leaf parsley leaves when blanching, to ensure a bright green oil. Herb oil adds the perfect finishing touch to a dish (page 67).

Milk and heavy cream We are big believers in using whole milk and full-fat cream for all our recipes. There is no place in our kitchen for low-fat or skim of any kind. As with butter, we prefer to use dairy in its original, unaltered form.

Mustard Burgundy is the mustard capital of France. If you want true Dijon, it's important that it comes from Burgundy's Côte d'Or. We proudly source some of our favorites from Edmond Fallot in Burgundy and Moutarde de Meaux Pommery not far from Paris. We keep several varieties on hand: regular, grainy, and *pompier* (spicy).

Olive oil We use organic extra-virgin, first-cold-pressed olive oil for everything, from sautéing meats and fish (being careful not to let it overheat or burn) to making vinaigrette, simply because it's clean and in its pure state. We often prefer the taste of a lighter, fruitier olive oil rather than a heavy, peppery one, so it doesn't overpower the dish. We source our house olive oil from a small organic producer in the South of France. Depending on the dish, we may also use an extra-virgin finishing olive oil from Tuscany. Finishing olive oils tend to be more expensive and are more delicate in flavor. They should not be used in cooking, as the delicate flavor will be lost. We drizzle sparingly over salads, meats, and vegetables just before serving. Look for good-quality olive oil and buy it in small quantities from a reliable source.

Organic flour and sugar We use organic, unbleached flour that we source locally from Babeth, our baker, and organic sugar from our local organic health-food store for our recipes. We prefer to use organic flour and sugar, as they are free of pesticides and synthetic chemicals. It's important to keep in mind that flours differ, depending on which country it is coming from. We recommend only using high-quality, organic, unbleached flour when making the recipes in this book.

Sea salt When cooking, it's important to use a clean, pure, and natural salt with no additives. We prefer to use fleur de sel, the delicate layer of sea salt hand-harvested from the surface of the sea, in all of our recipes. See page 67 for different ways to flavor sea salt.

Shallots and onions Shallots have a flavor all their own and can be enjoyed raw or cooked. We use shallots when making vinaigrettes and sauces. Onions are also essential in the kitchen. We use them for stocks, soups, and sauces. It's important to look for shallots and onions that are firm, not soft. Store them at room temperature, each in their own stone crock.

Spices When using dry spices, whole ones are best for freshness, and we prefer to grind them, as needed, in a mortar and pestle. We store them in our pantry in neatly arranged glass jars with tight-fitting lids.

Truffles The very best truffles come from France and Italy. The most prized black truffles can be found in the Dordogne and Périgord, in southwestern France. The famous white truffle comes from the Piedmont region of Italy. Both the black and white truffle varieties are harvested at the end of the year, each with their own distinctive aromas and flavors, and are highly prized in the culinary world.

In Burgundy, we are fortunate to find our own variety of black truffle. Not nearly as pungent and pricey as the Périgord and Piedmont varieties, they are still wonderful to have on hand to use as a garnish for autumn soups and salads. They are delicate and mild in flavor. We recommend enjoying them quickly, as they are at their best immediately after harvesting. For short-term storage, truffles must be wrapped in cloth and stored in a tightly sealed glass jar in the refrigerator for no longer than a few days. We rec-ommend eating them on everything until they are gone.

Vanilla beans When using vanilla beans, we prefer to use whole beans and keep them stored in a glass jar filled with vodka. The vodka softens the beans, and the alcohol helps to preserve them. You could use another spirit, such as brandy, but we prefer vodka for its neutral flavor. Whenever we need to use vanilla in a recipe, rather than tediously scraping the seeds out with a paring knife, we simply snip the bean in half and squeeze out the vanilla paste. When making Crème Anglaise (page 386), Crème Pâtissière (page 385), ice cream, or simple syrup, after we've removed the seeds into the milk or liquid, we also include the pod to help infuse the flavor. Once steeped, we remove the pod when straining and discard. The vanilla-infused vodka can also be used in place of vanilla extract (see page 263).

Vanilla sugar After using a vanilla bean (if it hasn't been steeped in milk or another liquid), we let the pod dry out by leaving it in an open jar for a few days before adding it to a jar of granulated sugar. As we continue to add dried vanilla pods to the sugar, it becomes infused with vanilla flavor, creating vanilla sugar.

Yeast In France, fresh yeast is readily available and it's possible to source from the neighborhood *boulangerie* (bakery). We enjoy experimenting with fresh yeast from time to time, but we usually opt for active dry yeast for our recipes.

Herb Oil

MAKES ABOUT 1 CUP (240 ML)

3 cups (90 g) fresh basil or other green herb
(plus ¾ cup (40 g) fresh flat-leaf parsley
leaves, if using thyme or rosemary as the
herb base)

1 cup (240 ml) fruity extra-virgin olive oil,
preferably French

Bring a large pot of salted water to a boil
and prepare a bowl of ice and water.

Add the herb to the boiling water and
blanch for about 15 seconds. If making
thyme or rosemary oil, add the parsley and
continue blanching for 10 more seconds.
Using a small fine-mesh strainer, lift the
herbs out of the boiling water and immediately plunge them into the ice water to stop
the cooking and preserve their color. Drain
and use your hands to squeeze as much
water as possible out of the leaves. You'll
end up with a compact mass that's about
the size of an egg.

Place the herbs in a blender, add the
olive oil, and blend on high until the herbs
are very small and the mixture is well
combined, 2 to 3 minutes. Transfer the
mixture to a glass container, cover, and
refrigerate overnight.

The next day, remove the mixture from
the refrigerator and let it come to room
temperature. Line a fine-mesh strainer
with two layers of cheesecloth and place
over a glass bowl to catch any drips. Add
the herb-oil mixture to the cheesecloth
and tie the ends with kitchen twine to
form a pouch. Remove the strainer and use
additional twine to attach the cheesecloth
pouch to the middle part of the handle of a
wooden spoon. Arrange the wooden spoon
so that the ends sit on two jars that are tall
enough to allow the pouch to hang from
the middle of the handle and drip into the
glass bowl. Let the herb oil slowly drain
from the cheesecloth pouch until it stops
dripping, about 30 minutes. Store the oil in
a glass container in the refrigerator; for the
best flavor, use within 5 days.

Flavored Sea Salts

MAKES ABOUT 1 CUP (220 G)

GARDENER'S FLEUR DE SEL
3 tablespoons lemon zest
3 tablespoons fresh chervil leaves or chopped
young fresh flat-leaf parsley leaves
1 cup (220 g) fleur de sel

BUTCHER'S FLEUR DE SEL
1 tablespoon fresh thyme leaves
1½ teaspoons finely chopped fresh rosemary
Pinch of piment d'Espelette
1 cup (220 g) fleur de sel

FISHMONGER'S FLEUR DE SEL
2 tablespoons lemon zest
1 small handful of fresh dill
1 small handful of fresh chervil
1 tablespoon fennel seeds, crushed
1 cup (220 g) fleur de sel

Line a baking sheet with parchment paper.
Spread the fresh herbs and zest, if using, on
the parchment and let them dry overnight at
room temperature.

In a glass jar, combine the ingredients
for the salt you are making with the fleur
de sel. Store the flavored fleur de sel at
room temperature; for the best flavor, use
within 6 months.

SPRING

Springtime is a fleeting moment in Burgundy. The weather still feels cool and damp, but all of a sudden, the trees start flowering, the tulips appear, and the vines begin to bud, and you know that it's here. After a long winter, these signs of spring remind us that warmer months are ahead.

The Beaune market is abuzz with signs of new life: wild cress, crisp little fingerling potatoes and delicate baby carrots, bundles of fresh peas and snap peas, fava beans, earthy morels, fragrant green garlic, turnips, and radishes. Crates of fat white asparagus show up for just a few weeks in April, and we cook with them as often as possible. When the tiny Gariguette strawberries appear, we buy huge boxfuls of them, and get busy making tarts and confiture. As the temperatures rise, bright red Burlat cherries and little Bergeron apricots appear at the market, and we find wild asparagus and woodland strawberries near the creek at Kendall and Laurent's house, just behind the potager.

After a winter hiatus, we look forward to the return of our favorite artisan food producers to the market, and enjoy buying their spring specialties: baby stinging nettles, wild garlic, freshly made sheep's-milk cheese, farm eggs (which happen to be at their most flavorful in the spring), and armfuls of lilacs and peonies. We purchase tiny starter plants, which we use to fill our kitchen window box with herbs and our garden full of vegetables.

This time of year, our cooking becomes lighter and our food more colorful. After a winter of hearty dishes, we welcome the bright flavors of barely cooked spring vegetables. We steam artichokes; make quick sautés of snap peas, spring peas, and asparagus; and serve radishes with curls of good butter and a sprinkling of fleur de sel.

On warm days, we leave the door open to the shop, and friends drop by after work for a glass of wine. The days grow longer, and, just as suddenly as it arrived, spring is gone.

SIMONE LOICHET | GARDENER

A Friday visit to Madame Loichet's garden, tucked behind a bright blue gate near the Beaune train station, is one of the highlights of our week. Simone Loichet, a vibrant woman in her eighties, can be found working in her garden every day, with her dog, Maya, by her side. Her life is centered around the rhythm of this garden. She wakes each morning with the sun and spends her day tending the earth.

Her garden is large, and the rows are neat and well cared for. In the cooler months, she starts her vegetables in a makeshift greenhouse to protect them from the elements. Depending on the season, she grows big heads of lettuces, tender *mâche*, fresh herbs (basil, thyme, tarragon, chives, parsley), heirloom tomatoes, baby carrots, green beans, potatoes, onions, and pumpkins. Her garden is full of old-fashioned flower varieties: irises, daffodils, and lilacs in the spring, zinnias, Marguerite daisies, and tiny bouquets of black-eyed Susans in the summer, and every color of dahlia imaginable in the early autumn. Every spring, little swallows return to nest in the rafters of the cool barn. They swoop in and out as we gather armfuls of lovely pale pink peonies to display in the shop.

Madame Loichet has been working in this garden ever since she was a child. Her parents were *maraîchers* (market gardeners), too, and she continues to use their vintage garden tools today to tend the rows. She still lives in the little stone house where she was born, right next to the garden. Every Friday, she sets out flat wooden crates of just-harvested vegetables and zinc buckets full of flowers in the old stone barn. It's sort of a secret "pre-market"—a chance for her favorite customers to stop by for a visit, and to shop from her before the hustle and bustle of the Saturday market.

We first met Madame Loichet at the market in 2009, and she quickly became our favorite artisan food producer. Her presence in Beaune is a link to the markets of years past, and our weekly visits to her garden remind us why we moved to Burgundy: to create a life rich in simplicity and to honor our devotion to good and well-made food.

YAN LAGOUGE | SHEPHERD

There's something meditative about walking through the Burgundian countryside with a herd of sheep and goats, listening to the rhythmic sounds of hooves and the clanking of bells. For our friend Yan, a shepherd who lives on a communal farm an hour southeast of Beaune, this is just part of his daily routine.

We first encountered Yan Lagouge at the market in 2010. A young guy with a big grin and a calm presence, he sells organic vegetables, lettuces, and herbs each week, along with sheep's- and goat's-milk cheeses from his farm, Ferme de Jointout. Yan, his companion, Alex, and their young daughter, Lila, live and work on the farm with four other couples, including Thomas, a German gardener who grows the vegetables, and Adele, an American cheese maker who runs the creamery. Each family has their own home, but they all share in the responsibilities of the farm: gardening, caring for the animals, making cheese and baking bread, and selling produce at the market.

Yan, currently in his mid-thirties, was always enamored with the idea of becoming a shepherd. Originally from Strasbourg, he first took the more conventional route, studying chemistry and working as a pharmacist for several years before finally deciding to give shepherding a try. He quit his job and became a shepherd's apprentice—first in France, and then in New Zealand. He later moved to the southwest of France to study agriculture and work on a farm. It was there that he met Thomas and Adele. After several years of working on farms in southwest France, they moved to Burgundy in 2009 and founded Ferme de Jointout.

Their day is built around the rhythm of the farm: They rise at dawn to milk the sheep and goats, and then take the milk to the creamery, where Adele transforms it into *tommes* of sheep's-milk cheese, soft goat's-milk cheese rounds, and jars of fresh yogurt. Thomas spends the day working in the garden. At midday, Yan leads his herd of sheep and goats out to pasture to graze for the afternoon. The community of Ferme de Jointout is an inspiring example of a growing number of young people in France embracing the traditions of old-world farming.

GARDEN DAY

Laurent, the kids, and I live in a village, about twenty minutes south of Beaune, along the route des Grands Crus. When we were first married, Laurent and I lived in a small apartment in Beaune, just down the street from Monsieur Vossot's butcher shop and my mom's original apartment (and first home of The Cook's Atelier). Once we found out we were pregnant with Luc, we started to look for a house. We hoped to find one in the country, but not too far from town, and one that we could call home forever. I pictured a small stone house with a fireplace and a spot for a small kitchen garden. Laurent, being from the South of France, insistently hoped for a house by water. At the time, the idea seemed too far-fetched to me, and probably way out of our budget. Surprisingly, we fell in love with the very first house we visited: It was a small, modest stone cottage in a tiny village with a big yard and, miraculously, a little creek out back. We knew right away that it would be the ideal place to raise our family.

The house itself was a bit rough. It had been empty for many years, the rooms were dark, and the only source of heat came from the fireplace. But we saw its potential and loved the original bread oven in the kitchen (which was once used to bake bread for the entire village), not to mention the garden and possibility for a kitchen potager. Next to the creek sat an old stone barn, originally part of a walnut mill. With its rough-hewn wooden beams and rustic charm, we envisioned it as the perfect setting for entertaining outside.

Today, after spending a morning working in the garden, we set up a table under the cherry tree. When lunch is ready, we grab the chilled bottles from the creek, fill our glasses, and gather around the table. These simple Sunday meals are one of the things we cherish most about living in France.

French Radishes AND *Butter* WITH *Gardener's Fleur de Sel* PAGE 82

Fava Bean AND *Sweet Pea Salad* WITH *Fennel* AND *Garden Herbs* PAGE 85

Savory Tart WITH *Spinach* AND *Mushrooms* PAGE 86

Almond-Cherry Galette PAGE 89

French Radishes and Butter with Gardener's Fleur de Sel

SERVES 6

Peppery fresh radishes, creamy butter, and a hint of sea salt—a favorite French apéritif—
are truly magical together. We like to put a little twist on the classic by serving
curls of good French butter, shaved from a larger block with a vegetable peeler,
and a sprinkling of our homemade Gardener's Fleur de Sel.

3 bunches small breakfast
   radishes with tops

4 to 8 tablespoons (½ to
   1 stick/55 to 115 g) unsalted
   butter

Gardener's Fleur de Sel
   (page 67)

Trim the radishes, leaving the green leaves attached.
Using a stainless-steel vegetable peeler, shave the butter
into thin curls and refrigerate them until ready to use.
Arrange the radishes and butter on a platter. Serve with
the gardener's salt.

Fava Bean and Sweet Pea Salad with Fennel and Garden Herbs

SERVES 6

Light and refreshing, this makes a perfect first course in the springtime.
The recipe is very versatile—feel free to mix up
the combination of herbs or add in thinly sliced garden radishes.

Fleur de sel

3 cups fresh shelled fava beans (from 3 pounds/1.4 kg in the pod)

2 cups fresh shelled sweet peas (from 2 pounds/910 g in the pod)

3 fennel bulbs

1 lemon, halved

Fruity extra-virgin olive oil, preferably French

1 bunch fresh chives, finely chopped

Handful of fresh mint leaves

Handful of fresh flat-leaf parsley leaves

Handful of fresh chervil leaves

Freshly ground black pepper

Bring a large pot of salted water to a boil and fill a bowl with ice and water.

Add the fava beans to the boiling water and blanch until just tender, 3 to 5 minutes, depending on the size. Immediately plunge the fava beans into the ice water to stop the cooking and preserve their color. Once the fava beans are cool, use a slotted spoon to scoop them out of the ice water, then pop off their pale green skins to release the bright green beans; reserve the ice water. Set the beans aside and discard the skins.

Fill the pot with fresh water, add salt, and bring it to a boil. Add more ice to the ice water. Add the peas to the boiling water and blanch just until tender, 2 to 3 minutes. Immediately plunge the peas into the ice water to stop the cooking and preserve their color. Once the peas are cool, drain and set them aside.

Trim the fennel bulbs, remove the tough outer layer, cut them in half, and remove the inner cores. Using a mandoline, thinly slice the fennel. Put it in a large bowl and squeeze one lemon half over the top to preserve the fennel's color.

Drizzle the fennel generously with olive oil and toss to coat. Add the peas, chives, mint, parsley, and chervil. Season with salt and pepper. Toss gently to combine, then taste and season with additional salt, pepper, and lemon juice, as needed. Serve on a large platter or individual salad plates and arrange the delicate fava beans around the finished salad.

Savory Tart with Spinach and Mushrooms

MAKES 1 (9-INCH/23-CM) TART OR 8 (4-INCH/10-CM) TARTLETS

Savory tarts are ideal for outdoor entertaining, as they can be made ahead of time and served at room temperature. There are endless seasonal variations for this recipe—just substitute the spinach, mushrooms, and chervil for whichever vegetables and herbs look good at your market.

FOR THE TART

Unbleached all-purpose flour, for dusting

½ recipe Pâte Brisée (page 379)

1 large egg yolk

3 tablespoons heavy cream

FOR THE CUSTARD

3 large eggs

½ cup (120 ml) heavy cream

½ cup (120 ml) crème fraîche

¼ tablespoon fresh thyme leaves

⅛ teaspoon freshly grated nutmeg

½ teaspoon fleur de sel

¼ teaspoon freshly ground black pepper

FOR THE FILLING

3 tablespoons unsalted butter

7 ounces (200 g) cremini mushrooms, thinly sliced

Fleur de sel and freshly ground black pepper

1 shallot, thinly sliced into rings

3 tablespoons dry white wine, such as Burgundy Chardonnay

2½ cups (50 g) baby spinach leaves

Handful of fresh chervil leaves, for garnish (optional)

Make the tart shell: On a lightly floured surface, use the pâte brisée to make the tart shell (see page 374). Freeze it for 15 to 20 minutes before baking.

Preheat the oven to 375°F (190°C).

In a small bowl, whisk together the egg yolk and heavy cream. Use a pastry brush to lightly brush the egg wash over the dough. Partially blind bake the tart shell (see page 333).

Make the custard: In a medium bowl, whisk together the eggs, heavy cream, crème fraîche, thyme, nutmeg, salt, and pepper until smooth. Set aside.

Make the filling: In a large heavy sauté pan, melt 2 tablespoons of the butter over medium heat and sauté the mushrooms until tender and caramelized, 7 to 10 minutes. Season with salt and pepper. Remove the mushrooms from the pan, reserving any liquid, and set aside. Do not clean the pan.

In the same pan, melt the remaining 1 tablespoon butter over medium heat. Add the shallot and sauté until soft, about 3 minutes. If there was any mushroom liquid, add it to the pan and sauté until it has been absorbed. Add the wine and use a wooden spoon to scrape up any bits from the bottom of the pan. Cook until the wine has reduced by half, about 1 minute. Add the spinach, season with salt and pepper, and sauté until just barely wilted, about 1 minute. Remove from the heat.

Assemble the tart: Place the cooled, partially baked tart shell on a baking sheet. Arrange the mushrooms and spinach mixture evenly in the tart shell. Carefully pour the custard into the tart shell just until it reaches the top—you may have a little left over. Bake until the custard is barely set, about 25 minutes. Let it cool on a wire rack. Garnish with fresh chervil, if desired, and serve warm or at room temperature. The tart is best eaten the day it is made.

Almond-Cherry Galette

SERVES 6

This rustic galette perfectly captures the ripe fruit of the season.
The recipe can be adapted using any seasonal fruit and can also be made into small
individual galettes. The almond flour in the dough pairs nicely with the cherries,
and would also work well with peaches in the summer and pears in the autumn.

1 tablespoon unbleached, all-
purpose flour, plus more for
dusting

½ recipe Galette Dough
(page 378)

¼ cup (50 g) sugar

Seeds of ½ vanilla bean
(see page 64)

1 tablespoon fresh lemon juice

3 cups (465 g) halved pitted
sweet cherries

1 tablespoon cold unsalted
butter, cut into small pieces

1 large egg yolk

3 tablespoons heavy cream

Preheat the oven to 350°F (175°C). Line a baking sheet
with parchment paper.

On a lightly floured surface with a floured rolling pin,
roll the galette dough into a large round, about 12 inches
(30.5 cm) in diameter and ¼ inch (6 mm) thick. Brush
off any excess flour with a pastry brush. Place the dough
round on the parchment-lined baking sheet. Sprinkle it
with 2 teaspoons of the sugar.

In a small bowl, combine 3 tablespoons of the sugar,
the vanilla seeds, flour, and lemon juice and stir to
combine. Place the cherries in a large bowl, sprinkle with
the sugar mixture, and gently toss until evenly coated.

Arrange the cherry mixture in the center of the dough
round, leaving a 1½-inch (4-cm) border. Scatter the butter
over the cherries. Fold the border over the cherry mixture,
overlapping as you go. Refrigerate for 15 minutes.

Remove the galette from the refrigerator. In a small
bowl, whisk together the egg yolk and heavy cream. Use
a pastry brush to lightly brush the egg wash over the
dough. Sprinkle the remaining 1 teaspoon of sugar over
the entire galette. Bake until the crust is golden and the
juices are bubbling, 35 to 40 minutes. Set on a wire rack
to cool. Serve it warm or at room temperature.

JAM DAY

On one of the first Saturdays in spring—before the season's cooking classes officially begin—we head to the market and fill our baskets with provisions for lunch. Our early spring lunches include absolutely everything we can find at the *marché* (market)—spring peas and wild garlic; baby leeks; white, green, and wild asparagus; morels; and beautiful black-feathered *pintade* (guinea hen). When we spot the very first strawberries of the season, we know spring has officially arrived.

In France, we are delighted to have many varieties of heirloom strawberries. There are floral Mara des Bois, ruby-red Charlottes, plump Ciflorettes, and tiny, wild Fraises des Bois—all extremely fragrant and each with their own unique flavor and perfume. But the very first to arrive are Gariguettes. These delicate berries are at the market for only a few weeks, and their arrival marks the start of our jam season. Sweet and delicious, like you'd imagine an old-fashioned strawberry might taste, Gariguettes are perfect for making confiture. We return to the Atelier with crates of them to begin our first small batch.

We start our jam-day ritual by preparing our old French copper confiture pot—the one that we purchased over a decade ago in Auxerre. This well-worn and patinaed copper pot is one of our favorites, and has been used to make scores of jam.

We slice the berries and pile them in the confiture pot with sugar and lemon (and sometimes vanilla), turn the heat on high, and pull up a stool so that Luc and Manon can take turns stirring. As galettes bake in the oven, and sweet pea soup simmers on the back of the stove, delicious aromas fill the kitchen. It's a wonderful way to spend an early spring Saturday.

Baby Leek Galettes with Goat Cheese and Wild Garlic

SERVES 6

Rustic and beautiful, these galettes are a wonderful beginning to a spring lunch. You can also make this as one large galette and serve it alongside a leafy green salad. Search your farmers' market for wild garlic leaves or fresh ramp leaves, as they complement the freshness of the goat cheese. If you can't find wild garlic or fresh ramps, garlic chives and garlic scapes are good alternatives.

12 to 14 baby leeks, white and light green parts only

3 tablespoons unsalted butter

Leaves from 6 sprigs thyme

½ cup (120 ml) dry white wine, such as Burgundy Chardonnay

½ cup (120 ml) crème fraîche

Fleur de sel and freshly ground black pepper

1 large egg, beaten

2 tablespoons finely chopped fresh flat-leaf parsley

½ recipe Pâte Brisée (page 379)

Unbleached all-purpose flour, for dusting

1 cup (115 g) crumbled fresh goat cheese

Handful of wild garlic leaves or ramp leaves, coarsely chopped

1 large egg yolk

3 tablespoons heavy cream

Preheat the oven to 400°F (205°C). Line a baking sheet with parchment paper.

Halve each leek lengthwise, then cut them crosswise into thin slices. Rinse the leeks in a large bowl of cold water, swishing to remove any sand. Using your hands, transfer the leeks to a colander to drain, leaving the sand in the bottom of the bowl.

In a large sauté pan, melt the butter over medium heat. Add the leeks, thyme, and ½ cup (120 ml) water and sauté until the leeks are tender, 10 to 12 minutes. Add the wine and cook until the liquid has reduced, 10 to 15 minutes more. Add the crème fraîche and stir to coat the leeks. Season with salt and pepper. Remove from the heat and let cool for 10 minutes. Add the beaten egg and parsley and stir to incorporate. Set aside.

Divide the pâte brisée into six equal pieces. On a lightly floured surface with a floured rolling pin, roll each piece into a round about 6 inches (15 cm) in diameter and ¼ inch (6 mm) thick. Brush off any excess flour with a pastry brush. Arrange the galette rounds on the parchment-lined baking sheet. Divide the leek mixture among the galettes, spreading it in the center and leaving a 1½-inch (4-cm) border. Sprinkle with the goat cheese and wild garlic leaves. Gently fold the border over the leek mixture, overlapping it as you go. In a small bowl, whisk together the egg yolk and heavy cream. Use a pastry brush to lightly brush the egg wash over the dough. Bake until the pastry is golden and the cheese is just starting to brown, 25 to 30 minutes. Serve warm.

Sweet Pea Soup with Crispy Bacon and Herbed Cream

SERVES 6

This bright-green soup can be made the day before you serve it, and is delicious served warm or cold. If you make it ahead, keep in mind that it will thicken—just add a little water or vegetable stock to thin the soup to your desired consistency.

3 tablespoons unsalted butter

1 large yellow onion, chopped

4 cups (960 ml) Vegetable Stock (page 355)

6 cups fresh shelled sweet peas (from 6 pounds/2.7 kg in the pod)

½ cup (25 g) fresh flat-leaf parsley leaves

¼ cup (13 g) fresh mint leaves

Fleur de sel and freshly ground black pepper

1 (¼- to ½-inch-/6- to 12-mm-thick) slice *lard fumé* or 2 slices thick-cut bacon, cut into lardons

¼ cup (60 ml) crème fraîche

2 tablespoons heavy cream

2 tablespoons finely chopped fresh chives

Chive blossoms or pea shoots (optional)

In a large heavy pot, melt the butter over medium heat. Add the onion and sauté until soft and translucent, about 5 minutes. Add 2 cups (480 ml) of the vegetable stock and bring it to a boil. Add the peas and simmer gently, adjusting the heat as needed, until tender, about 5 minutes. Remove from the heat and add the parsley, mint, and the remaining 2 cups (480 ml) vegetable stock. In a blender, puree the soup in batches until smooth, then strain through a chinois. Season with salt and pepper and set aside.

In a small sauté pan, cook the lardons over medium heat until crispy and cooked through, 5 to 8 minutes. Transfer them to the paper towel–lined plate to remove excess grease and set aside.

In a small bowl, whisk together the crème fraîche, heavy cream, and chives.

Divide the soup among bowls and top each with a spoonful of the crème fraîche mixture. Garnish with the lardons and chive blossoms, if using, and serve immediately.

Pintade with Green Asparagus and Morels

SERVES 6

Pintade, or guinea hen, is a black-feathered fowl that is popular in France.
Though sometimes compared to a farm chicken, its meat is darker and leaner and, in our
opinion, more flavorful. It pairs very nicely with tender asparagus and the first morels
of the season. If you can't find guinea hen, use a small, farm-and-pasture-raised chicken.

FOR THE GUINEA HEN

1 (3¼- to 3½-pound/1.5- to
1.6-kg) guinea hen

Fleur de sel and freshly ground
black pepper

2 tablespoons extra-virgin olive
oil, preferably French

6 sprigs thyme

2 fresh bay leaves

**FOR THE ASPARAGUS AND
MORELS**

1½ pounds (680 g) green
asparagus, trimmed

1 tablespoon extra-virgin olive
oil, preferably French

3 tablespoons unsalted butter

1 cup (110 g) fresh morels,
halved if large

Fleur de sel and freshly ground
black pepper

FOR THE PAN SAUCE

¼ cup (60 ml) dry white
wine, such as Burgundy
Chardonnay

1 cup (240 ml) Chicken Stock
(page 357)

Fleur de sel and freshly ground
black pepper

1 teaspoon unsalted butter

Make the guinea hen: Preheat the oven to 450°F (230°C).

Remove the guinea hen from the refrigerator and
let it come to room temperature before cooking. Rinse
and thoroughly dry the guinea hen inside and out. Use
kitchen tweezers to remove any pin feathers or quills as
needed. Cut the guinea hen into pieces (see page 348)
and season with salt and pepper.

In a large sauté pan, heat 1 tablespoon of the olive
oil over medium-high heat until hot but not smoking.
Working in batches, without crowding the pan, add about
half of the guinea hen pieces, skin-side down, and sear,
turning once or twice, until golden brown on all sides, 4 to
5 minutes. Transfer them to a large platter, and repeat with
the remaining pieces and olive oil.

Remove the pan from the heat and pour off the fat. Add
the dark meat back into the pan, leaving the breast meat
on the platter. Add the thyme and bay leaves. Place the pan
in the oven and roast until the dark meat is almost cooked
through, about 20 minutes. Add the breast meat to the pan
and continue roasting until a meat thermometer inserted
in the thickest part of the breast reaches 160°F (70°C),
about 15 minutes more. The internal temperature will rise
to 165°F (75°C) upon standing. Let the guinea hen rest on a
warm platter while you prepare the vegetables and the pan
sauce. Reserve the pan with the meat juices.

Make the asparagus and morels: Bring a large pot of
salted water to a boil and fill a bowl with ice and water.

Add the asparagus to the boiling water and blanch
until tender, 3 to 4 minutes, depending on the size. The
asparagus are done when you can put the tip of a paring
knife into a spear and it's tender throughout.

Recipe continues on page 100

Immediately plunge the asparagus spears into the ice water to stop the cooking and preserve their color. Once the asparagus is cool, set on a clean kitchen towel to drain. Set aside.

Heat the olive oil and 1 tablespoon of the butter in a small sauté pan over medium heat. Add the morels and a ½ cup (120 ml) water and season with salt and pepper. Cover and simmer for 2 to 3 minutes. Add another 1 tablespoon butter and cook, uncovered and stirring occasionally, until the morels are tender and the liquid has evaporated, 2 to 3 minutes. Season with salt and pepper and keep warm.

In a medium sauté pan, melt the remaining 1 tablespoon butter over medium heat. Add the asparagus and sauté until the spears are warmed through and the butter is nutty brown, 3 to 5 minutes, depending on the size. Season with salt and pepper and keep warm.

Make the pan sauce: Remove all but 1 teaspoon of the fat from the pan used to roast the guinea hen, making sure to leave any bits of meat. Place the pan over medium-high heat. Add the white wine and use a wooden spoon to scrape any little bits off the bottom. Simmer until the wine is reduced by half, about 1 minute. Add the chicken stock and bring to a simmer. Continue simmering, adjusting the heat as needed, until reduced by half, about 5 minutes. Strain through a fine-mesh strainer into a medium saucepan and place over medium heat. Bring to a simmer and continue simmering until reduced to the desired consistency. Season with salt and pepper, then remove from the heat, add the butter, and swirl the pan until it's incorporated.

Add the morels to the serving dish or platter with the guinea hen and drizzle some of the pan sauce over both. Serve with the asparagus and the rest of the pan sauce.

Shortcakes with Homemade Strawberry Confiture

SERVES 8

Light and crumbly, with just a hint of sweetness, these shortcakes pair perfectly with any number of seasonal fruit jams. In spring, we make shortcakes using strawberries and apricots. In the summer months, we use peaches, blueberries, raspberries, blackberries, and nectarines. We recommend using a 2½-inch (6-cm) round pastry cutter, but feel free to use a different size if you like.

FOR THE STRAWBERRIES

1 pound (455 g) very ripe strawberries, hulled and halved

3 tablespoons granulated sugar

1½ tablespoons fresh lemon juice

FOR THE SHORTCAKES

3 cups (375 g) unbleached all-purpose flour, plus more for dusting

⅓ cup (65 g) granulated sugar, plus more for sprinkling

1 tablespoon baking powder

½ teaspoon fleur de sel

¾ cup (1½ sticks/170 g) cold unsalted butter, cut into small pieces

1 tablespoon lemon zest

1 cup (240 ml) heavy cream, plus more as needed

1 cup (240 ml) Gariguette Strawberry Confiture (page 390)

FOR THE WHIPPED CREAM

½ cup (120 ml) heavy cream

1 tablespoon confectioners' sugar

Make the strawberries: In a medium bowl, gently toss together the strawberries, granulated sugar, and lemon juice. Set aside.

Make the shortcakes: Preheat the oven to 425°F (220°C). Line a baking sheet with parchment paper.

In a large bowl, whisk together the flour, granulated sugar, baking powder, and salt. Add the butter. Using your hands, gently work the butter into the flour mixture until it resembles coarse cornmeal, with some pieces of butter visible. Add the lemon zest and toss to incorporate.

Drizzle the heavy cream over the dough and use a fork to gently toss just until the mixture comes together. Be careful not to overwork the dough—it should appear soft, but crumbly, with no signs of dry flour. If the dough looks too dry, add a little more cream.

On a lightly floured surface with a lightly floured rolling pin, roll the dough to a 1 inch (2.5 cm) thickness. Using a 2½-inch (6-cm) round pastry cutter, cut the dough into circles. Gather up the remaining dough, roll it to a 1 inch (2.5 cm) thickness, and cut out more circles. Repeat until all the dough is used. Place the shortcakes 2 inches (5 cm) apart on the parchment-lined baking sheet. Refrigerate for 1 hour.

Using a pastry brush, brush the top of each shortcake with a little heavy cream, then sprinkle with granulated sugar. Bake until the shortcakes are golden brown, about 15 minutes. Transfer them to a wire rack to cool.

Make the whipped cream: In a large bowl, combine the heavy cream and confectioners' sugar, then use a balloon whisk to beat until soft peaks form.

Assemble the shortcakes: Cut the shortcakes in half horizontally. Create layers, alternating with the strawberry confiture, fresh strawberry mixture, and whipped cream, and a final drizzle of confiture. Serve immediately.

DINNER IN THE WINE SHOP

The addition of the wine shop at The Cook's Atelier has become an extended living space for us, as we enjoy having friends from town stop in for an impromptu visit and a glass of wine. After the market on Saturdays, we have regulars who stop in for coffee, and perhaps pick up a bottle or two of wine to take home for dinner. In late spring and throughout summer, we leave the door open and often sit outside, enjoying a glass of wine after a busy day of cooking. The kids play out on the sidewalk, and we chat with friends and neighbors as they pass by.

Throughout the season, we host private dinner parties in the shop, both for friends and for clients. With its stone walls, hand-wrought iron wine racks, and hanging copper pots, the shop creates a lovely and inviting ambiance for a dinner party. We host Thanksgiving here every year, as well as an annual wine dinner in November during the Hospices de Beaune celebration. We select local wines to pair with each course, pulled directly from the racks surrounding the table. On occasion, we'll invite a local winemaker as our guest of honor, and feature wines from his or her domaine.

The shop has become a neighborhood gathering place, which was an unexpected but welcome surprise.

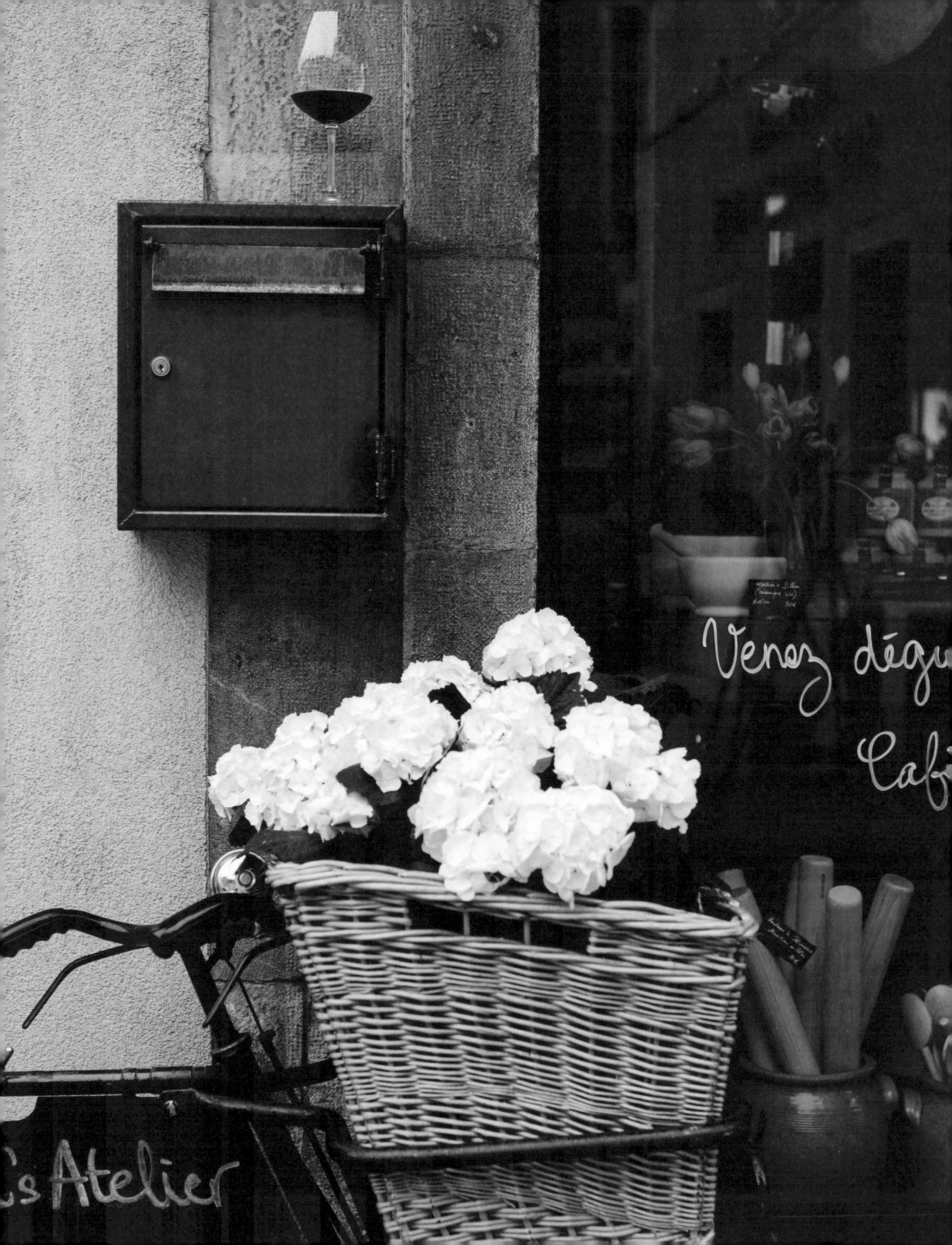
Venez dégu
Caf
Atelier

White Asparagus with Hollandaise and Garden Chervil

SERVES 6

White asparagus and lemony hollandaise are practically made for each other. This classic sauce is the perfect accompaniment to tender asparagus or the first artichokes of the season.

1½ pounds (680 g) white asparagus

Fleur de sel

1 tablespoon unsalted butter

Freshly ground white pepper

1 recipe Sauce Hollandaise (page 368), warm

Small handful of fresh chervil leaves, for garnish

Peel the asparagus, then use your hands to snap off the tough ends. Using a paring knife, cut the bottoms on an angle, making a clean edge.

Bring a large pot of salted water to a boil and fill a bowl with ice and water.

Add the asparagus to the boiling water and blanch until tender, 6 to 10 minutes, depending on the size. The asparagus is done when you can put the tip of a paring knife into a spear and it's tender throughout. Immediately plunge the asparagus into the ice water to stop the cooking. Once the asparagus is cool, set the spears on a clean kitchen towel to drain.

In a medium sauté pan, melt the butter over medium heat. Add the asparagus and sauté until the spears are warmed through and the butter is nutty brown, about 5 minutes. Season with salt and pepper. Place the asparagus on warm plates, drizzle with the warm hollandaise, and garnish with the chervil.

Green Garlic Soufflé

SERVES 8

Our savory soufflé begins with a béchamel base and is inspired by Julia Child. The base can be adapted using a variety of ingredients as flavorings. In the springtime, we like to infuse the milk with fresh green garlic, ramps, or even a bouquet garni before preparing the béchamel.

5 tablespoons (30 g) freshly grated Parmesan cheese

1¼ cups (300 ml) whole milk

8 stalks young, green garlic, white and pale-green parts only, halved lengthwise

3 tablespoons unsalted butter, plus more for the mold

¼ cup (30 g) unbleached all-purpose flour

½ teaspoon fleur de sel

¼ teaspoon freshly ground black pepper

4 large egg yolks

¾ cup (85 g) coarsely grated Comté or Gruyère cheese

A pinch of freshly grated nutmeg

1 teaspoon dry mustard (optional)

7 large egg whites

Set a rack in the middle of the oven and preheat the oven to 425°F (220°C). Butter the inside of a 6-cup (1.4-L) soufflé mold or eight individual 1-cup (240-ml) ramekins. Sprinkle the inside of the mold(s) with some of the Parmesan, reserving any excess. Set aside.

In a saucepan, combine the milk and green garlic. Place over medium heat and bring to just under a boil. Remove from the heat and steep for about 15 minutes to infuse the garlic into the milk. When ready to prepare the soufflé, bring the milk back to just under a boil, then strain out and discard the garlic.

In a medium saucepan, melt the butter over medium heat. Add the flour and stir briskly with a wooden spoon until the butter and flour come together, being careful not to let the mixture brown, about 1 minute. Add the hot milk, all at once, and whisk to blend well. Add the salt and pepper, whisking continuously, until the béchamel becomes thick, about 1 to 2 minutes. Remove from the heat and add the egg yolks, one at a time, until incorporated. Add the Comté, nutmeg, and dry mustard (if using) and stir until fully combined. Transfer the soufflé base to a large bowl and let cool slightly.

In a large, very clean, preferably copper bowl, use a large balloon whisk to beat the egg whites until firm peaks form. Stir a large spoonful of the whipped egg whites into the base to begin lightening it. Using a rubber spatula, gently fold in the remaining egg whites, working quickly to keep the base light and airy.

Pour the finished mixture into the prepared mold(s), filling it just below the top rim. Sprinkle the top with the remaining Parmesan. Bake on the middle rack of the oven until the top is golden brown and lifted about 2 inches (5 cm) over the edge of the mold, 25 to 30 minutes (15 to 18 minutes for the ramekins). Do not be tempted to open the oven during baking or the soufflé will fall. Serve immediately.

Roasted Leg of Lamb with
Fava Beans, Rosemary, Sage, and Lemon

SERVES 8 TO 10

Lamb is at its very best in the spring, and we make this dish at least once a year
in celebration of the season. Surprisingly simple to prepare,
this roasted leg of lamb is perfect for large gatherings around the table.

FOR THE LAMB

1 (6-pound/2.7-kg) whole
   bone-in leg of lamb

10 sprigs rosemary, plus more
   for garnish

Fleur de sel and freshly ground
   black pepper

Extra-virgin olive oil, preferably
   French

1 tablespoon unsalted butter

8 cloves garlic, smashed

1 lemon, thinly sliced, for
   serving

1 small handful of fresh sage,
   for serving

FOR THE FAVA BEANS

6 cups fresh shelled fava beans
   (from 6 pounds/2.7 kg in the
   pod)

Fruity extra-virgin olive oil,
   preferably French

Fleur de sel and freshly ground
   black pepper

Make the lamb: Remove the leg of lamb from the refrigerator and let it come to room temperature before roasting. Remove any fell, the papery membrane covering the leg of lamb, plus any thick sections of fat. Be sure to leave a thin layer of the fat, so the lamb doesn't dry out while roasting. Pat the lamb dry.

Preheat the oven to 400°F (205°C).

Using kitchen twine, tie the roast to secure the meat for even roasting (see page 345). Place the sprigs of rosemary under the twine. Season with salt and pepper.

In a large roasting pan, heat a drizzle of olive oil over medium-high heat until hot but not smoking. Add the lamb and sear, turning, until browned and caramelized on all sides, 6 to 8 minutes. Add the butter and garlic and, as soon as the butter melts, use a spoon to baste the lamb for a few minutes. Place the pan in the oven and roast until a meat thermometer inserted in the thickest part of the meat reaches 130°F (55°C) for medium-rare, about 1 hour. The internal temperature will rise to 145°F (63°C) upon standing. Let the leg of lamb rest on a warm cutting board for about 20 minutes before carving.

Make the fava beans: Bring a large pot of salted water to a boil and fill a bowl with ice and water.

Add the fava beans to the boiling water and blanch until just tender, 3 to 5 minutes. Immediately plunge the fava beans into the ice water to stop the cooking and preserve their color. Once the fava beans are cool enough to handle, remove them, then pop off their pale green skins to release the bright green beans. Discard the skins. Place the beans in a large bowl and drizzle with the olive oil and season with salt and pepper.

Serve the lamb whole on a large platter surrounded with the fava beans, lemon slices, and sage. Garnish with rosemary.

Rustic Apricot Tart

MAKES 1 (9-INCH/23-CM) TART OR 8 (4-INCH/10-CM) TARTLETS

At the market in Beaune, we have the most beautiful rose-colored Bergeron apricots
in the late spring and early summer. They are perfect for this tart, as they are sweet
and delicate, yet still hold their shape well. If you can't find the Bergeron variety,
feel free to use any type of small apricot. Be sure to work quickly after adding the sugar
and lemon mixture to the apricots, so they don't lose too much of their juice.

Unbleached all-purpose flour,
   for dusting

½ recipe Pâte Sucrée (page 378)

1 large egg yolk

3 tablespoons heavy cream

½ cup (100 g) granulated sugar,
   plus more for sprinkling

Seeds of ½ vanilla bean
   (see page 64)

¼ teaspoon fleur de sel

2 pounds (910 g) Bergeron
   apricots

Confectioners' sugar, for
   dusting

Crème fraîche or whipped
   cream, for serving

On a lightly floured surface, use the pâte sucrée to make
the tart shell (see page 374). Freeze it for 15 to 20 minutes
before baking.

Preheat the oven to 375°F (190°C).

In a small bowl, whisk together the egg yolk and
heavy cream. Use a pastry brush to lightly brush the egg
wash over the dough. Partially blind bake the tart shell
(see page 333).

Raise the oven temperature to 400°F (205°C).

In a small bowl, combine the sugar, vanilla seeds, and
salt. Set aside.

Cut the apricots in half and remove the pits. If the
apricots are small, cut them into quarters; if they're large,
cut them into eighths. Place the apricots in a large bowl,
sprinkle with the sugar mixture, and gently toss until
evenly coated.

Working quickly, arrange the apricot slices, tightly
overlapping, on the bottom of the tart shell, forming a
tight, compact circle. The apricots will shrink as they
cook, so try to fit as much fruit in the tart shell as possible.
Scrape any remaining sugar mixture left in the bowl over
the apricots, then lightly sprinkle them with more sugar.
Bake until the pastry is golden and the fruit is cooked
through and slightly caramelized, 40 to 45 minutes. The
finished tart should have a jamlike consistency, with a
golden, flaky crust. The liquid will be bubbling. Let the
tart cool to room temperature before serving and then
dust with confectioner's sugar. Serve with a dollop of
crème fraîche. The tart is best eaten the day it is made.

THE LITTLE ONES

Luc and Manon have always been a very important part of the adventure. We knew before they even arrived that we wanted The Cook's Atelier to be an extension of their home, and a place to which they would enjoy coming. At the beginning of the journey, on rue Maufoux, Luc was right at home in the kitchen, just a week after his birth. Cradled in his baby sling, he peacefully slept amid the rhythmic clank of copper pots during the cooking class, and continued on while the plates were served and the wine was poured. Guests loved the family atmosphere and marveled at the sweet, quiet baby who never made a peep.

Luc was the tiny age of two when we moved to the shop on rue de Lorraine. His little sister, Manon, arrived shortly after in the spring. As with all new beginnings, the first few months at the new Atelier were hectic. But she, too, fell right into sync and nestled up in the baby sling as we went about our day setting up shop and cooking in the kitchen.

Both being born on market days—Luc on a Saturday and Manon on a Wednesday—it's only fitting that we sometimes celebrate their birthdays at the shop with a simple menu, appropriate for little ones. We've set up two little wooden chairs for them underneath our display of copper cookware where, after school, they'll sit and greet guests with an exuberant "*Bonjour!*" During a cooking class, they are sure to pop into the kitchen for warm gougères. On Wednesdays, they spend the afternoon with us in the kitchen making bread or cookies, or "working" with Papa (aka Laurent) in the wine shop.

On any given day, you may see Luc flying around on his vintage red tricycle or Manon "cooking" with her tiny copper pots, or you may find them sitting on the shop's front steps together, enjoying an ice cream cone. Our tiny cooks in training will always have a spot at The Cook's Atelier.

Limonade with Fresh Mint

MAKES ABOUT 4 QUARTS (3.8 L)

Full of fresh-squeezed lemons and mint leaves from the garden, this lemonade
is refreshing on a warm spring or summer day.

3 cups (720 ml) fresh lemon
juice (from about 16 lemons)

1½ cups (300 g) sugar, plus
more if needed

3 quarts (208 L) cold water

1 lemon, sliced

Handful of fresh mint leaves

In a large bowl, combine the lemon juice and sugar and
stir until the sugar is dissolved. Add the cold water and
stir, then taste for tartness and add more sugar, as needed.

Pour the lemonade into a large pitcher or jug and
chill it. Serve over ice and garnish with the lemon slices
and mint.

Spring Vegetables with Aïoli

SERVES 6

Aïoli is a classic, garlicky sauce from the south of France. We prefer to make ours the old-fashioned way, by hand. When making aïoli, it's important to use the freshest eggs you can find. Serve it alongside any crisp raw vegetables, shellfish, or grilled meats and fish.

3 very fresh cloves garlic, smashed

½ teaspoon fleur de sel, plus more as needed

1 large egg yolk, preferably from a farm egg, at room temperature

1½ cups (360 ml) fruity extra-virgin olive oil, preferably French

1½ tablespoons fresh lemon juice, plus more as needed

Radishes, carrots, and blanched green asparagus (see page 339), for serving

In a heavy mortar, mash together the garlic and salt using the pestle, until they form a smooth paste. Set aside. In a bowl, add the egg yolk. While whisking continuously, begin to very slowly drizzle in the olive oil, just a few drops at a time, until the mixture begins to thicken. Be careful not to add too much olive oil at once or the mixture will break. Continue whisking until all the olive oil has been incorporated. Whisk in the garlic paste and lemon juice. Taste and season with additional lemon juice or salt as needed.

Serve the aïoli with the vegetables.

New Potato Pissaladières with Jambon Cru and Green Onions

MAKES 4 FLATBREADS; SERVES 8

Pissaladière is the equivalent of a French pizza, originating in the South of France.
We make ours in our bread oven year-round using seasonal, fresh ingredients from the market.

FOR THE DOUGH

1½ cups (360 ml) warm (about 110°F/43°C) water

2¼ teaspoons active dry yeast

¼ cup (60 ml) extra-virgin olive oil, preferably French, plus more for the bowl

4 cups (500 g) unbleached all-purpose flour, plus more as needed

2 teaspoons fleur de sel

1 teaspoon freshly ground black pepper

2 tablespoons fresh thyme leaves (optional)

FOR THE TOPPING

1½ pounds (680 g) new potatoes, scrubbed

4 green onions, trimmed

Extra-virgin olive oil, preferably French

16 slices jambon cru (dry-cured ham) or prosciutto

Leaves from 2 sprigs rosemary, finely chopped

Fleur de sel and freshly ground black pepper

Handful of fresh chervil leaves, for garnish

Make the dough: In a large bowl, combine the warm water and yeast and whisk to dissolve the yeast. Let the yeast proof for 10 to 15 minutes. Add the olive oil and stir to combine.

In a second large bowl, whisk together the flour, salt, pepper, and thyme, if using. Add this mixture to the proofed yeast and stir until smooth.

Lightly oil a large bowl. Turn the flour and yeast mixture onto a lightly floured work surface. Use a bench scraper and your hands to bring the dough together. It will be a little sticky. Knead, adding flour, as needed, until the dough becomes mostly uniform and easier to handle, about 5 minutes. Shape the dough into a ball and place it in the oiled bowl, turning to coat the dough in the oil. Cover with a damp kitchen towel and let rest in a warm, dry place until doubled in size, 2 to 3 hours.

Make the topping: Preheat the oven to 400°F (205°C). Line two baking sheets with parchment paper.

Bring a large pot of salted water to a boil. Using a mandoline, thinly slice the potatoes. Add the potatoes to the boiling water and blanch until tender but still holding their shape, about 8 minutes. Drain the potatoes, then place them on a clean kitchen towel to remove any excess moisture.

Cut the green onions crosswise into thin slices, reserving the greens. In a medium sauté pan, heat a drizzle of olive oil over medium heat. Add the whites of the green onions and sauté just until tender, about 8 minutes. Set aside.

Make the pissaladières: Remove the dough from the bowl and divide it into four equal pieces. Using your hands, gently shape each piece into a rough oval shape and place two on each parchment-lined baking sheet. Drizzle the dough with olive oil. Arrange the potatoes, green onions, and jambon cru on top of each piece of dough. Sprinkle with the rosemary and season with salt and pepper. Bake until the crust is golden brown and the onions are caramelized, 15 to 20 minutes.

Scatter the chervil and the reserved green onion greens on top and serve warm.

Chocolate Layer Cake

MAKES 1 THREE-LAYER CAKE

This chocolate layer cake is a favorite. We bake the cake the day before we plan to frost it, to be sure it is completely cool before assembling. For special birthdays, we sometimes double the cake batter to make a six-layer cake. If you end up with extra ganache, store it in the refrigerator and reheat it in a heatproof glass bowl over boiling water to make chocolate-covered strawberries or cherries for another day.

FOR THE CAKE

2 cups (250 g) unbleached all-purpose flour

1 cup (95 g) unsweetened cocoa powder, plus more for the pans

1½ teaspoons baking powder

1 teaspoon fleur de sel

1 cup (240 ml) whole milk

½ cup (120 ml) crème fraîche

1 cup (2 sticks/225 g) unsalted butter, at room temperature, plus more for the pans

2 cups (400 g) sugar

5 large eggs

Seeds of 1 vanilla bean (see page 64)

FOR THE GANACHE

2 pounds (910 g) high-quality bittersweet chocolate (at least 70% cacao), finely chopped

4 cups (960 ml) heavy cream

Make the cake: Preheat the oven to 350°F (175°C).

Place a piece of parchment paper on a cutting board and set an 8-inch (20-cm) round cake pan on top. Holding the pan securely with one hand, use a paring knife to trace around the pan and create a parchment circle to fit in the bottom of the pan. Repeat for the remaining two cake pans.

Butter the cake pans, then place a parchment circle in the bottom of each. Butter the parchment. Dust the cake pans with cocoa powder, tapping out any excess.

Sift the flour, cocoa powder, baking powder, and salt into a medium bowl and set aside.

In a small bowl, combine the milk and crème fraîche. Set aside.

In the bowl of an electric stand mixer fitted with the paddle attachment, cream the butter on medium-high speed until pale and light in color. Add the sugar and continue to beat until creamy. Add the eggs, one at a time, incorporating each egg before adding the next and scraping the sides of the bowl with a rubber spatula as needed. Add the vanilla seeds and mix to combine. Lower the speed of the mixer and add the flour mixture, a third at a time, alternating with the milk mixture. Scrape down the sides of the bowl and mix until just combined.

Pour the batter into the prepared cake pans and use an offset spatula to spread it evenly (if doubling the batter to make a six-layer cake, you'll fill each of the cake pans with more batter). Tap each pan on the counter to remove any air bubbles. Bake until a paring knife inserted in the center comes out clean, about 25 to 30 minutes. Set the pans on a wire rack and let the cakes cool completely. Run an offset spatula or small knife around the edges of

Recipe continues on page 128

the pans to loosen the cakes. Set a wire rack on top of one of the cakes and carefully flip it over to release the cake. Remove the pan and parchment. Place a second wire rack on top of the cake and carefully flip it again. Repeat with the remaining two cakes. Once completely cooled, wrap the cakes in plastic wrap and set aside.

Make the ganache: Place the chocolate in a large heatproof bowl. In a medium saucepan, heat the heavy cream over medium heat until just under a boil. Be careful not to boil the cream or it will scald. Pour the hot cream over the chocolate and let it stand for a few minutes to melt the chocolate. Stir with a rubber spatula until smooth and glossy. Allow the mixture to cool at room temperature until it thickens slightly.

Assemble the cake: Using a long serrated knife, carefully cut a small amount off the top of each cake to make them flat, if necessary. (If making a six-layer cake, cut each cake horizontally in half to make two layers—you should have a total of six layers.)

Place a small spoonful of ganache in the center of a cake stand, then set the first cake layer on top, cut-side up. Add a large dollop of ganache and use a small offset spatula to spread it evenly over the top of the cake layer. Continue adding cake layers and ganache until you have three or six layers, with the last being cut-side down. Don't spread ganache on top of the final cake layer. If the cake appears to be sliding, use long wooden skewers to hold it straight until the ganache has a chance to firm up. Refrigerate the cake until set, about 1 hour.

Remove the skewers from the cake, if using. Frost the top and the sides of the cake with the remaining ganache, leaving some for decoration, if desired. In a pastry bag fitted with a decorative tip, pipe little stars around the bottom and top edges of the cake. At this point, the ganache should be firm enough to pipe, but if it's too soft, refrigerate it briefly until it's the right consistency. This cake keeps well covered with plastic wrap or under a cake dome at room temperature for a couple of days.

SUMMER

Summertime in Burgundy is a season of abundance. The cool, rainy spring gives way to hot, sunny days and balmy evenings. The rolling farmland surrounding Beaune is lush and green, dotted with sunflower fields, and the vineyards are full of grapes awaiting harvest. The market is at its busiest, full of vendors and shoppers, and the surrounding village *marchés aux puces* (flea markets) are bustling.

The market overflows with fresh produce: plump eggplants, striped green zucchini and yellow pattypan squash, speckled lemon cucumbers, fennel and green onions, bunches of peppery roquette, and all different varieties of basil. There are piles of red- and yellow-stemmed Swiss chard, crisp heads of lettuce, fragrant Charentais melons, sweet peaches, and rose-tinged white nectarines. We buy perfectly ripe berries—red currants, blackberries, white and red raspberries, blueberries, and wild woodland strawberries—to make into fruit tarts, and bouquets of sunflowers and daisies for the shop. We eagerly await the arrival of heirloom tomatoes, grown in every color and shape imaginable. They are so flavorful that you need little more than a sprinkle of fleur de sel and a drizzle of good French olive oil to make them into a meal.

Summer meals aren't cooked so much as they are assembled: composed salads, chilled soups, grilled meats, and vegetables find their place at our table. Desserts are simple and based around fresh fruit. We take advantage of the warm weather by eating outdoors as much as possible. Though Burgundy is known for its Pinot Noir and Chardonnay, in the summertime, we enjoy drinking dry, pale rosé from the South of France.

Summer is the busiest season of the year for us. When we're not shopping at the market, teaching classes, or working in the potager, we are preserving the summer's bounty, allowing us to savor the flavors of summer all year long.

BÉRENGÈRE POULET & CYRIL PAGÈS | BIODYNAMIC FARMERS

When you first meet Bérengère Poulet, you can't help but notice her bright blue eyes and her warm smile. We met her at the market in 2013, when she first started selling her produce, and we now visit her stand every Saturday morning. Her organic fruits and vegetables and handmade products—confitures, *gelées* (jellies), and raw honey from her bees—are of the highest quality, all grown and made on her farm.

The meticulous fifteen-acre (six-ha) farm that Bérengère runs with her partner, Cyril Pagès, is situated twenty miles (thirty-two km) southwest of Beaune. Their farm has no tractors, no fancy equipment, and no pesticides. All the work is done by hand, with an old-fashioned plow and a pair of donkeys, Narcisse and Nougat. They live in a small, slate-roofed stone farmhouse attached to their barn. Their dwelling is humble but pristine. Lace curtains hang in the windows, and a little wooden table for two sits out front, topped with potted plants. Their tiny kitchen is filled with rows of perfectly stacked jars of homemade confiture, pickles, elderberry syrup, *tisanes* (herbal tea), and honey.

The couple follows the tenets of biodynamics, a holistic approach to farming. Their goal is to grow the most delicious, pristine produce, while creating a diversified, balanced ecosystem on their land.

The pair purchased the farm—named Zacheries after the stream that flows through the property—in 2011. With her background in flowers and wine, and his experience working in an organic co-operative in Dijon, they both loved working outdoors and wanted to grow their own products.

They grow flawless vegetables, along with the freshest mesclun, wild garlic and tender salads greens, and a variety of herbs and edible flowers. In the spring, they hand-harvest baby stinging nettles, and in the summertime, they sell the most gorgeous berries—red and black currants, blueberries, tiny red and white strawberries, and colorful raspberries—that we make into fruit tarts and confiture.

CÉLINE & THÉO LOUBET | URBAN GARDENERS

In a nondescript industrial lot on the edge of town sits a large greenhouse and city garden where some of the best heirloom tomatoes in Burgundy are grown. Outside, a large plot of land overflows with summer vegetables: eggplant, zucchini, squash, peppers, green beans, tender lettuces, mizuna, green onions, and peppery dandelion greens. Large wooden wine barrels line the garden, planted with fresh herbs. We source from this city garden spring, summer, and autumn, and plan our menu around their offerings.

Welcome to Les Loups 'Bio, a second-generation biodynamic farm run by Céline and Théo Loubet. For this twentysomething brother-sister pair, the ability to grow plants is second nature. Born into a family of five children, the siblings grew up helping out on the farm and working at the market with their father, Yannick, who was one of the first producers at the market to obtain the AB—*Agriculture Biologique*—or organic certification. Céline and Théo continue this tradition and grow top-quality produce.

Céline and Théo took over the small farm in 2014, and they now oversee two locations: one in Beaune and one ten minutes away in Varennes. The pair spends most days in the summertime working in the greenhouse or in the garden, planting, watering, pruning, harvesting, and stacking produce in wooden crates to take to the market. The siblings share most duties on the farm, but Céline handles all the marketing and has grown the family business from a small market stand to direct-sourcing produce to some of the best restaurants in town.

SUPPER IN THE VINES

Living in Burgundy, everything is connected to wine, as the town of Beaune is quite literally surrounded by vines. To celebrate the long days of summer, we've often thought about how beautiful a dinner in the vineyards could be. So, we hatched a plan to throw a sunset barbecue in a vineyard for thirty of our closest friends. We soon realized, however, that hosting a supper amidst the vines in Burgundy is not quite that simple. These small parcels of land are privately owned and highly prized, and the idea of throwing a dinner in one of these noble *vignobles* (vineyards) is not something anyone would usually think to do. But we kept envisioning this beautiful vineyard dinner in our minds, and contacted a few winemaker friends to present the idea. After scouting the possible options, a Grand Cru vineyard, co-owned by a very good friend of ours and Jean-Nicolas Méo (see pages 49–50) of Domaine Méo-Camuzet, was the vineyard of choice. Somehow, we convinced both of them to let us proceed with our far-fetched plan.

Over the years, we've gotten comfortable with organizing and hosting large dinner parties. But it took quite a bit of planning to orchestrate a dinner of this magnitude outside the comfort of our Atelier, not to mention without a kitchen. We managed to pull it off, though, with the help of a few willing friends. We began the preparation several days before the party, and made sure to create a menu including some items that could be prepared ahead of time. The day of the event, we rented a big truck and loaded long wooden tables and Tolix chairs from the shop. We packed countless boxes of our tableware, French linens, candles, and all the necessary items we would need to prepare a dinner for thirty on-site. There were buckets of fresh market flowers from Madame Loichet (see page 74), and cases and cases of wine. We set up a makeshift grill, made out of an old steel barrel, just down the vineyard road.

As the sun set, we lit the candles and the guests began to arrive. We offered them chilled glasses of bubbly and, as they mingled, we set to work preparing our simple menu. We served each course with one of Jean-Nicolas's wines, and the main course was paired with wine from the very vineyard where the dinner party was held.

In true French fashion, the guests lingered well into the night, enjoying wine and conversation by candlelight. We look back on this very special, and probably once-in-a-lifetime summertime evening, and have to laugh. As well prepared as we were, even down to the smallest of details, neither of us took into consideration just how long the party would go on, and that we would have to pack everything up by moonlight.

Cucumber Salad with Strawberries and Lemon Vinaigrette

SERVES 8 TO 10

This simple salad makes for a refreshing amuse-bouche or first course on a hot summer day.
It is all about the quality of ingredients, so look for a variety of heirloom cucumbers ranging in
colors, shapes, and sizes. We like to use Fraises des Bois, tiny woodland strawberries gathered
from the woods near our kitchen potager. You can also use small, organic strawberries.

About 2 pounds (910 g) heirloom cucumbers in various sizes and colors

4 radishes

1 shallot, thinly sliced into rings

Fleur de sel and freshly ground black pepper

1 cup (145 g) red and yellow Fraises des Bois or tiny strawberries, hulled

Small handful of small fresh basil leaves

Small handful of small fresh purple basil leaves

1 (3½-ounce/100-g) wedge Parmesan cheese

1 recipe Vinaigrette (page 354), using the lemon juice variation

1 tablespoon finely chopped fresh chives

8 to 10 lemon wedges, for garnish

Using a mandoline, slice some of the larger cucumbers into long, thin ribbons and the rest into thin rounds. Cut any smaller cucumbers into wedges. Thinly slice the radishes lengthwise using a stainless-steel vegetable peeler. Transfer the cucumbers and radishes to a large bowl, add the shallot, season with salt and pepper, and toss to combine.

Arrange the cucumber mixture on chilled salad plates, overlapping and curling the cucumbers around each other for a pretty presentation. Divide the strawberries and basil leaves among the salads. With a stainless-steel vegetable peeler, shave the Parmesan into thin ribbons and divide it among the salads. Drizzle the salads with the vinaigrette and sprinkle with the chives. Garnish each plate with a lemon wedge and serve.

Heirloom Tomato Soup

SERVES 8 TO 10

In the height of summer, the Beaune market overflows with every shape, size,
and color of tomato imaginable. This soup is only as good as the tomatoes that
you use, so look for ripe, juicy ones. You can use any type or color of tomato, but we
strongly recommend that you purchase heirloom varieties at your farmers' market,
or source them from a friend with a garden. This soup is best served very cold.

FOR THE SOUP

4 pounds (1.8 kg) ripe heirloom
  tomatoes

2 medium cucumbers, peeled,
  seeded, and coarsely
  chopped

3 cloves garlic, coarsely
  chopped

¼ cup (60 ml) sherry vinegar

⅓ cup (80 ml) extra-virgin olive
  oil, preferably French

Fleur de sel and freshly ground
  black pepper

FOR THE GARNISH

1 medium cucumber, peeled,
  seeded, and finely diced

1 cup (150 g) finely diced
  assorted sweet peppers

1 cup (145 g) tiny heirloom
  tomatoes, halved or
  quartered, depending on
  their size

¼ cup (35 g) finely diced red
  onion or shallot

¼ cup (15 g) thinly sliced green
  onion greens

Small handful of small fresh
  basil leaves and blossoms
  (optional)

Fruity extra-virgin olive oil,
  preferably French, for
  drizzling

Make the soup: To peel the tomatoes, bring a large pot
of water to a boil and fill a bowl with ice and water. Use
a sharp paring knife to make a tiny X on the bottom of
each tomato. Working in batches, add the tomatoes to
the boiling water and blanch just until the skin is starting
to peel away, 30 to 60 seconds. Use a slotted spoon to
lift the tomatoes out of the boiling water and immediately plunge them into the ice water. Gently peel off the
tomato skins and coarsely chop the tomatoes, removing
and discarding the cores, but reserving the juices. Transfer
the chopped tomatoes and their juices to a large bowl and
add the cucumbers and garlic.

Working in batches, in a blender, puree the tomato
mixture, adding enough sherry vinegar and olive oil to
allow the mixture to spin. Blend until smooth, then strain
through a chinois into a 2-quart (2-L) container. Repeat
until all the soup is blended. Season with salt and pepper,
then cover and refrigerate until completely cold, or preferably overnight.

Make the garnish: In a small bowl, combine the
cucumbers, sweet peppers, tomatoes, red onion, and most
of the onion greens and most of the basil (if using). Divide
the garnish among 8 to 10 chilled, shallow soup bowls,
arranging it in the center. Remove the soup from the refrigerator and carefully ladle it into the bowls over the garnish.
Sprinkle with the remaining onion greens and basil (if
using), drizzle with olive oil, and serve immediately.

La Pièce de Boucher with Grilled Leeks, Pan-Roasted Tomatoes, and Summer Pesto

SERVES 8 TO 10

In France, *la pièce de boucher* (the butcher's cut) is a favorite cut of meat, and ideal for grilling. Traditionally, this was the leftover meat that the butcher would take home to his family—either a piece of meat that was too small to sell, or leftover beef trimmings, often including bits of filet, entrecôte, bavette, or various other pieces. We like maintaining the tradition of cooking la pièce de boucher, as it allows guests to sample different cuts of meat. When grilling, we cook over wood embers or grapevines, as it adds a nice aromatic note to the beef. Cooking time will vary, depending on the size and cut of meat you get from your butcher. This is a great dish for a gathering, as it can be easily adjusted depending on the size of your group.

FOR THE BEEF

3 pounds (1.4 kg) assorted beef cuts, such as filet, rib eye, sirloin, or flank

Extra-virgin olive oil, preferably French

Butcher's Fleur de Sel (page 67)

Freshly ground black pepper

FOR THE LEEKS

24 baby leeks

Extra-virgin olive oil, preferably French

Fleur de sel and freshly ground black pepper

FOR THE TOMATOES

24 red cherry tomatoes on the vine

Extra-virgin olive oil, preferably French

Fleur de sel and freshly ground black pepper

1 recipe Summer Pesto (page 151)

Make the beef: Remove the beef from the refrigerator and let it come to room temperature before grilling.

Prepare a grill for high-heat (450° to 500°F/230° to 260°C) cooking.

Drizzle the beef all over with olive oil and use your hands to rub the oil into the meat. Season the beef all over with the butcher's salt and pepper. Grill over high heat, flipping occasionally, until a meat thermometer inserted in the thickest part of each piece of meat reaches 120° to 130°F (50° to 55°C) for medium-rare. The internal temperature will rise to 145°F (63°C) upon standing. Let the beef rest on a warm cutting board.

Make the leeks: Trim the leeks, keeping only the white and palest green parts, then rinse and thoroughly dry them. Drizzle the leeks with olive oil, season with salt and pepper, and toss to coat.

Grill the leeks over high heat, turning occasionally, until tender, 5 to 8 minutes.

Make the tomatoes: Trim the tomatoes from the vine, keeping the stems intact. Place the tomatoes in a medium cast-iron pan, drizzle with olive oil, season with salt and pepper, and toss to coat.

Place the cast-iron pan on the grill over high heat and cook the tomatoes, shaking the pan as necessary to evenly cook, until the skins begin to split, 5 to 8 minutes.

To serve, thinly slice the beef. Arrange the beef, leeks, and tomatoes on large platters and serve them family-style, along with the pesto.

Summer Pesto

Pesto, the fragrant summer sauce of fresh basil, garlic, toasted pine nuts, Parmesan, and extra-virgin olive oil, is classically made by hand with a mortar and pestle. Making pesto in a food processor not only reduces flavor, but it bruises the basil and overheats the ingredients. The mortar and pestle version creates a much more authentic sauce with bold flavors and a bright green color. Pesto pairs well with beef or fish just off the grill and homemade pastas. Before you add the basil to the mortar, be sure to chop it first with a sharp knife or mezzaluna.

½ cup (65 g) pine nuts, toasted

5 cloves garlic

4 cups (160 g) fresh basil leaves

1 cup (240 ml) fruity extra-virgin olive oil, preferably French, plus more for storing

1 cup (100 g) freshly grated Parmesan cheese

Fleur de sel and freshly ground black pepper

In a large, heavy mortar, mash together the pine nuts and garlic using the pestle, until they form a rough paste with no large chunks of garlic. Chop the basil leaves with a mezzaluna or sharp knife. Add the chopped basil, a little at a time, to the garlic paste and continue to mash. As the mixture thickens, gradually drizzle in the olive oil, continuing to blend the mixture into a paste. Once the paste is mostly smooth and the ingredients are combined, stir in the Parmesan and any remaining oil, and season with salt and pepper.

To store, transfer the pesto to a glass jar, drizzle the surface with olive oil, cover, and refrigerate it until ready to use. The pesto will keep for several days in the refrigerator; bring it to room temperature before serving.

Butter Cake with Peaches and Raspberries

MAKES 1 (9-INCH/23-CM) CAKE; SERVES 8 TO 10

This is the perfect simple butter cake recipe. The fruit can be adapted, depending on the season
and the availability at the market. In early spring, we use the very first Gariguette strawberries.
In the summer months, we use a variety of stone fruits, as well as an assortment of fresh berries.
For the autumn and winter months, we like to use barely sautéed buttery pears or apples.
In the cooler months, be sure to let the sautéed fruit cool slightly before adding it to the top of the cake.
We often serve this with a dusting of confectioners' sugar and a dollop of whipped cream.

1 cup (240 ml) whole milk

¼ cup (60 ml) crème fraîche

1¾ cups (220 g) unbleached
all-purpose flour, plus more
for the pan

1 tablespoon baking powder

½ teaspoon fleur de sel

½ cup (1 stick/115 g) unsalted
butter, at room temperature,
plus more for the pan

¾ cup (150 g) granulated sugar

1 large egg

Seeds of 1 vanilla bean (see
page 64)

2 medium peaches, halved,
pitted, and thinly sliced

¼ cup (30 g) fresh raspberries

1 to 2 teaspoons vanilla sugar
(see page 64)

Preheat the oven to 350°F (175°C). Place a piece of parchment paper on a cutting board and set a 9-inch (23-cm) round cake pan on top. Holding the pan securely with one hand, use a paring knife to trace around the pan and create a parchment circle to fit in the bottom of the pan. Butter the cake pan, then place the parchment circle in the bottom. Butter the parchment. Dust the cake pan with flour, tapping out any excess.

In a medium bowl, whisk together the milk and crème fraîche.

In a large bowl, whisk together the flour, baking powder, and salt.

In a separate large bowl, use a wooden spoon to cream the butter until soft. Add the granulated sugar and continue creaming until well combined. Add the egg and vanilla seeds and continue creaming until fully incorporated.

Add the flour mixture and the milk mixture, alternating each addition, until smooth and combined.

Pour the batter into the prepared cake pan and use an offset spatula to spread it evenly. Arrange the sliced peaches in an overlapping, circular pattern, being careful not to let the fruit touch the side of the pan. Arrange the raspberries over and in between the peaches. Sprinkle with the vanilla sugar. Bake until the cake is golden and a paring knife inserted in the center comes out clean, about 45 minutes. Set the pan on a wire rack and let it cool completely. Serve.

FRENCH ROSÉ

When the weather turns warm in France, no matter where you go, rosé is often the beverage of choice. We first took a liking to it when Kendall was teaching English in the South of France, the year after she graduated from college. We've always been drawn to the bold flavors of the Provençal table and have fond memories of the local market in Nîmes, where she lived when she first arrived in France. Market stalls were full of salted capers, olives, sun-dried tomatoes, fresh anchovies, and other fish from the morning's catch. Some vendors sold their own rosé in bulk, and the locals would stand in line to refill old bottles to the brim.

As a nod to Laurent's Provençal roots and Kendall's memorable days in the South, each summer we host a gathering celebrating the food and wine of Provence, using what we find locally here in Burgundy. Pale, dry, and crisp, Provençal rosés, such as those originating from the town of Bandol, are the perfect complement to this menu.

Whether we are celebrating inside at the Atelier or outside at Kendall and Laurent's house, we serve the menu family-style, for a relaxing and leisurely French meal.

Chilled Zucchini Soup

SERVES 6 TO 8

This chilled summer zucchini soup becomes light and velvety, thanks to the addition
of butter and a little cream. It can be served hot or cold, but we prefer it cold with a tiny
dollop of savory whipped cream and a sprinkling of finely chopped garden chives and
lemon zest to brighten the flavors. This soup is best served on the day you make it.
We enjoy serving this soup as an amuse-bouche in small vintage glassware.

2 tablespoons unsalted butter

1 medium yellow onion, finely
  chopped

3 cloves garlic, finely chopped

2½ pounds (1.2 kg) zucchini,
  cut into very thin rounds

1 bouquet garni (see page 61)

Fleur de sel and freshly ground
  black pepper

1 quart (960 ml) Vegetable
  Stock (page 355)

1 teaspoon fresh lemon juice

1 cup (240 ml) heavy cream

Finely chopped fresh chives, for
  sprinkling

Pinch of lemon zest, for
  sprinkling

Fruity extra-virgin olive oil,
  preferably French, for
  drizzling

In a large heavy-bottomed saucepan, melt the butter
over medium heat. Add the onion and garlic and sauté
until the onion is soft and translucent, about 5 minutes.
Add the zucchini and the bouquet garni, season with
salt and pepper, and sauté until the zucchini starts to
soften, about 2 minutes. Add the vegetable stock, raise the
heat to medium-high, and bring it to a simmer. Simmer
gently, reducing the heat, as needed, until the zucchini is
very tender, about 15 minutes. Remove and discard the
bouquet garni.

Fill a bowl large enough to accommodate a 2-quart
(2-L) container with ice and water.

Working in batches, ladle the soup into a blender and
puree it until smooth. Strain the soup through a chinois
into a 2-quart (2-L) container. Stir in the lemon juice to
help preserve the color. Place the container inside the
bowl of ice water and let it cool, stirring occasionally,
until completely chilled. Taste and season as needed, then
stir in ½ cup (120 ml) of the heavy cream.

In a large bowl, use a balloon whisk to beat the
remaining ½ cup (120 ml) of heavy cream until it holds
soft peaks. Set aside.

Divide the soup among six to eight bowls (or six to
eight small vintage glasses) and top each with a dollop of
the savory whipped cream. Sprinkle with the chives and
lemon zest, drizzle with olive oil, and serve immediately.

Watermelon and Vineyard Peach Salad

SERVES 6 TO 8

This salad, with a surprising mix of colors, flavors, and textures, makes for a beautiful presentation whether served family-style or plated for individual servings. The ingredients represent the bounty of a Burgundian garden midsummer—the key is to source perfectly ripe fruit and garden vegetables. We dress this salad with a classic white wine vinaigrette, and finish it with a handful of crumbled creamy Charbonnat chèvre, a mild goat cheese from the region, although you can easily substitute a favorite mild goat cheese from a cheese maker in your area.

1 small watermelon (about 4 pounds/1.8 kg)

3 perfectly ripe vineyard (donut) peaches

1 medium cucumber, cut into thin rounds

1 small red onion, thinly sliced into rings

Handful of fresh raspberries

Large handful of tiny yellow tomatoes, halved or quartered

Small handful of small fresh green and purple basil leaves

Small handful of fresh flat-leaf parsley leaves

1 fresh Charbonnat chèvre, or 1 cup (115 g) crumbled mild fresh goat cheese

Fleur de sel and freshly ground black pepper

1 recipe Vinaigrette (page 354), using the white wine vinegar variation

Cut the watermelon into small wedges, removing the rind and the seeds if necessary. Cut the peaches in half, remove the pits, and cut them into wedges. Arrange the watermelon and peaches on a platter or divide them among six to eight individual salad plates—there should be 2 or 3 watermelon wedges and 3 or 4 peach wedges per plate. Tuck the cucumber, red onion, raspberries, and tomatoes in and around the watermelon and peaches and sprinkle with the basil and parsley. Crumble the chèvre over the salads and season with salt and pepper.

Drizzle the vinaigrette over the salads and serve immediately.

Pan-Seared Veal Chop with White Wine Jus

SERVES 6 TO 8

Every summer, we source amazing veal chops from our local butcher, Monsieur Vossot. This preparation makes for a wonderful summer main course, as it is light in flavor and can be served at room temperature. We like to pair veal with lemon, either fresh in wedges or halved and charred, served alongside our Vegetable Tian with Fried Basil (page 167).

FOR THE VEAL CHOPS

3 double (2-bone) veal chops, about 2 pounds/910 g each, Frenched (optional; see page 345)

Fleur de sel and freshly ground black pepper

Extra-virgin olive oil, preferably French

1 lemon, halved or cut into wedges

FOR THE PAN SAUCE

1 shallot, finely chopped

3 sprigs thyme

1 fresh bay leaf

½ cup (120 ml) dry white wine, such as Burgundy Chardonnay

2 cups (480 ml) White Veal Stock (page 359)

Fleur de sel and freshly ground black pepper

1 teaspoon unsalted butter

Preheat the oven to 375°F (190°C).

Make the veal chops: Remove the veal chops from the refrigerator and let them come to room temperature before cooking. Pat the veal dry, then season with salt and pepper.

In a large cast-iron skillet, heat a drizzle of olive oil over medium heat until hot but not smoking. Working in batches, add the veal chops and sear, turning, until nicely caramelized, 3 to 4 minutes per side.

Transfer the veal chops to a large roasting pan. Either add the lemon halves to the pan to char them or reserve the lemon wedges for serving. Place the pan in the oven and roast until a meat thermometer inserted in the thickest part of the meat reaches 130°F (55°C) for medium-rare, about 30 minutes. The internal temperature will rise to 145°F (63°C) upon standing. Let the veal chops rest on a warm cutting board for about 15 minutes before carving. Reserve the pan with the meat juices.

While the veal is resting, make the pan sauce: Remove all but 1 teaspoon of the fat from the pan used to roast the veal, making sure to leave any bits of meat. Heat the pan over medium-high heat. Add the shallot, thyme, and bay leaf and sauté until the shallots are soft and translucent, about 1 minute. Add the white wine and 1 cup (240 ml) of the veal stock and use a wooden spoon to scrape any little bits off the bottom. Simmer until the liquid is reduced by half, 5 to 10 minutes. Add the remaining 1 cup (240 ml) veal stock and bring to a simmer. Continue simmering, adjusting the heat as needed, until reduced by half, about 5 minutes. Strain through a fine-mesh strainer into a medium saucepan and place over medium heat. Bring to a simmer and continue simmering until reduced to the desired consistency. Season with salt and pepper, then remove from the heat, add the butter, and swirl the pan until it's incorporated.

When ready to serve, cut the veal chops, parallel to the bones, into thin slices. Serve the veal with the pan sauce and lemon wedges or charred lemon alongside.

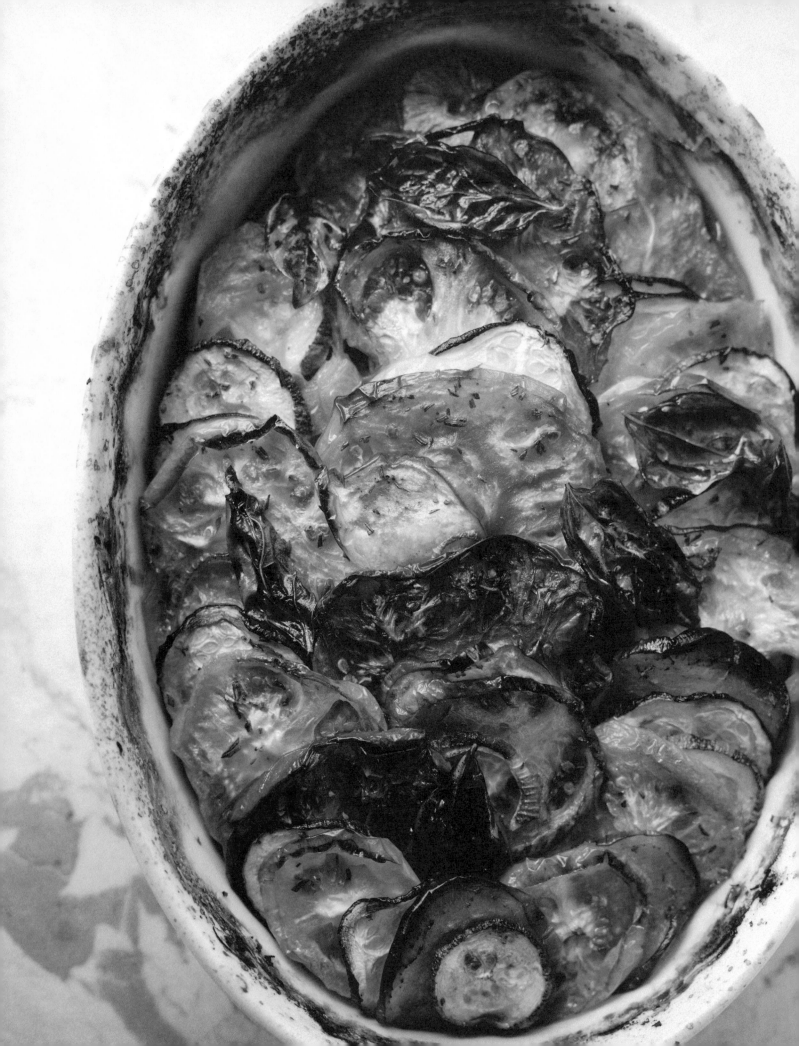

Vegetable Tian with Fried Basil

SERVES 6 TO 8

This tian can be served hot or at room temperature. We recommend that all the vegetables are roughly the same size, so that the slices have a uniform appearance in the finished dish. This would also be lovely as a main course with a leafy green salad.

FOR THE TIAN

1 clove garlic, smashed

6 assorted small heirloom tomatoes, cut into very thin rounds

2 small yellow zucchini, cut into very thin rounds

2 small green zucchini, cut into very thin rounds

2 small red onions, cut into very thin rounds

1 small purple striped or regular eggplant, cut into very thin rounds

Finely chopped fresh thyme, tarragon, rosemary, and oregano

Fleur de sel and freshly ground black pepper

Extra-virgin olive oil, preferably French

FOR THE FRIED BASIL

Organic canola oil, for frying

Handful of fresh basil leaves

Fleur de sel

Make the tian: Preheat the oven to 350°F (175°C).

Rub the bottoms and sides of a large gratin dish with the smashed garlic. Layer the tomatoes, zucchini, onions, and eggplant in the gratin dish, alternating the vegetables and fitting them very snugly into the dish. As you build each layer, sprinkle with fresh herbs and season with salt and pepper. Once the dish is full, drizzle with olive oil. Bake until the vegetables are tender, about 45 minutes.

Meanwhile, make the fried basil: Fill a 4-quart (3.8-L) heavy-bottomed saucepan with enough canola oil to come a quarter of the way up the sides. Heat the oil over medium heat until it registers 350°F (175°C) on a deep-fat thermometer. Line a baking sheet with paper towels.

Once the oil is hot, working in batches, carefully drop the basil leaves one at a time into the oil—the oil may splatter due to the moisture in the leaves. The basil will turn brilliant green and crisp in seconds. Use a slotted spoon to scoop the basil leaves from the oil and place them on the paper towel–lined baking sheet to absorb any excess oil. Sprinkle with salt. Repeat with the remaining basil, letting the oil return to 350°F (175°C) between batches. Sprinkle the tian with the fried basil and serve.

Summary Berry Tart

MAKES 1 (9-INCH/23-CM) TART OR 8 (4-INCH/10-CM) TARTLETS

When making this fresh fruit tart or tartlets, we use a colorful array of summer berries.
Look for any kind of fresh, seasonal berry at your local market, but don't forget to make the pastry
cream in advance, as it needs to set for about two hours in the refrigerator.

Unbleached all-purpose flour,
for dusting

½ recipe Pâte Sablée (page 377)

1 large egg yolk

½ cup (120 ml) plus
3 tablespoons heavy cream

1 tablespoon confectioners'
sugar

1 recipe Crème Pâtissière
(page 385)

1 cup (145 g) fresh blueberries

1 cup (125 g) fresh yellow
raspberries

1 cup (125 g) fresh red
raspberries

½ cup (82 g) fresh red currants

½ cup (82 g) fresh white or pink
currants

¼ cup (35 g) fresh white
woodland strawberries or
tiny strawberries, hulled

On a lightly floured surface, use the pâte sablée to make the tart shell (see page 374). Freeze it for 15 to 20 minutes before baking.

Preheat the oven to 375°F (190°C).

In a small bowl, whisk together the egg yolk and 3 tablespoons of the heavy cream. Use a pastry brush to lightly brush the egg wash over the dough. Blind bake the tart shell (see page 333).

In a large bowl, combine the remaining ½ cup (120 ml) heavy cream and the confectioners' sugar, then use a balloon whisk to beat them until soft peaks form. Add a spoonful of the whipped cream to the pastry cream and stir to lighten it.

Using an offset spatula or small knife, spread the pastry cream in the cooled tart shell. Top it with the fruit and serve immediately with the whipped cream alongside.

BASTILLE DAY

Bastille Day and the Fourth of July are equally important national holidays for our Franco-American family, so we combine them into one big Independence Day fête. We celebrate on a weekend in mid-July with flags, sparklers, and a summery meal, served under the eaves of the old barn near the creek at our house, not far from the potager. It's a casual, outdoor family affair, which often starts in the late afternoon. We gather greens from the garden, prepare the meal together, and set the table. If it's particularly warm, we'll take some time to sit by the creek, enjoying wine and an apéritif and watching the kids play. As the sun dips lower in the sky, we sit down for an al fresco meal.

By the time we have finished the last bites of dessert, the candles are burning low and the kids are fast asleep.

Little Croques Madames

SERVES 6 TO 8

Our take on the classic *croque madame*, a traditional French sandwich with ham,
melted cheese, béchamel, and a fried egg on top, this miniature version features tiny quail eggs.
If you can't find quail eggs, skip them and add another dollop of béchamel along with a
sprinkling of cheese to the top before baking, as one does when making a *croque monsieur*.
Be generous with the cheese, and be sure to use the best-quality ham available.

3 tablespoons unsalted butter, plus more, as needed

1 loaf country bread, sliced, crusts removed, and cut into 16 (2-inch/5-cm) squares

1 cup (110 g) coarsely grated Comté or Gruyère cheese

4 thin slices of high-quality ham, torn into pieces

1 recipe Sauce Béchamel (page 368), warm

8 quail eggs, cracked and placed in small individual prep bowls

Fleur de sel and freshly ground black pepper

2 tablespoons finely chopped fresh chives

Preheat the oven to 425°F (220°C). Line a baking sheet with parchment paper.

In a medium sauté pan, melt 2 tablespoons of the butter. Dip the bread into the melted butter to coat one side. Place the bread squares, buttered-side up, on the parchment-lined baking sheet and toast in the oven until just golden, 3 to 4 minutes. Don't clean the sauté pan.

Flip the toast squares over so that the buttered sides face down. Sprinkle ½ cup (55g) of the cheese evenly on eight of the toast squares. Arrange one or two pieces of ham on top of each toast, then spoon a generous amount of béchamel over the ham. Using half the remaining cheese, sprinkle each toast with additional cheese. Top the sandwiches with the remaining toast squares, buttered-side up. Sprinkle with the remaining cheese and bake until the cheese is melted and bubbling, about 5 minutes.

While the sandwiches are baking, place the sauté pan over medium heat and melt the remaining 1 tablespoon of butter. Working in batches, fry the quail eggs sunny-side up, spooning the butter over the eggs as they cook, just until the whites are set, 1 to 2 minutes. Repeat with the remaining eggs, adding more butter, as needed. Season with salt and pepper.

Top each sandwich with a quail egg, sprinkle with the chives, and serve on a warm platter.

Heirloom Tomato Tartelettes

MAKES 8 (4-INCH/10-CM) TARTLETS OR 1 (9-INCH/23-CM) TART

Heirloom tomatoes play the starring role in the summer months here in Beaune.
They come in a variety of colors, shapes, and sizes, and we eat them as often as possible.
These tartlets make a beautiful first course and can be made as a large tart as well. For a variation,
we often add ¼ cup (25 g) freshly grated Parmesan and a few grinds of black pepper to our
Pâte Brisée dough to give it a little extra flavor. The tartlet shells and the filling can be prepared
ahead of time; assemble them right before serving and top with tomatoes, herbs, and herb oil.

Unbleached all-purpose flour, for dusting

½ recipe Pâte Brisée (page 379)

1 large egg yolk

3 tablespoons heavy cream

¾ cup (85 g) crumbled fresh goat cheese

¼ cup (60 ml) crème fraîche

2 tablespoons extra-virgin olive oil, preferably French

1 tablespoon lemon zest

1 tablespoon fresh lemon juice

Fleur de sel and freshly ground black pepper

1 to 1¼ pounds (455 to 570 g) various small heirloom tomatoes, sliced and quartered or halved, depending on their size

Small fresh basil leaves and blossoms, for garnish (optional)

1 bunch fresh chives, finely chopped

Herb Oil (page 67), for drizzling

On a lightly floured surface, use the pâte brisée to make the tartlet shells (see page 374). Freeze them for 15 to 20 minutes before baking.

Preheat the oven to 375°F (190°C).

In a small bowl, whisk together the egg yolk and heavy cream. Use a pastry brush to lightly brush the egg wash over the dough. Blind bake the tartlet shells (see page 333).

In a large bowl, stir together the goat cheese, crème fraîche, olive oil, lemon zest, and lemon juice. Season with salt and pepper.

Remove the cooled tartlet shells from the pans, then spoon the cheese filling into them, spreading it evenly. Arrange the tomatoes neatly in an overlapping circular pattern, covering the filling and alternating the tomatoes by color. Arrange the quartered and halved tomatoes beautifully on top of the sliced tomatoes. Tuck the basil and blossoms (if using) in between the tomatoes to form a pretty pattern. Garnish with chives, drizzle with herb oil, and serve immediately.

Poitrine de Porc with Sweet Peppers, Petites Courgettes, and Summer Greens

SERVES 6 TO 8

Poitrine de porc, or pork belly, is a summer favorite in France, served with or without the bone. It is ideal for large gatherings because much of the work is done the day before serving. Rich and fatty, this is the cut of pig that produces bacon, so just a taste will do. We pair it with barely roasted sweet peppers and *petites courgettes* (tender baby zucchini) along with crisp, fresh, summer greens like mizuna, roquette, or barely wilted mustard greens to lighten the dish.

FOR THE POITRINE DE PORC

1 (2-pound/910-g) piece of boneless pork belly with skin

2 tablespoons Butcher's Fleur de Sel (page 67)

4 tablespoons (60 ml) extra-virgin olive oil, preferably French

1 large yellow onion, diced

2 fresh bay leaves

1 cup (240 ml) dry white wine, such as Burgundy Chardonnay

3 sprigs flat-leaf parsley

About 6 cups (1.4 L) Brown Veal Stock (page 359)

FOR THE SWEET PEPPERS

8 to 12 mixed red, yellow, and purple heirloom bell peppers

2 tablespoons extra-virgin olive oil, preferably French

Fleur de sel and freshly ground black pepper

5 sprigs thyme

FOR THE PETITES COURGETTES

1 tablespoon unsalted butter

1 tablespoon extra-virgin olive oil, preferably French

16 green and yellow baby zucchini, sliced lengthwise

Fleur de sel and freshly ground black pepper

FOR THE SUMMER GREENS

2 tablespoons extra-virgin olive oil, preferably French

1 large bunch mizuna, wild roquette (arugula), or mustard greens, stemmed and leaves coarsely chopped

Fleur de sel and freshly ground black pepper

Make the poitrine de porc: Preheat the oven to 325°F (165°C).

Place the pork belly on a baking sheet and pat dry. Season with the butcher's salt, cover with plastic wrap, and refrigerate for 1 hour.

In a Dutch oven large enough to hold the pork belly, heat 3 tablespoons of the olive oil over medium-high heat until hot but not smoking. Carefully add the pork belly, skin-side down, and sear on all sides until golden brown and crispy, 10 to 12 minutes total.

Transfer the pork belly to a platter. Remove all but 1 to 2 teaspoons of fat from the Dutch oven, making sure to leave any bits of meat. Place the Dutch oven over medium-high heat. Add the onion and bay leaves and sauté until the onions are soft and translucent, 3 to 5 minutes. Add the wine and use a wooden spoon to scrape up any little bits from the bottom of the pan. Simmer until reduced by half, about 5 minutes.

Return the pork belly to the Dutch oven, skin-side up. Tuck the parsley around the pork belly, then add enough

Recipe continues on page 180

stock to come almost to the top of the pork, leaving the crispy skin uncovered. Cover and braise in the oven until tender, about 3 hours.

Let the pork belly cool completely in the braising liquid. Once the pork belly is at room temperature, transfer it to a baking sheet, cover with plastic wrap, and refrigerate overnight. Discard the braising liquid.

Make the sweet peppers: Preheat the oven to 350°F (175°C).

Place the peppers in a large gratin dish, drizzle with the olive oil and season with salt and pepper. Add the thyme and roast until tender, 15 to 18 minutes. The peppers should be tender but still retain their shape and bright color.

Finish the poitrine de porc: Cut the pork belly into six to eight pieces. Line a baking sheet with paper towels.

In a large sauté pan, heat the remaining 1 tablespoon olive oil over medium-high heat until hot but not smoking. Sear the pork belly on all sides, until caramelized and warmed through, 8 to 10 minutes. Place the pork belly on the paper towel–lined baking sheet to absorb any excess fat. Season with salt.

Make the petites courgettes: In a large sauté pan, melt the butter with the olive oil over medium heat. Add the zucchini and season generously with salt and pepper. Sauté just until tender and golden on all sides, about 5 minutes.

For the greens: If using mizuna or wild roquette, drizzle with olive oil and season with salt and pepper. If using mustard greens, in a large sauté pan, heat the olive oil over medium heat. Add the mustard greens and sauté just until tender, 1 to 2 minutes. Season with salt and pepper.

To serve, arrange the poitrine de porc, peppers, and greens on a large platter, and place the petites courgettes on a second platter.

Nectarine and Blueberry Tart

MAKES 1 (9-INCH/23-CM) TART OR 8 (4-INCH/10-CM) TARTLETS

This is an ideal dessert for summer picnics, as you can bake the tart shell with the almond cream ahead of time and add the fruit just before serving. Remember to make the almond cream in advance, as it needs to set for about three hours in the refrigerator. It's bright and colorful, not too sweet, and the almond filling complements the fresh fruit. Peaches and raspberries make a nice variation.

Unbleached all-purpose flour, for dusting

½ recipe Pâte Sucrée (page 378)

1 recipe Crème d'Amande (page 386)

1 large egg yolk

3 tablespoons heavy cream

¼ cup (60 ml) Apricot Confiture (page 391)

4 ripe nectarines

¾ cup (110 g) fresh blueberries

Confectioners' sugar, for dusting

On a lightly floured surface, use the pâte sucrée to make the tart shell (page 374). Freeze it for 15 to 20 minutes before baking.

Preheat the oven to 375°F (190°C).

Take the almond cream out of the refrigerator and let it soften slightly at room temperature.

In a small bowl, whisk together the egg yolk and heavy cream. Use a pastry brush to lightly brush the egg wash over the dough. Partially blind bake the tart shell (see page 333).

Using an offset spatula or small knife, carefully spread the almond cream evenly in the tart shell. Bake until the tart shell is golden and the almond filling is just set, about 20 minutes. Set on a wire rack to cool.

Using an offset spatula, spread the apricot jam on top of the cooled almond cream. Cut the nectarines in half, remove the pits, and thinly slice the fruit. Carefully arrange the nectarine slices, tightly overlapping, around the edge of the tart shell, forming a tight, compact circle. Repeat to create an inner circle going in the opposite direction. Scatter the blueberries on top, lightly dust with confectioners' sugar, and serve immediately.

SUNFLOWER PICNIC

In the height of summer, when Burgundy's sunflower fields begin to bloom in mid-July, we all carve out one special day on a weekend to make an annual journey. We pack a lunch and a few bottles of rosé in Madeleine, our quirky, but iconic vintage Citroën 2CV (or, *Deudeuche*, as the French call them) and quintessential picnic car, and head out to find the perfect spot in the sunflower fields. Picnicking is the ultimate French pasttime (it's practically engrained in the French mindset) and the French take their picnics very seriously. They'll find any and every excuse to pack a blanket, a baguette, some cheese, and a bottle of wine to enjoy outdoors when the weather warms up and the sun is shining bright. And so, we join in, too, and have happily embraced this intentional outing. Our picnic menu is always simple, emphasizing the abundance of summer, and is easy to transport. It's become a memorable and much-anticipated tradition.

Pickled Cucumbers PAGE 390

Charentais Melon Salad WITH *Jambon* DE *Bayonne* AND *Basil* PAGE 189

Niçoise Pan Bagnat PAGE 190

Mixed Berry Pies PAGE 194

Charentais Melon Salad
with Jambon de Bayonne and Basil

SERVES 8

This salad is an ideal first course for a summertime picnic. We prefer to use sweet, fragrant Charentais melons. If you can't find them, make sure to use small, perfectly ripe cantaloupes. *Jambon de Bayonne* is a dry-cured ham from the Basque region where the pig is fed on chestnuts and hickory nuts. If this is not available, use another high-quality ham, such as prosciutto di Parma, San Daniele, or Serrano. The addition of different varieties of freshly picked garden basil makes a beautiful presentation and adds a sweet perfume.

4 ripe Charentais melons, or 3 small perfectly ripe cantaloupes, halved and seeded

8 thin slices jambon de Bayonne or prosciutto

2 shallots, thinly sliced into rings

Handful of fresh basil leaves in different colors and sizes

1 recipe Vinaigrette (page 354), using balsamic and sherry vinegar variation

Herb Oil (page 67), for drizzling (optional)

Fleur de sel and freshly ground black pepper

Cut each melon half into thirds. Remove the rind from each wedge. Arrange the melon wedges on a platter or divide them among individual salad plates—there should be two or three wedges per plate. Drape the slices of ham over the melon wedges and sprinkle the shallots and basil over the salad. Drizzle with the vinaigrette and the herb oil (if using). Season with salt and pepper and serve immediately.

Niçoise Pan Bagnat

SERVES 8

As an ode to Laurent's Provençal origins, we enjoy highlighting the cuisine of the South
of France in the warm summer months, bringing a little bit of Provence to Burgundy.
Aïoli and tomatoes find their places on our table, and we favor outdoor dining. For picnics,
we enjoy bringing along a hearty *Niçoise pan bagnat*, a traditional Provençal sandwich.
Crunchy on the outside and soft on the inside, pan bagnat is made by slicing a boule
(a rustic round loaf of bread common in France) in half and layering it with a green salad
dressed in Anchovy Vinaigrette, boiled eggs, seared tuna, capers, and tomatoes.

½ cup (120 ml) fruity extra-virgin olive oil, preferably French, plus more for drizzling

2 tablespoons fresh lemon juice

3 cloves garlic, smashed

Fleur de sel and freshly ground black pepper

4 (4- to 5-ounce/115- to 140-g) sushi-grade tuna steaks, 1½ inches (4 cm) thick

Handful of green beans, ends trimmed

1 small bunch of radishes

1 cup (155 g) pitted Niçoise olives

1 recipe Anchovy Vinaigrette (page 354)

8 small or 2 large country boules, or rustic round loaves of bread

Handful of mesclun or baby lettuce

4 medium heirloom tomatoes, cut into ½-inch- (12-mm-) thick rounds

4 large hard-boiled eggs, cut into wedges

¼ cup (30 g) salt-packed capers, rinsed

Handful of fresh basil leaves

In a gratin dish large enough to hold the tuna steaks in a single layer, combine the olive oil, lemon juice, and garlic. Season with salt and pepper. Place the tuna steaks in the marinade and turn to coat. Cover and refrigerate, turning occasionally, for 1 hour.

Blanch and shock the green beans to preserve their color and drain on a clean kitchen towel. Thinly slice the radishes lengthwise using a stainless-steel vegetable peeler.

Heat a large heavy-bottomed sauté pan over medium-high heat. Remove the tuna steaks from the marinade and place them directly in the pan. Sear, flipping once, until browned on the outside but still rare on the inside, about 2 minutes per side. Transfer them to a cutting board and cut into thin slices.

In a large bowl, combine the green beans, radishes, and olives. Drizzle with the anchovy vinaigrette, and gently stir to evenly coat.

Slice the boules in half horizontally. Drizzle both insides with a little olive oil. Layer the mesclun, tomatoes, tuna, eggs, and green bean mixture on the bottom slices of bread and top with the capers and basil. Season with salt and pepper, finish with the sandwich tops, and serve.

Mixed Berry Pies

SERVES 8

These little pies are perfect for picnics, as they can be prepared ahead of time. Feel free to switch out the fruit, depending on what's in season and what looks fresh at the market.

Unbleached all-purpose flour, for dusting

1 recipe Pâte Brisée (page 379)

1 cup (140 to 150 g) mixed berries, such as blueberries, blackberries, and red and white raspberries

1½ tablespoons fresh lemon juice

2 tablespoons sugar, plus more for sprinkling

1 tablespoon cornstarch

⅛ teaspoon fleur de sel

1 tablespoon unsalted butter, cut into small pieces

1 large egg yolk

3 tablespoons heavy cream

Preheat the oven to 375°F (190°C). Line a baking sheet with parchment paper.

On a lightly floured work surface with a floured rolling pin, roll the pâte brisée into a 12-inch (30.5-cm) square that's ⅛ inch (3 mm) thick. Brush off any excess flour with a pastry brush. Cut the dough into 16 (3-inch/7.5-cm) squares and place the squares on the parchment-lined baking sheet. Using a very small cookie cutter, cut a shape into the center of eight of the squares—the decorative squares will be the tops of the pies. Refrigerate the dough while preparing the berries.

In a large bowl, gently toss together the berries, lemon juice, sugar, cornstarch, and salt. Set aside for 15 minutes.

Remove the pastry squares from the refrigerator. Place 1 heaping tablespoon of the berry mixture in the center of each of the eight solid pastry squares and sprinkle with a couple pieces of the butter. In a small bowl, whisk together the egg yolk and heavy cream. Use a pastry brush to moisten the edges of each pastry square with the egg wash. Arrange a decorative pastry square on top of each pie and use the tines of a fork to seal the edges together. Lightly brush the top of each pie with egg wash, then sprinkle with sugar.

Bake until golden brown, about 30 minutes. Serve warm or at room temperature. These are best eaten the day they are made.

AUTUMN

In the autumn, we welcome the crisp chill in the air and the bright blue skies. The kids head back to school, and we relish the slower rhythms of the season. We bundle up in our sweaters and scarves, gather wood to make fires at home, and prepare the soil in our garden to rest for the winter months ahead.

After the first autumn rain, wild mushrooms begin to sprout up in the woods. Many of our producers forage for mushrooms and Burgundian truffles, and bring their treasures to the market. The market fills with pears and crisp red apples from nearby orchards; bright orange pumpkins and taupe-colored butternut squash; bitter greens like escarole, frisée, and chicory; and big bouquets of mixed-colored dahlias. Hand-harvested nuts, like walnuts and hazelnuts, make their appearance, along with perfectly ripe local figs. We look forward to buying and cooking duck—*magret de canard* (duck breast) and foie gras—as they both are particularly good in the autumn months. Autumn is a time for braising and roasting, and for enjoying hearty Burgundian dishes.

In Burgundy, after a long year of grape-growing, there is much to celebrate. Everyone comes together to fête the wine harvest, with post-harvest parties at every domaine. And in mid-November, France celebrates the release of the new Beaujolais wine. But the biggest party of the season takes place around the third Sunday of November, when visitors from around the world flock to town for the Hospices de Beaune wine auction, along with a three-day food and wine festival. Lights twinkle over the streets, and crowds of people wander through town enjoying glasses of Burgundy wine, oysters, escargots, and frog's legs. After November, the festivities wind down and the town settles into a restful calm, before winemakers begin to prepare for the next year's harvest.

PASCAL LAPRÉE | DUCK FARMER

If you drive an hour northwest of Beaune, through lush green farmland dotted with grazing cows and crisscrossed by low stone walls, you'll find yourself in the medieval village of Mont-Saint-Jean, on the outskirts of the Morvan Forest. Drive past the ancient church and château and follow the arrow-shaped sign that says "Foie Gras." Just down the road, in the tiny hamlet of Mairey, you'll find one of the best duck producers in Burgundy, Pascal Laprée.

Monsieur Laprée lives on his family's sprawling farm, along with some two hundred sheep and several hundred ducks. Three generations of the Laprée family work in the business, and everything is done by hand, taking care to preserve traditional methods. He grew up on this farm, working with his father to raise sheep. In his mid-twenties, after a stint working in Québec, Canada, he returned home and decided to start raising ducks to make foie gras.

An integral part of the gastronomic culture and heritage in France, foie gras appears—either preserved as a terrine or as foie gras entier that is quickly pan-seared—at nearly every holiday celebration and festive gathering. When we asked Monsieur Laprée how he learned to make this delicacy, he laughed and said, "From an expert! A friend's grandmother in the southwest of France taught me how to produce foie gras over the telephone." She was clearly a good teacher, as he has now been producing some of the best foie gras and magret de canard in Burgundy for more than thirty years.

Everything he does—from raising his ducks to making foie gras—follows the same good animal husbandry practices that have been used in France for centuries. His ducks are of the Moulard breed, a cross between White Pekin and Muscovy, and are specifically raised to make foie gras. He purposely keeps his production very small, only raising ducks in the spring and autumn, and they roam freely on the land. He uses every single part of the duck (not just the breasts and livers), including the neck and wings for *rillettes* (pâté) and the legs and thighs for confit. Nothing is wasted.

We enjoy visiting him at the market every week, and showing our guests what artisanal France truly looks like.

BABETH CHARBOUILLOT | ARTISAN BAKER

Babeth Charbouillot, a petite woman with unruly gray hair, lives in the small town of Chagny, twenty minutes south of Beaune. She converted a wooden gypsy caravan, parked behind an organic beer brewer, into a wood-fired oven where she bakes big, crusty boules of whole wheat, spelt, and flaxseed bread. She begins her morning at 4:30 A.M., heating the oven, making and shaping the dough, and baking the bread. In the afternoon, she hand-delivers her artisanal loaves to shops and restaurants in neighboring towns, relying on word of mouth to sell her bread.

Babeth became enamored by breadmaking when she took time off from work to raise her four children. She began experimenting with different flours and baking techniques at home, and eventually asked her favorite local baker, Arnaud Marin, if she could work with him. He made his bread in an old wood-fired bread oven in the tiny village of Sacquenay, using locally grown wheat and ancient grains, which Babeth found especially intriguing.

After nine years of learning everything she could about artisanal breadmaking, she decided to branch out and start her own business, Babeth et Ses Fours. She works with a small, local farmer in Montliot-et-Courcelles, who grows old wheat varieties and mills them into flours that she uses for baking. "It's very important to me how the grain is grown and how the flour is made," she says. "Industrial white flour is too refined and has lost many of its nutrients." The locally produced flour she uses in her bread is much higher in nutrients, minerals, and protein, and lower in gluten than typical bread flour. She doesn't use commercial yeast in her bread, but instead uses a twenty-year-old *levain* (sourdough starter) that she "feeds" daily.

Babeth is a true artisan baker, and you can taste her commitment to her craft in every single wood-fired boule. We use her bread for all of our cooking classes, workshops, and dinner parties, and love its crusty exterior and nutty depth of flavor.

MARKET LUNCH

Lunch at The Cook's Atelier is more than just a meal—it's an all-day affair, including a morning trip to the market, followed by a cooking session and a convivial meal around our zinc-topped farm table. Guests join us from around the world, drawn together by a shared love of food, wine, and France. Our guests get swept up in the magic of the place, and after a day spent cooking, dining, and drinking wine together, the same group who started out as strangers ends up leaving as friends.

We meet our guests and stroll through the morning market. We chat with our favorite producers and gather all of our provisions before winding our way back to the Atelier to prepare lunch.

We climb the old, wooden stairs leading from the wine shop to the second-floor kitchen, and unpack our market baskets. Everyone dons an apron and we talk through the day's menu, explaining and demonstrating classic French culinary techniques used in each recipe. Then we all get to work prepping the ingredients. Delicious aromas fill the air, and appetites grow in anticipation of the lunch to come.

Once the cooking is finished, aprons come off, we sip Champagne, and everyone gets a chance to enjoy the fruits of their labor. Guests find a seat, we pour the wine, and we bring up the first course. The menu is always changing and is based on the season's offerings. Conversation and laughter fill the air, and glasses clink as the meal continues late into the day.

Sautéed Cèpes on Toasts

When the first *cèpes* (porcini mushrooms) arrive in autumn, we can't get enough of them.
Our friend Frédéric forages for cèpes near the Morvan and brings them to the Saturday market in
Beaune. We buy as many as we can, and use them often in our recipes. We like to sauté them simply
with shallots, thyme, and white wine, and serve them on toasts for an autumn apéritif.

1 loaf rustic bread, such as *pain de mie* or Brioche (page 371)

4 tablespoons (½ stick/55 g) unsalted butter

5 ounces (140 g) small cèpes, thinly sliced lengthwise

1 shallot, finely chopped

Leaves from 3 sprigs thyme, plus more for garnish

½ cup (120 ml) dry white wine, such as Burgundy Chardonnay

Fleur de sel and freshly ground black pepper

1½ ounces (40 g) dry sheep's-milk cheese, shaved

Preheat the oven to 350°F (175°C).

Cut the bread into rectangular slices 2 to 3 inches (5 to 7.5 cm) long—depending on the size of the mushrooms—and remove the crusts. In a medium sauté pan, melt 3 tablespoons of the butter over medium-high heat. Dip the bread in the melted butter to coat both sides. Do not clean the pan. Place the bread slices on a baking sheet and toast, flipping them once, until golden, 8 to 10 minutes. Set aside.

Add the remaining 1 tablespoon of butter to the hot pan over medium-high heat and sauté the mushrooms, 1 to 2 minutes, until caramelized. Add the shallot, thyme, and wine and cook until the wine has reduced and slightly thickened and the mushrooms are tender, 2 to 3 minutes. Season with salt and pepper.

Arrange the mushroom slices on the prepared toasts and drizzle with a little of the shallot mixture. Top with the shaved cheese and serve immediately.

Roasted Potimarron Soup with Beurre Noisette

SERVES 8 TO 10

This autumn soup highlights the abundance of potimarron in our market.
It has a beautiful orange color and velvety texture, and we garnish it with a dollop of crème fraîche, fresh parsley, a few shavings of Burgundian truffle, and a drizzle of *beurre noisette* (brown butter). This recipe can be adapted to use other squash varieties that you might find in your own market, such as Blue Hubbard or butternut. Feel free to substitute vegetable stock for the chicken stock for a lighter version. If Burgundian truffles are not available, we sometimes garnish the soup with tiny sautéed chanterelles.

5 pounds (2.3 kg) potimarron (about 6 medium), halved and seeded

6 tablespoons (90 ml) extra-virgin olive oil, preferably French

Fleur de sel and freshly ground black pepper

12 fresh sage leaves

6 sprigs thyme

6 large leeks, white and light green parts only

4 medium carrots, chopped

2 medium yellow onions, chopped

3 cloves garlic, coarsely chopped

½ cup (120 ml) white wine, such as Burgundy Chardonnay

1 bouquet garni (see page 61)

4 to 6 cups (960 ml to 1.4 L) Chicken Stock (page 357)

½ cup (120 ml) crème fraîche

Small handful of finely chopped fresh flat-leaf parsley

1 recipe Beurre Noisette (page 352), warm

1 Burgundian truffle (optional)

Preheat the oven to 350°F (175°C).

Place the squash halves, cut-side up, on a baking sheet and drizzle with 3 tablespoons of the olive oil. Using your hands, rub the olive oil all over the exposed flesh of the squash to prevent burning, then season with salt and pepper. Scatter the sage leaves and thyme sprigs over the squash and roast until a paring knife can be easily poked through the skin of the squash, about 20 minutes. Set aside until cool enough to handle. Remove and discard the sage and thyme. Once cooled, use a large spoon to scoop the cooked flesh away from the tough skin. Discard the skin and place the flesh in a large bowl.

Meanwhile, halve each leek lengthwise, then cut them crosswise into 1-inch (2.5-cm) pieces. Rinse the leeks in a large bowl of cold water, swishing to remove any sand. Using your hands, transfer the leeks to a colander to drain, leaving the sand in the bottom of the bowl.

In a large Dutch oven, heat the remaining 3 tablespoons olive oil over medium-high heat. Add the leeks, carrots, onions, and garlic and sauté until soft, 6 to 8 minutes. Add the wine and cook until the liquid has evaporated, 2 to 3 minutes. Add the squash, bouquet garni, and enough stock to just cover the squash. Bring it to a gentle simmer and cook, adjusting the heat, as needed, until the flavors meld, 20 to 25 minutes.

Remove and discard the bouquet garni. Working in batches, carefully ladle the soup into a blender and puree until smooth. Strain the soup through a chinois. Season with salt and pepper.

Serve the soup in warmed soup bowls topped with a dollop of crème fraîche, parsley, a drizzle of beurre noisette, and thin shavings of truffle (if using).

Magret de Canard with Celery Root Puree and Chanterelles

SERVES 8 TO 10

Magret de canard is the breast from a Moulard duck, a cross between White Pekin and Muscovy, the breed used in France to make foie gras. Magret de canard cooks like a steak and should be served rare to medium-rare. It is important to note that the breast is very lean, and overcooking it will cause it to be tough. Unlike other types of red meat, which are first brought to room temperature and quickly seared over high heat, duck is added to a cold pan directly from the refrigerator, and cooked slowly so the fat renders, creating a crisp, golden brown skin. The cooled rendered fat can be stored in a glass jar in the refrigerator and used at another time to sauté vegetables, potatoes, or leafy greens.

FOR THE CELERY ROOT PUREE

2 medium celery roots

Fleur de sel

8 tablespoons (1 stick/115 g) unsalted butter

4 pounds (1.8 kg) russet potatoes

½ cup (120 ml) whole milk

½ cup (120 ml) heavy cream

Freshly ground black pepper

2 tablespoons finely chopped fresh flat-leaf parsley

FOR THE DUCK

4 or 5 (14-ounce/400-g) Moulard duck breasts

Fleur de sel and freshly ground black pepper

FOR THE PAN SAUCE

1 shallot, finely chopped

3 sprigs thyme

1 fresh bay leaf

1 cup (240 ml) red wine, such as Burgundy Pinot Noir

1 tablespoon Demi-Glace (optional; page 363)

Fleur de sel and freshly ground black pepper

1 teaspoon unsalted butter

FOR THE CHANTERELLES

2 tablespoons unsalted butter

30 small chanterelles

Fleur de sel and freshly ground black pepper

FOR THE MIZUNA

8 small handfuls of green and purple mizuna

Extra-virgin olive oil, preferably French

Fleur de sel and freshly ground black pepper

Make the celery root puree: Cut a circle of parchment paper slightly larger than a medium saucepan.

Peel the celery roots and cut them into small pieces. Place in a medium saucepan and cover with cold water. Add a large pinch of salt and 2 tablespoons of the butter. Arrange the parchment round on top of the saucepan, then gently push it into the pan so it touches the celery root and the edges go up the sides of the pan. Bring the celery root to a boil, then reduce the heat and simmer until tender, 20 to 25 minutes. Drain and set aside.

Peel the potatoes and cut them into small pieces. Place them in a large saucepan and cover with cold water. Add a large pinch of salt and bring to a boil. Reduce

Recipe continues on page 217

the heat and simmer until tender, 15 to 20 minutes. Drain.

Using a ricer or food mill, puree the cooked celery root and potatoes together into a large bowl. Combine the milk and heavy cream in a small saucepan over medium heat and bring to just under a boil. Remove from the heat, add the remaining 6 tablespoons butter, and stir until melted. Gradually add the milk and heavy cream mixture to the celery root and potato mixture, stirring gently to incorporate and adding only enough to reach the desired creamy consistency. Season with salt and pepper and keep warm.

Make the duck: Preheat the oven to 400°F (205°C).

Rinse and thoroughly dry the duck breasts, then place them, fat-side up, on a wooden cutting board. Check the fat sides for pin feathers and quills and use kitchen tweezers to remove them, if needed. Turn the duck breasts over so they're meat-side up, and use a thin, sharp knife to remove any silver skin. Flip the duck breasts back over so they're fat-side up, and use the knife to score the fat in a diagonal crisscross pattern, making incisions ¼ to ½ inch (6 to 12 mm) apart, and being careful not to go all the way through to the meat. Season with salt and pepper.

Working in batches, place the duck breasts, fat-side down, in a large heavy sauté pan that's cold and dry. Turn on the heat to medium and slowly render the fat. As you're rendering, use a small spoon to occasionally baste the breast meat with the rendered fat. Render until the fat side is golden brown, 8 to 10 minutes. Place the breasts, fat-side up, on a baking sheet and set aside. Repeat with the remaining duck breasts. Reserve the pan with the meat juices. Place the baking sheet

in the oven and roast the duck breasts until a meat thermometer inserted in the thickest part of the meat reaches 130°F (55°C) for medium-rare, 8 to 10 minutes. The internal temperature will rise to 145°F (63°C) upon standing. Let the duck rest on a warm cutting board while you make the pan sauce.

Remove all but 1 teaspoon of the fat from the pan used to render the duck fat, making sure to leave any bits of meat. Place the pan over medium-high heat. Add the shallot, thyme, and bay leaf and sauté until the shallots are soft and translucent, about 1 minute. Add the red wine and use a wooden spoon to scrape any little bits off the bottom. Simmer until reduced by half, about 5 minutes. Strain through a fine-mesh strainer into a small saucepan and place over medium heat. Bring to a simmer and continue simmering until reduced to the desired consistency. Add the demi-glace, if using, and simmer until slightly reduced, 2 to 3 minutes. Season with salt and pepper, then remove from the heat, add the butter, and swirl the saucepan until it's incorporated. Keep warm.

Make the chanterelles: In a large sauté pan, melt the butter over medium-high heat and sauté the mushrooms, 3 to 4 minutes, until tender and caramelized. Season with salt and pepper. Keep warm.

Make the mizuna: In a large bowl, drizzle the mizuna with olive oil and toss to combine. Season with salt and pepper.

To serve, divide the mizuna among warmed plates. Cut each duck breast in half on an angle, then in half on an angle again and place it on top of the mizuna. Arrange the chanterelles around the duck and drizzle with the pan sauce. Garnish the celery root puree with the parsley and serve it alongside the duck.

Plum Tarte Tatin

SERVES 8 TO 10

Inspired by a classic apple tarte tatin, we enjoy using brilliantly colored yellow, red, and purple autumn plums for a beautiful presentation. You can easily adapt the recipe by using apples, pears, and even peaches in the summer. Use a well-seasoned cast-iron skillet or a traditional tarte tatin pan.

½ recipe (1 sheet) Pâte Feuilletée (page 379)

3 pounds (1.4 kg) yellow, red, and purple plums, halved and pitted

1 cup (200 g) vanilla sugar (see page 64)

Unbleached, all-purpose flour for dusting

10 tablespoons (1¼ sticks/ 140 g) unsalted butter, cut into small pieces

⅛ teaspoon fleur de sel

Preheat the oven to 375°F (190°C).

Remove the pâte feuilletée from the freezer and let it thaw on the counter.

In a large bowl, sprinkle the plums with 2 tablespoons of the vanilla sugar and let stand for 30 minutes.

Once the pâte feuilletée is workable, lightly dust a work surface with flour and use a rolling pin to roll the dough into a ¼-inch- (6-mm-) thick rectangle. On one end of the rectangle, cut a circle that's slightly larger in diameter than the pan you plan to cook the tarte tatin in.

Heat a 10- to 12-inch (25- to 30.5-cm) cast-iron skillet or tarte tatin pan over medium-high heat. Add the butter. Once the butter is melted and foaming, sprinkle the salt and the remaining vanilla sugar around the pan. Cook, swirling the pan often but not stirring, until the sugar has dissolved and the mixture turns a golden caramel color but doesn't get too dark, 10 to 12 minutes. Remove the pan from the heat.

Carefully arrange the plums, slightly overlapping and alternating between the three colors, around the edge of the pan, forming a tight, compact circle. Repeat to create an inner circle going in the opposite direction. Depending on how tightly you layer them, you may have leftover plums.

Place the pan back on the stove and cook over medium heat until caramelized and jammy, about 15 minutes. Remove the pan from the heat and let it cool slightly.

Carefully arrange the pâte feuilletée on top of the plums, gently tucking the edge in between the fruit and the sides of the pan. Bake until the pastry is golden, 30 to 35 minutes. Remove from the oven and let the tart cool to room temperature before serving.

When ready to serve, place a plate or wire baking rack on top of the pan and carefully flip both over, so the pastry ends up on the bottom. Leave the pan on top for a few minutes to allow the fruit to naturally release itself from the pan. Serve immediately.

Madeleines

MAKES ABOUT 36 MADELEINES

These small, buttery cakes, forever associated with the French writer Marcel Proust, are baked in fluted tins, giving them their unforgettable, shell-like shape—one of the true sweet representations of France. When baked in a hot oven, they puff up to create the classic "hump" on their backs. We serve warm madeleines with coffee after every class at The Cook's Atelier.

⅔ cup (150 g) unsalted butter

1 tablespoon lemon zest

1 tablespoon fresh lemon juice

3 large eggs, at room temperature

1 large egg yolk, at room temperature

¾ cup (150 g) granulated sugar

½ teaspoon fleur de sel

1½ cups (190 g) unbleached all-purpose flour, plus more for the pans

1 teaspoon baking powder

Confectioners' sugar, for dusting

In a small saucepan, melt the butter over low heat. Let it cool slightly, then use a pastry brush to generously coat two or three madeleine tins with butter. Dust the pans with flour, tapping out any excess, and refrigerate to set.

Add the lemon zest and lemon juice to the remaining butter and set aside.

In the bowl of a stand mixer fitted with a whisk attachment, combine the eggs, egg yolk, sugar, and salt. Beat on medium-high speed until the mixture is pale and has doubled in volume, about 5 minutes. It will have a ribbonlike consistency when the batter is picked up with the whisk and drizzled over the remaining batter.

Sift the flour and baking powder into the egg mixture and use a large rubber spatula to gently fold until just combined. Slowly drizzle the melted butter into the batter, folding gently until fully incorporated. Cover and refrigerate for at least 1½ hours or up to 12 hours.

Set a rack in the upper third of the oven and preheat the oven to 375°F (190°C).

Place the madeleine batter in a pastry bag fitted with a large round tip. Starting near the "base," pipe into the bottom of each mold, filling them about two-thirds of the way and not spreading the batter. Bake until the madeleines feel set to the touch, 7 to 8 minutes. Let them cool slightly, dust with confectioners' sugar, then serve immediately. Madeleines are best served warm and eaten the day they are made.

WINE HARVEST PARTY

For winemakers in Burgundy, the harvest is the busiest time of the year. Depending on the weather, the harvest can begin as early as August or as late as October, but typically occurs mid- to late September. Once the grapes have been safely picked, pressed, and stored, every domaine throws a big party. Burgundians are quite jovial by nature and love a celebration. Traditionally, they gather for *la paulée*, a convivial dinner celebrating the end of the harvest, which represents a year's worth of hard work and good fortune. They feast and drink and take time to appreciate what they've achieved. This annual gathering is relaxed and festive, and very much a part of Burgundian heritage that has been carried on for centuries.

For la paulée, we create a menu *à la bourguignonne*. Hearty and humble, traditional Burgundian fare evokes a real sense of terroir. Regional specialties highlight the region's celebrated Charolais beef, wild game, escargots, free-range duck, and the famed Bresse chicken. Though we enjoy the rustic classics of Burgundy, we often adapt the flavors in a slightly lighter, more-refined manner.

The wine harvest party is an ode not only to the talents of the winemaker and the efforts of the vineyard workers, but also a toast to nature and to the many elements that are beyond our control.

Gougères

MAKES ABOUT 24 GOUGÈRES

Gougères are part of a classic Burgundian apéritif, served with a glass of bubbly or wine.
Our recipe was mastered at La Varenne and is adapted from Anne Willan's classic version.
These airy little cheese puffs are made from savory pâte à choux dough (pages 376–77),
utilizing the same technique used to make sweet éclairs and profiteroles.

4 large eggs

6 tablespoons (¾ stick/85 g) unsalted butter

½ teaspoon fleur de sel

⅔ cup (80 g) unbleached all-purpose flour

½ cup (55 g) coarsely grated Comté or Gruyère cheese

½ teaspoon Dijon mustard (optional)

½ teaspoon ground mustard (optional)

Freshly ground black pepper

¼ cup (25 g) finely grated Comté or Gruyère cheese

Preheat the oven to 350°F (175°C).

In a small bowl, whisk one of the eggs and set aside. Crack the remaining three eggs into a separate bowl or measuring cup with a spout. Do not mix; set aside.

In a small heavy-bottomed saucepan, combine ⅔ cup (165 ml) water, butter, and salt over medium heat. Cook until the butter has melted, then bring the mixture to a full boil. Immediately add the flour all at once and beat vigorously with a wooden spoon. Stir until the mixture forms a smooth ball that pulls away from the sides of the pan and a film forms on the bottom of the pan, at least 2 minutes. Reduce the heat to low and beat the mixture to remove any excess moisture and dry out the dough, at least 1 minute.

Remove the pan from the heat and let it cool slightly. Add the remaining three eggs, one at a time, beating thoroughly with a wooden spoon after each addition. The dough should be shiny and smooth. Stir in the coarsely grated cheese, along with the Dijon mustard and ground mustard (if using). Season with the pepper.

Transfer the choux paste to a pastry bag fitted with a large round tip. Pipe a very small amount of dough in the corners of a baking sheet to hold down the paper, then line the baking sheet with parchment paper.

Pipe roughly 1½-inch (4-cm) rounds onto the parchment-lined baking sheet, allowing enough room for them to double in size.

Use your fingertips to gently brush the tops of the gougères with a small amount of the reserved beaten egg, being careful not to smash them or let any excess egg fall on the parchment. Sprinkle the tops with the finely grated cheese. Bake until the gougères are puffed, nicely golden, and feel light for their size, 20 to 22 minutes. Serve immediately. Gougères are best the day they are made. You can make them early in the day and warm them in the oven for 1 to 2 minutes right before serving.

Escargots

SERVES 6 TO 8

Escargots are a very traditional first course in a Burgundian menu. It's important to use best-quality snails, either canned or jarred, as frozen ones will have a rubbery quality to them. They can be served in a savory broth without the shell, but we prefer to serve them the old-fashioned way, in shells with a flavorful garlic-parsley butter.

36 to 48 best-quality French snails, canned or jarred

¾ to 1 cup (180 to 240 ml) cognac or dry white wine, such as Burgundy Chardonnay

36 to 48 escargot shells

1 recipe Herb Butter (page 352)

Crusty baguette, for serving

Preheat the oven to 400°F (205°C).

Rinse the snails in cold water, drain, and set aside.

Place 1 teaspoon of the cognac or white wine in each shell, followed by a single snail. Using a teaspoon, add a generous dollop of the herb butter to each shell. Place the filled shells in individual escargot pans or in one or two large gratin dishes. If there is any herb butter remaining, distribute it in the dish. (The escargots can be prepared to this point and refrigerated for up to 12 hours before baking and serving.) Bake until the butter is bubbling, 5 to 8 minutes.

Serve immediately with a crusty baguette.

Coq au Vin

SERVES 8 TO 10

Coq au vin is a classic Burgundian preparation. Originally a peasant dish,
it was traditionally prepared using a rooster and red wine. We lighten and brighten up
this dish by using dry white wine, such as a Burgundy Chardonnay, and finish the dish with
barely blanched vegetables and small new potatoes. This same method can be
used to prepare the classic dish bœuf bourguignon as well (see the variation on page 235).

FOR THE CHICKEN

2 (3- to 4-pound/1.4- to 1.8-kg) farm-and-pasture-raised chickens, cut into 10 pieces each (see page 348)

Fleur de sel and freshly ground black pepper

1 tablespoon extra-virgin olive oil, preferably French

1 (¼- to ½-inch-thick/6- to 12-mm-thick) slice lard fumé, or 2 slices thick-cut bacon, cut into lardons

2 cups (280 g) coarsely chopped carrots

2 medium onions, coarsely chopped

3 cups (720 ml) dry white wine, such as Burgundy Chardonnay

About 5 cups (1.2 L) Chicken Stock (page 357)

1 bouquet garni (see page 61)

FOR THE FINISHING VEGETABLES

24 to 30 small new potatoes, such as Yukon Gold, peeled

Fleur de sel and freshly ground black pepper

24 white pearl onions

Boiling water

¼ cup (60 ml) dry white wine, such as Burgundy Chardonnay

3 sprigs thyme

1 fresh bay leaf

5 or 6 whole black peppercorns

20 small carrots, trimmed, leaving some of the green stems attached

½ pound (225 g) white button mushrooms

2 tablespoons unsalted butter

Handful of fresh chervil leaves, for garnish

Make the chicken: Preheat the oven to 350°F (175°C).

Rinse and thoroughly dry the chicken pieces. Season with salt and pepper and set aside.

Heat a large Dutch oven over medium heat. Add the olive oil and heat until hot but not smoking. Add the lardons and sauté until crispy and cooked through, 5 to 8 minutes. Use a slotted spoon to transfer the lardons to a small bowl and set aside. Do not wash the Dutch oven.

Place the Dutch oven over medium-high heat and add six or seven pieces of chicken, skin-side down, being careful not to overcrowd the pan (work in batches, as necessary). Sear, turning the chicken and adjusting the heat as needed, until the chicken is nicely caramelized on all sides, 10 to 12 minutes. As you're searing, be careful that the pan doesn't overheat and burn on the bottom. If this happens, you must stop, wash the pot, and start again. Otherwise, the finished sauce will have a burnt taste.

Place the Dutch oven over medium-high heat. Add the carrots and onions and sauté until the onions are soft and

Recipe continues on page 234

translucent, about 5 minutes. Add the wine and use a wooden spoon to scrape up any little bits from the bottom of the pan. Turn off the heat. Arrange a large, double-layered piece of cheesecloth in the Dutch oven so that it covers the cooked vegetables and hangs over the sides of the pot. Carefully place the seared chicken on the cheesecloth and tie the ends of the cheesecloth to create a bundle. Add enough stock to cover the chicken. Add the bouquet garni, cover, and bring to a simmer. Transfer the pot to the oven and braise until the chicken is cooked through, 45 to 50 minutes.

Make the finishing vegetables: Place the potatoes in a large saucepan and cover with cold water. Add a large pinch of salt and bring to a boil. Reduce the heat and simmer until tender, 15 to 20 minutes. Drain and set aside.

Using a small paring knife, make an X on the root end of each pearl onion. Place them in a large heatproof bowl and add just enough of the boiling water to cover. Let them stand until the skins soften, 10 to 15 minutes. Drain the onions and let them stand until cool enough to handle. Using a small, sharp knife, trim the nonroot ends, then peel back and remove the skins; discard the skins.

Place the onions in a small saucepan. Add the wine, thyme, bay leaf, and peppercorns and place over medium heat. Simmer until the wine has reduced slightly, then add just enough water to barely cover the onions and continue to simmer, adjusting the heat, as needed, until the onions are tender, about 15 minutes. Using a slotted spoon, transfer the onions to a small bowl, then season with salt and pepper and set aside.

Bring a large pot of salted water to a boil and fill a bowl with ice and water.

Cut the carrots in half lengthwise (if necessary depending on their size), then add them to the boiling water and blanch until tender, 2 to 3 minutes. Immediately plunge the carrots into the ice water to stop the cooking and preserve their color. Remove and set them on a clean kitchen towel to drain.

Using a paring knife, gently peel back the top layer of each mushroom by holding it upside-down, gently catching the edge of the cap, and carefully peeling it back to remove the clean mushroom cap. Quarter the mushrooms. In a large sauté pan, melt the butter over medium-high heat and sauté the mushrooms until tender and caramelized, 1 to 2 minutes. Set aside.

Remove the chicken pot from the oven. Carefully lift out the cheesecloth bundle with the chicken and place it on a platter or in a large bowl. Remove the cooked vegetables and bouquet garni and discard. Strain the sauce through a chinois into another pot large enough to hold the chicken pieces.

Depending on how thick the sauce is, it may be necessary to reduce the sauce further. If so, place the pot over medium-high heat and bring it to a simmer. Simmer, adjusting the heat as needed, until slightly reduced. To create a slightly thicker sauce, you can add a beurre manié (see page 367). Simmer until the sauce reaches the desired consistency, 1 to 2 minutes. Season with salt and pepper.

Return the chicken to the sauce. Add the lardons, pearl onions, carrots, and mushrooms, cover, and simmer for a few minutes to meld the flavors. Season with salt and pepper.

To serve, divide the potatoes among eight to ten warm, flat soup bowls. Add some sauce to cover and warm the potatoes. Arrange the chicken and vegetables neatly in the bowls, adding a bit more sauce. Garnish with the fresh chervil.

Variation: The same technique and method in this recipe can be applied when making bœuf bourguignon, the quintessential Burgundian beef stew braised in red wine. Although the traditional recipe calls for a rump roast or chuck roast slowly braised and cooked for several hours, until the meat is tender, we prefer to make our version of it using a beef tenderloin as it speeds up the cooking process and ensures a very flavorful and tender stew. Simply replace the chicken here with a 3-pound (1.4-kg) beef tenderloin (cut into 1½- to 2-inch/4- to 5-cm pieces), sear it as you would the chicken, and use a bottle of Burgundy Pinot Noir in lieu of Chardonnay, as well as beef stock in lieu of the chicken stock.

Chocolate-Hazelnut Tart

MAKES 1 (9-INCH/23-CM) TART OR 8 (4-INCH/10-CM) TARTLETS

We generally save chocolate desserts for the colder months, and we especially like this tart because it is decadent, without being too sweet. Use the best-quality chocolate you can find, ideally with at least 70 percent cacao. You can make this recipe with a classic pâte sucrée, though we love adding ground hazelnuts to the dough for added flavor.

Unbleached all-purpose flour, for dusting

½ recipe Pâte Sucrée (page 378), nut dough variation

1 large egg yolk

1½ cups plus 3 tablespoons (405 ml) heavy cream

12 ounces (340 g) high-quality bittersweet chocolate (at least 70% cacao), finely chopped

¾ cup (100 g) hazelnuts, toasted, skinned, and coarsely chopped

On a lightly floured surface, use the pâte sucrée to make the tart shell (page 374). Freeze it for 15 to 20 minutes before baking.

Preheat the oven to 375°F (190°C).

In a small bowl, whisk together the egg yolk and 3 tablespoons of the heavy cream. Use a pastry brush to lightly brush the egg wash over the dough. Blind bake the tart shell (see page 333).

To make the ganache: Place the chocolate in a large heatproof bowl. In a small saucepan, heat the remaining 1½ cups (360 ml) heavy cream over medium heat until just under a boil. Pour over the chocolate, then gently stir with a rubber spatula just until the chocolate is melted and smooth.

Pour the ganache into the cooled tart shell and use an offset spatula to spread it evenly. Top with the toasted hazelnuts, either all over the tart or in a decorative pattern. Let the tart stand in a cool, dry place (don't refrigerate) until the chocolate is set, then serve. This tart is best served the day it is made.

APPLE PICKING

In the autumn, the orchards surrounding Beaune teem with apples. We load up our 2CV with baskets, blankets, and a picnic lunch, and head south to visit a friend's apple orchard. We have a few apple trees at our own house not far from Beaune, but there's something nostalgic about picnicking in a big orchard, surrounded by rows and rows of apple trees. Luc and Manon climb the tall ladder and pick the apples, and before we know it, we've filled up an entire basket with these crisp red and golden beauties that we'll bring home to make into apple tarts, cakes, and compotes. Sometimes, we end up with so many apples that we set out big baskets of them in front of the shop, so people can help themselves as they walk by. Once the apple gathering is done, we enjoy a simple autumnal picnic lunch outdoors, while the kids play in the rows nearby.

Hot Cider

SERVES 6 TO 8

When making this hot cider, be sure to look for crisp, sweet apple varieties.
For a festive touch, you can add a splash of Calvados or apple brandy for the adults if you like.

6 to 8 cups (1.4 to 2 L) organic apple juice

6 to 8 star anise pods

6 to 8 cinnamon sticks

Pinch of freshly grated nutmeg

2 or 3 sweet red apples, halved, cored, and thinly sliced

Calvados (optional)

In a medium saucepan, warm the apple juice, star anise, cinnamon sticks, and nutmeg over medium heat. Strain and then serve the cider in warm mugs with sliced apples and a splash of Calvados (if using).

Curly Escarole with Apples and Comté

SERVES 6 TO 8

Our autumn market is full of crisp chicories, endive, frisée, and escarole. We prefer to select small tender heads, as the flavor is less bitter. As lettuce becomes scarce in the cooler months, escarole makes for a beautiful salad, especially when paired with sweet apple slices and nutty Comté cheese. We like to use local varieties of apples, such as Melrose and Opale, though you can use any kinds that are available at your local market. We prepare this salad onsite, tearing the escarole leaves and slicing the apples before tossing them into the vinaigrette.

2 small heads escarole

1 recipe Vinaigrette (page 354), using the apple cider vinegar variation

2 sweet red apples, halved, cored, and thinly sliced

Handful of fresh flat-leaf parsley leaves

4 ounces (115 g) Comté or Gruyère cheese, thinly shaved

Fleur de sel and freshly ground black pepper

Tear the escarole into small pieces and add it to the bowl with the vinaigrette. Add the apple slices and parsley and toss to coat them in the vinaigrette. Using a stainless-steel vegetable peeler, thinly shave the cheese and gently toss again. Season with salt and pepper. Serve immediately.

Duck Pâté en Croûte

MAKES 1 (9½ BY 4-INCH/24 BY 10-CM) PÂTÉ; SERVES 6 TO 8

It is very rewarding for a cook to be able to master classic French terrines and pâtés, which are served all over France. This beautiful pastry-covered pâté, often part of the traditional French charcuterie board, works great for parties, as it can be made in steps several days in advance. When making a French-style pâté, you will use a mix of lean and fatty meat—in this case, both duck and pork. Be sure to source your meat from a high-quality local butcher. Rather than using a meat grinder as most butcher shops do, we prefer to hand-chop the meat with a large chef's knife or sharp cleaver. This makes for a more rustic and moist pâté. After it's cooked, we add in a layer of aspic between the meat and the dough for a pretty presentation. Aspic is typically made by adding gelatin (in sheet or powdered form) to warmed consommé. Serve with crisp cornichons and Dijon mustard.

FOR THE FILLING

17 ounces (480 g) duck breast, fat removed

7 ounces (200 g) pork loin

10½ ounces (300 g) tender pork fat (also called fatback; not lard)

1 tablespoon extra-virgin olive oil, preferably French, plus more as needed

1 large yellow onion, finely chopped

3 cloves garlic, finely chopped

3 sprigs thyme

3 whole juniper berries

Pinch of ground allspice

3 tablespoons dry white wine, such as Burgundy Chardonnay

Fleur de sel and freshly ground black pepper

5¼ ounces (150 g) chicken livers

1 tablespoon unsalted butter

1 shallot, finely chopped

¼ cup (60 ml) cognac

1 recipe Aspic (page 364), unset and slightly warm

FOR THE DOUGH

3 cups (375 g) unbleached all-purpose flour

1 teaspoon fleur de sel

1 cup (2 sticks/225 g) cold unsalted butter, cut into small pieces

5 large egg yolks

½ cup (120 ml) heavy cream

1 teaspoon distilled white vinegar

Dijon mustard, for serving

Cornichons, for serving

Make the filling: Using a sharp chef's knife or cleaver, chop the duck and pork loin into roughly ¼-inch (6-mm) pieces. Cut the tender pork fat into slightly smaller pieces. Transfer the duck, pork loin, and pork fat to a large bowl and set aside.

In a large sauté pan, heat the olive oil over medium heat. Add the onion and sauté until soft and translucent, about 5 minutes. Add the garlic and thyme and sauté until the garlic softens, about 1 minute. Set aside to cool.

Using a heavy mortar and pestle, crush the juniper berries.

Add the onion mixture to the meat mixture. Add the juniper berries, allspice, and wine and stir to combine.

Recipe continues on page 246

Season with salt and pepper, then cover and refrigerate overnight, or for up to 2 days.

Rinse the chicken livers, remove any membranes or veins from the exterior, and pat dry. Season all over with salt and pepper.

In a medium sauté pan, melt the butter over medium-high heat. When the butter starts to foam, add the chicken livers and sauté until caramelized but still rare on the inside, 2 to 3 minutes. Add the shallot and sauté for 1 minute more. Turn off the heat and add the cognac to the pan. Turn the heat back on and very carefully tip the pan to ignite the cognac and flambé the chicken livers. The flame will go out by itself once all the alcohol has burned off. Let it stand for a few minutes to cool, then chop the chicken livers into ¼-inch (6-mm) pieces, add to the cold meat mixture, and mix well to combine. Cover and refrigerate for several hours, preferably overnight.

Make the dough: In a large bowl, whisk together the flour and salt. Add the butter. Using your hands, gently toss to coat the butter in the flour mixture. Scoop the mixture in your hands and gently press the flour and butter between your fingertips until the mixture looks grainy, with some small pieces of butter still visible. Work quickly to ensure that the butter stays cold.

In a small bowl, whisk together four of the egg yolks, 6 tablespoons (90 ml) of the heavy cream, and the vinegar. Drizzle over the dough and use a fork to gently toss until incorporated. Continue working the dough, gently squeezing it between your fingertips until it comes together and there is no dry flour visible. Be careful not to overwork the dough. It is ready as soon as you can squish the dough in one hand and it stays together.

Divide the dough into two pieces: two-thirds of the dough will be used to line the terrine mold and one-third will be used for the top and decorations. Wrap each piece in plastic wrap and refrigerate for at least 1 hour.

In a small bowl, whisk together the remaining egg yolk and the remaining 2 tablespoons heavy cream. Set aside.

Preheat the oven to 350°F (175°C).

Roll the larger piece of dough into a roughly 15 by 10-inch (38 by 25-cm) rectangle, about ¼ inch (6 mm) thick. Place a 9½ by 4-inch (24 by 10-cm) mold in the center of the dough and gently press down to indent the bottom of the mold into the dough. Using the base as a guide, turn the mold on its side to mark the side and end dimensions. Cut the dough about 2 inches (5 cm) larger than the markings to allow the dough to hang over the sides of the mold. Roll the smaller piece of dough into a roughly 12 by 6-inch (30.5 by 15-cm) rectangle, about ¼ inch (6 mm) thick, and turn the mold upside down to mark the dimensions of the top. Cut the dough about ¼ inch (6 mm) larger than the dimensions of the top—it should measure about 10 by 4½ inches (25 by 11 cm). Reserve any dough scraps.

Fold the larger rectangle of dough using the marking as a guide and gently place it inside the (9½ by 4-inch /24 by 10-cm) mold, letting the excess dough fall over the sides. Using your hands, gently press the dough into the mold, making sure it fits snugly along the bottom, inside edges, and corners.

Remove the meat mixture from the refrigerator. To check for seasoning, form a small piece of the meat mixture (about 2 tablespoons) and form it into a patty. Cook the patty in a little olive oil in a small sauté pan over medium-high heat until browned and cooked through, 4 to 5 minutes. Taste to check the seasoning (then enjoy or discard), and adjust the seasoning, as needed. The pâté will be served at room temperature, so it's important to make sure it's properly seasoned. Then, using a large spoon, gently fill the mold and press the meat mixture tightly, filling it to the top of the mold.

Gently fold one long side of the dough over the meat mixture. Lightly brush the dough with the egg wash, then fold the second long side over the top. Trim the short ends so that only about ¼ inch (6 mm) hangs over the ends. Lightly brush the dough with the egg wash, then fold the short sides over. Place the smaller rectangle of dough on top of the terrine, folding the edges under to create a neat appearance. Using a paring knife, cut a small circle through the center of the dough to allow steam to escape when baking. Cut a small piece of foil (about 6 by 4-inch/15 by 10-cm), roll it into a cylinder, and place it in the hole. Roll and cut any dough scraps to create decorations (such as in leaf shapes) for the top. Lightly brush the entire top surface of the dough with the egg wash, then arrange the decorative pieces of dough on top. Lightly brush the decorations with egg wash.

Place the mold on a baking sheet and bake until a meat thermometer inserted into the center registers 165°F (75°C), about 1 hour. Remove from the oven and let it cool for 1 hour. Remove the foil cylinder.

Once the pâté is cooled, insert a small funnel into the hole where the foil cylinder was, then slowly and gradually pour the slightly warm aspic into the funnel, allowing it to spread throughout the pâté. It can take a while for the aspic to spread, so you may need to add it in stages. It also helps to tip the mold from side to side to help move the aspic around the meat. Continue adding more aspic until it fills the opening. The pâté will continue to cool while you add the aspic. Once you've added as much aspic as possible and the pâté is at room temperature, cover and refrigerate it overnight. Reserve any leftover aspic for another use.

When ready to serve, remove the mold from the refrigerator and let the pâté come to room temperature. Carefully remove the pâté from the mold and cut it into slices. Serve with Dijon mustard and cornichons. The pâté can be covered and refrigerated for up to 5 days.

Apple Tart

There is nothing more classic than a French apple tart.
Serve it with a dollop of crème fraîche or Crème Anglaise (page 386).

Unbleached all-purpose flour, for dusting

½ recipe Pâte Sucrée (page 378)

1 large egg yolk

3 tablespoons heavy cream

7 Golden Delicious apples

4 tablespoons (½ stick/55 g) unsalted butter

2 tablespoons granulated sugar

Seeds of 1 vanilla bean (see page 64)

2 tablespoons vanilla sugar (see page 64), for sprinkling

Confectioners' sugar, for dusting

On a lightly floured surface, use the pâte sucrée to make the tart shell (see page 374). Freeze it for 15 to 20 minutes before baking.

Preheat the oven to 375°F (190°C).

In a small bowl, whisk together the egg yolk and heavy cream. Use a pastry brush to lightly brush the egg wash over the dough. Partially blind bake the tart shell (see page 333).

Peel three of the apples, then cut them in half, remove the cores, and dice. Put the diced apples in a medium saucepan. Add 2 tablespoons of the butter, the granulated sugar, vanilla seeds, and ¼ cup (60 ml) water and place them over low heat. Cook, stirring occasionally, until the apples are tender and most of the water has evaporated, about 30 minutes. Transfer to a small bowl and mash with a fork until the mixture is mostly smooth and resembles thick applesauce. Set aside to cool.

Peel the remaining four apples, then cut them in half, remove the cores, and cut into ⅛-inch- (3-mm-) thick slices.

In a large, deep sauté pan, melt the remaining 2 tablespoons butter over medium heat. Add the apple slices and sauté, stirring gently so they don't break, until just softened, about 5 minutes.

Using an offset spatula or small spoon, spread the apple puree evenly in the partially baked tart shell. Reserve 8 to 10 of the thinnest apple slices. Carefully arrange the remaining apple slices, tightly overlapping, around the edge of the tart shell, forming a tight, compact circle. Repeat to create an inner circle going in the opposite direction. Depending on how tightly you layer them, you may have leftover apple slices. Carefully curl the reserved, thin apple slices so they resemble roses and arrange them vertically in the center of the tart. Sprinkle with the vanilla sugar.

Bake until the apples are tender and just starting to brown, 35 to 40 minutes. Serve warm or at room temperature, dusted with confectioners' sugar.

Beaujolais

BEAUJOLAIS NOUVEAU

On the third Thursday of November, France celebrates the arrival of Beaujolais Nouveau, the new vintage of Beaujolais wine. Made from Gamay grapes grown in Beaujolais, just south of the Côte d'Or, this fresh, fruity but dry wine ferments for just a few weeks before being bottled and released for sale. From Paris to Marseille, people flock to bars *à vin* (wine bars) at midnight to have a first taste of the new vintage. It's a festive French occasion, and we join in the celebration with an intimate Beaujolais Nouveau dinner party at the Atelier each year. We set our table and invite friends to join us for a relaxed dinner, served family-style.

The menu—rustic, hearty, and satisfying—is the perfect companion for any Beaujolais Nouveau wine celebration.

House-Made Chicken Liver Pâté PAGE 254

Warm Frisée Salad WITH *Bacon, Shallots,* AND *Poached Farm Egg* PAGE 257

Pan-Seared Quail WITH *Potato Gratin* AND *Glazed Carrots* PAGE 258

Chocolate Mousseline PAGE 263

House-Made Chicken Liver Pâté

SERVES 8 TO 10

We make this smooth, flavorful pâté often to enjoy as an apéritif. It's a classic inspired by Michael Field. Be sure to bring it to room temperature and sprinkle the top with fleur de sel before serving, and accompany it with plenty of warm toasted bread.

1 cup (2 sticks/225 g) unsalted butter

1 small onion, finely chopped

1 small shallot, finely chopped

2 cloves garlic, finely chopped

3 sprigs thyme

1 fresh bay leaf

1 small Granny Smith apple, peeled, cored, and finely chopped

¼ cup (60 ml) dry white wine, such as Burgundy Chardonnay

1 pound (455 g) chicken livers

Fleur de sel and freshly ground black pepper

¼ cup (60 ml) cognac

About 4 tablespoons (60 ml) heavy cream

1 to 2 teaspoons fresh lemon juice

½ recipe Clarified Butter (page 352), warm

Warm toasted bread, pickled vegetables, and cornichons, for serving

In a large sauté pan, melt 2 tablespoons of the butter over medium heat. Add the onion and shallot and sauté until soft and translucent, about 5 minutes. Add the garlic, thyme, and bay leaf and sauté until the garlic is softened, 1 to 2 minutes, being careful not to brown the garlic. Add the apple and wine and cook until the apple is soft and the white wine has evaporated, 2 to 3 minutes. Remove the thyme sprigs and bay leaf and discard. Transfer the mixture to a food processor. Do not clean the pan.

Rinse the chicken livers, remove any membranes or veins from the exterior, and pat dry. Season all over with salt and pepper.

In the same large sauté pan, melt 3 tablespoons of the remaining butter over medium-high heat. When the butter starts to foam, add the chicken livers and sauté until caramelized but still pink on the inside, about 4 minutes. Turn off the heat and add the cognac to the pan. Turn the heat back on and very carefully tip the pan to ignite the cognac and flambé the chicken livers. The flame will go out by itself once all the alcohol has burned off.

Add the livers, along with the pan juices, to the onion mixture in the food processor. Add 2 to 3 tablespoons of the heavy cream and puree until very smooth. Add the additional cream, as needed, to create a completely smooth mixture. Push the mixture through a small fine-mesh strainer into a large bowl, then set aside to cool to room temperature.

Cut the remaining 11 tablespoons (155 g) butter into small pieces and let them soften at room temperature. Once the pâté mixture has cooled completely, use a wooden spoon to gradually beat in the softened butter, 1 tablespoon at a time, until well combined. Add the lemon juice and season with salt and pepper. Transfer the pâté to a 4-cup (960-ml) ceramic terrine mold and smooth the top with an offset spatula or small spoon. Pour the warm clarified butter over the top of the terrine, cover, and refrigerate overnight. It can be stored in the refrigerator for up to 5 days.

Warm Frisée Salad with Bacon, Shallots, and Poached Farm Egg

SERVES 8 TO 10

This is a classic salad served in bistros and brasseries all over France. The frisée wilts slightly when drizzled with a warmed vinaigrette and topped with a poached farm egg and crispy lardons. It is nice as a first course and can easily be adapted for a simple weeknight supper. Make sure to use the freshest eggs you can find, as the whites will be firmer and they will poach better.

1 tablespoon distilled white vinegar

8 to 10 fresh large farm eggs

Extra-virgin olive oil, preferably French

2 (¼- to ½-inch-/6- to 12-mm) thick slices lard fumé or 4 slices thick-cut bacon, cut into lardons

2 shallots, thinly sliced into rings

2 tablespoons white wine vinegar

1 teaspoon Dijon mustard

8 to 10 small or 4 to 5 large heads frisée, tough stems removed

Fleur de sel and freshly ground black pepper

Fill a medium saucepan with water, add the distilled white vinegar, and bring it to a boil. Reduce the heat to maintain a simmer. Crack each egg into a small bowl, keeping them separate. Dip a large ladle into the simmering water to warm it. Lift the ladle out of the water and pour out most, but not all, of the water. Add an egg to the ladle, then lower the ladle so it's submerged in the simmering water and hold it there until the white is set, 30 seconds to 1 minute. As the white begins to set, lower the ladle all the way into the water and release the egg. If the egg sticks, use a small spoon to gently release the egg from the ladle. Cook, swirling the water as the egg cooks, until the white is set, 1 to 2 minutes. Use a slotted spoon to gently transfer the egg to a plate or platter covered with a clean, dry kitchen towel. Continue with the remaining eggs and set aside. Reserve the hot water.

In a large deep sauté pan, heat a drizzle of olive oil over medium heat. Add the lardons and sauté until crispy and cooked through, 5 to 8 minutes. Using a slotted spoon, transfer the lardons to a paper towel–lined plate to remove excess grease and set aside. Remove all but 3 tablespoons of the fat from the pan and place the sauté pan over low heat. Add the shallots and sauté until soft, about 3 minutes. Add the white wine vinegar and mustard and use a wooden spoon to scrape any little bits off the bottom. Add the frisée and toss to coat. Season with salt and pepper. Divide the frisée among eight to ten warmed salad plates and sprinkle with the lardons.

To rewarm the eggs, use a slotted spoon to dip each egg in the reserved hot water and hold until the egg is warm, 15 to 30 seconds. Transfer the egg to a plate or platter covered with a clean, dry kitchen towel and repeat with the remaining eggs. Season the eggs with salt and pepper, arrange them on top of the salads, and serve immediately.

Pan-Seared Quail with Potato Gratin and Glazed Carrots

SERVES 8 TO 10

A little more festive and flavorful than a simple roasted chicken, these tender little birds are quick to prepare. We sauté them on top of the stove to get a nice crispy skin before finishing them in the oven. It is important to truss and tie them when preparing for roasting, as this will ensure even cooking. With the addition of a beautiful potato gratin and buttery glazed carrots, this is the perfect rustic bistro dish to celebrate the arrival of Beaujolais Nouveau.

FOR THE POTATO GRATIN

1 clove garlic, smashed

½ cup (120 ml) heavy cream

½ cup (120 ml) whole milk

2 pounds (910 g) Yukon Gold potatoes (about 4 medium), peeled

1 tablespoon fresh thyme leaves

Fleur de sel and freshly ground black pepper

Freshly grated nutmeg

2 cups (220 g) coarsely grated Comté or Gruyère cheese

2 tablespoons unsalted butter, cut into small pieces, plus more for the dish

FOR THE QUAIL

8 to 10 (4- to 5-ounce/115- to 140-g) quail

Fleur de sel and freshly ground black pepper

2 tablespoons extra-virgin olive oil, preferably French

2 tablespoons unsalted butter

3 medium yellow onions, thickly sliced into rounds

6 sprigs thyme

3 fresh bay leaves

Small handful of fresh flat-leaf parsley leaves, plus more for garnish

1 clove garlic, halved horizontally

FOR THE GLAZED CARROTS

16 to 20 small carrots, trimmed, leaving some of the green stems attached, and halved lengthwise

2 tablespoons unsalted butter

Fleur de sel and freshly ground black pepper

FOR THE PAN SAUCE

1 shallot, finely chopped

3 sprigs thyme

1 fresh bay leaf

1 cup (240 ml) dry white wine, such as Burgundy Chardonnay

1 cup (240 ml) Chicken Stock (page 357)

Fleur de sel and freshly ground black pepper

1 teaspoon unsalted butter

FOR THE CRESSON

8 to 10 tiny handfuls of cresson or watercress

Extra-virgin olive oil, preferably French

Fleur de sel and freshly ground black pepper

Make the potato gratin: Preheat the oven to 350°F (175°C).

Rub the bottom and sides of a 13 by 9-inch (33 by 23-cm) gratin dish with the smashed garlic. Butter the dish and set aside.

In a small bowl, whisk together the heavy cream and milk.

Recipe continues on page 260

Using a mandoline, slice the potatoes into paper-thin rounds, about ⅛ inch (3 mm) thick. Arrange the potatoes in an overlapping layer in the gratin dish and continue until the bottom is completely covered. Sprinkle with a few thyme leaves and season with salt, pepper, and nutmeg. Scatter some cheese over the potatoes and dot with a few pieces of butter. Continue this layering process until the gratin is full, finishing with grated cheese on top. Place the gratin dish on a baking sheet to prevent spills in the oven, drizzle with the heavy cream and milk mixture, and bake until the potatoes are tender and the top is golden brown, about 45 minutes. Cover to keep warm while you roast the quail.

Make the quail: Raise the oven temperature to 425°F (220°C).

Remove the quail from the refrigerator and let them come to room temperature before cooking. Rinse and thoroughly dry the quail inside and out. Use kitchen tweezers to remove any pin feathers or quills, as needed. Season the inside of the quail with salt and pepper, then truss them (see page 348) and season the outside with salt and pepper.

In a large, oven proof sauté pan, heat 1 table-spoon of the olive oil and 1 tablespoon of the butter over medium-high heat. Add half the quail and sear on all sides, until the skin is crisp and nicely browned, 4 to 5 minutes. Transfer the quail to a plate, then use the remaining 1 tablespoon of olive oil and butter to sear the remaining quail. Transfer the second batch of quail to the plate; do not clean the pan.

Arrange the sliced onion rounds in the sauté pan, then place the quail, breast-side up, on top of the onions. Depending on the size of your pan and the number of quail, you may need to do this in two pans. Sprinkle the thyme, bay leaves, parsley, and garlic over the quail. Place the pan in the oven and roast until the juices run clear when you cut in between the breast and thigh, 15 to 18 minutes. Transfer the quail to a warm cutting board and let them rest. Keep the onion rounds warm for serving. Reserve the pan(s) with the meat juices. Reduce the oven temperature to 350°F (175°C).

While the quail is roasting, make the glazed carrots: Bring a large pot of salted water to a boil and fill a bowl with ice and water.

Add the carrots to the boiling water and blanch until tender, 2 to 3 minutes, depending on the size. Immediately plunge the carrots into the ice water to stop the cooking and preserve their color. Once the carrots are cool, set them on a clean kitchen towel to drain.

When ready to serve, melt the butter in a large sauté pan over medium-high heat. Once the foam subsides, add the carrots and sauté, gently tossing, until caramelized, 2 to 3 minutes. Season with salt and pepper. Keep warm.

Place the potato gratin in the oven to rewarm while you make the pan sauce.

Make the pan sauce (see page 334) with the ingredients, as listed.

Make the cresson: In a medium bowl, drizzle the cresson with olive oil and toss to combine. Season with salt and pepper.

To serve: Place the roasted onion rounds on warm plates and top with the roasted quail. Arrange the cresson and carrots on the plates, drizzle with the pan sauce, and garnish with fresh parsley leaves. Serve immediately with the potato gratin and the remaining pan sauce.

Chocolate Mousseline

SERVES 8 TO 10

We infuse our chocolate mousseline with vanilla vodka and pipe it into chilled pot de crème pots. When ready to serve, we add a dollop of homemade whipped cream and a dusting of cocoa powder.

1 cup (240 ml) heavy cream

8 ounces (225 g) high-quality bittersweet chocolate (at least 70% cacao), finely chopped

½ teaspoon unsweetened cocoa powder, plus more for dusting

1 cup (2 sticks/225 g) unsalted butter, cut into pieces, at room temperature

1 tablespoon vanilla vodka (see page 64) or orange liqueur

5 large egg yolks

½ cup plus 1 teaspoon (104 g) vanilla sugar (see page 64)

⅛ teaspoon fleur de sel

3 large egg whites

In a medium bowl, whip the heavy cream until it holds soft peaks. Cover and refrigerate until ready to use.

Place the chocolate in a medium heatproof bowl. Set the bowl over a saucepan of barely simmering water (do not let the bottom of the bowl touch the water) and melt the chocolate, stirring with a rubber spatula until completely smooth. Remove from the heat; reserve the barely simmering water. Sift the cocoa powder over the chocolate mixture, then slowly add the butter, stirring with a rubber spatula until completely smooth. Stir in the vanilla vodka.

In another medium heatproof bowl, whisk together the egg yolks, ½ cup (100 g) of the vanilla sugar, and the salt until pale yellow. Place the bowl over the pan of barely simmering water and whisk until the mixture is thickened and the sugar has completely dissolved, 3 to 4 minutes. Remove from the heat, then transfer it to a large bowl, being careful not to include any of the cooked eggs or solid pieces that may be stuck on the side of the bowl.

In a clean, copper bowl, using a whisk, whip the egg whites and the remaining 1 teaspoon vanilla sugar until they hold soft peaks.

Slowly add the chocolate mixture to the egg yolk mixture and stir until well combined. Reserve ½ cup (120 ml) of the chilled whipped cream for garnish and refrigerate it until ready to serve. Gently fold the rest into the chocolate mixture. Add a large spoonful of the whipped egg whites to the chocolate mixture and gently fold to lighten it. Add the remaining whipped egg whites and fold just until there are no streaks left. Cover and refrigerate until set, at least 1 hour.

When ready to serve, transfer the mousse to a pastry bag with a large round tip and pipe into chilled pot de crème pots or small individual ramekins. Top with a dollop of the reserved whipped cream, dust with cocoa powder, and serve.

WINTER

After a busy year of classes, we welcome the quiet calm of winter. By December, the crowds of tourists have disappeared, the Christmas lights are strung up in the streets, and we begin preparing for cozy celebrations *en famille*.

Winter days in Burgundy are short and chilly. We relish the frosty mornings and snow-dusted vines, though it's rare to get a serious snowfall. Barren vineyards sit quietly until January, when the pruning and the burning of freshly cut branches from the previous year begins.

We spend this slow season preparing for the year to come—thinking of new ideas for the shop, testing recipes and developing new menus, and taking time to reflect. Winter is a season for slow cooking—simmering pots of stock, soups, and stews, and firing up the bread oven at Kendall and Laurent's house to make roasted chicken or rustic boules of bread.

During the winter months, the Wednesday and Saturday markets are much calmer than usual. All the same, we bundle up and trek to the Saturday market to see what's available. We can always count on fresh celery root and other root vegetables like turnips, parsnips, and beets, as well as hearty greens, spinach, cabbages, Brussels sprouts, and persimmons. There's a beautiful selection of citrus from Corsica, and we can still buy bread, cheese, charcuterie, meat, and fish from our favorite producers. Autumn and winter are hunting seasons in Burgundy, and butchers work directly with local hunters to source fresh game such as venison, and game birds like pheasant and quail.

We often spend cozy winter Sundays cooking and eating by the fire at home. These moments remind us to slow down, breathe, and respect the rhythm of the seasons.

RAPHAËL VOSSOT | ARTISAN BUTCHER

We'll never forget the first time we met our favorite butcher. We had just moved to Beaune, and we had heard through the grapevine that Raphaël Vossot was the best butcher in town. On one of our first visits, we entered his shop, and around the corner came a gentle giant of a man. He set to work preparing *tête de veau*, a classic French dish of veal cheeks, head meat, and tongue, slowly simmered and served with a mustard sauce. A specialty of Lyon, the butcher capital of France, tête de veau takes the skill of an artisan butcher to properly prepare.

Monsieur Vossot began his career as a butcher at seventeen years old. Born just outside of Beaune, he earned his CAP (*le certificat d'aptitude professionnelle*) in charcuterie and butchery, and went on to apprentice with a butcher in Dijon for five years. From there, he worked as a butcher all over France, from Paris to the Jura to Carpentras, as well as stints in Switzerland, French Guiana, and the Reunion Island.

His little shop, situated on rue Maufoux for eighteen years, is truly a nose-to-tail operation, and he uses nearly every single part of the animal. It is everything you'd expect from an old-fashioned French butcher shop: Aging sausages hang from the ceiling and a long display case is packed with various cuts of poultry and meats, butchered in-house, as well as a large selection of house-made terrines and pâtés, *mousse de canard*, *confit de foie de volaille* (various duck and chicken liver mousses), an elaborate pâté en croûte (a pâté surrounded by a pastry crust), and the Burgundian specialty *jambon persillé* (a ham and parsley terrine), covered with a thick layer of aspic.

His shop is ideal for a cook: He cuts meat to order, and can get just about any type you need. He sources all of his meat and poultry from France, including the best of Burgundy.

Monsieur Vossot seeks to preserve the art and tradition of French butchery skills that were the norm thirty years ago, and keeps his craft alive by training young apprentices eager to learn more.

VIRGINIE BROUANT | FISHMONGER

Virginie Brouant is the proprietor of our favorite fish shop in Beaune. She opened in 2009, and her shop (bearing her name) has quickly gained a loyal following, thanks to her beautiful array of fresh fish and seafood. Every item in the shop is labeled with its origin—the majority of which comes from France—and whether or not it's line-caught.

Her selection is extensive, and everything she sells is seasonal. We usually rely on her to tell us what's best on any particular day. Large, flat turbot, *lotte* (monkfish), *bar* (sea bass), bright pink *rouget barbet* (red mullet), delicate sole, *St. Pierre* (John Dory), *cabillaud* (cod), and *sandre* (zander) are arranged on beds of ice. Tiny frog's legs line up neatly next to the cod. In a separate display sit baskets of oysters from Brittany and Normandy, along with cockles and mussels, *coquilles St. Jacques* (scallops) still in their shells, and all manner of shrimp varieties, from tiny *crevettes grises* to giant *gambas*. Though we don't live anywhere near the ocean, you'd never know it, looking around Virginie's shop.

Every Tuesday morning, she and her father drive nearly three hours to Rungis, the enormous wholesale market just south of Paris, to buy fresh fish for the shop. They arrive at 2 A.M. to make their selection, before returning to Beaune in time to open the shop at 7:30 A.M.

Virginie got her passion for fish from her uncle, a fishmonger with a shop in Paris. When she was young, he would take her to Rungis to buy fish with him, and she fell in love with the profession. She trained in Paris, earning her CAP degree as a *poissonnier* (fishmonger). In 2007, Virginie was awarded the elite title "*Meilleur Ouvrier de France*" (MOF) or "Best Craftsman in France" in the category of *Poissonnier Écailler* (fishmonger and *fruits de mer* [seafood] expert). This title is awarded every three years to the country's most outstanding artisans in more than one hundred creative trades. There are very few female fishmongers, and Virginie was one of the first women ever to win the MOF award for poissonnier écailler, a fact of which she is quite proud.

NOËL

Christmas in Burgundy is a lovely time of year. It's festive, yet understated in the most beautiful way—twinkling white lights arc through the streets and local shops feature bare pine trees, natural garlands, and wreaths tied with simple satin bows. On the Saturday market before Christmas, we gather our ingredients for the holiday meal and often stop, in the midst of our shopping, to enjoy a glass of mulled wine with old friends. People line up at the local pâtisserie to order their *bûche de Noël* (Yule log cake), and the market teems with Christmas specialties: tall white and red amaryllis, roasted chestnuts, artisan terrines of foie gras, plump *chapons* and *poulardes* (young roosters and hens from the Bresse region)—with their famous soft white plumes, wrapped in muslin and tied with ribbon like packages. There's a buzz in the air, as everyone prepares for the festivities to come.

For us, the holiday is all about family, and we've made an effort to create our own special traditions for Luc and Manon. We make chocolate truffles and *mendiants* (chocolate candies) with them, and decorate the tree together on Christmas Eve, always keeping in mind the spirit of the season.

On the special day, we gather at Kendall and Laurent's house, spending the day cooking and preparing the holiday meal. Though the menu may change from year to year, as it depends on our whims as cooks, we are always sure to pair it with a nice bottle of Burgundy and finish with the Thirteen Desserts, a Provençal tradition. It's a leisurely day that often finishes by candlelight.

Gravlax with Crème Fraîche Blinis and Caviar

SERVES 6 TO 8

Tiny blinis with house-made gravlax, crème fraîche, and caviar are the ultimate festive apéritif. In France, people love smoked and cured salmon, and it is always part of the holiday celebration. It's so popular that even local butchers sell their own cured salmon during the holidays. We buy a whole wild salmon from Virginie, our local fishmonger, and cure it ourselves. Surprisingly simple to prepare, gravlax adds an elegant touch to the holiday menu—especially when served with a glass of bubbly.

FOR THE GRAVLAX

2 teaspoons whole fennel seeds

1 teaspoon whole coriander seeds

1 cup (220 g) fleur de sel

1 cup (200 g) sugar

2 tablespoons lemon zest

2 tablespoons freshly ground black pepper

2 large bunches fresh dill, coarsely chopped

1 (3-pound/1.4-kg) sushi-grade, skin-on wild salmon, cleaned and filleted, with fatty belly and pin bones removed

¼ cup (60 ml) vodka

FOR THE BLINIS

2¼ teaspoons active dry yeast

¼ cup (60 ml) warm water (about 110°F/43°C)

¾ cup (180 ml) warm (about 110°F/43°C) whole milk

1⅓ cups (165 g) unbleached all-purpose flour, plus more as needed

2 large eggs, separated, whites kept at room temperature

½ teaspoon fleur de sel

3 tablespoons unsalted butter, melted, plus more for cooking

¼ cup (60 ml) crème fraîche

Small tin of high-quality caviar, for garnish

Small handful of fresh chervil leaves, for garnish

1 tablespoon lemon zest, for garnish

Make the gravlax: In a mortar and pestle, crush the fennel and coriander seeds. Transfer them to a large bowl. Add the salt, sugar, lemon zest, and pepper and stir to combine. Set aside.

Line a large, glass dish with plastic wrap, leaving a 5-inch (12-cm) overhang. Place about one-third of the chopped dill in the center of the dish, arranging it so it's roughly the size of one salmon fillet. Set aside.

Place the salmon fillets, skin-side down, on a piece of parchment. Using your hands, rub the spice mixture all over the salmon, making sure to completely cover the fillets, including the skin. Place one of the fillets, skin-side down, on top of the dill on the dish. Drizzle the flesh side with half the vodka, then top with another one-third of the dill. Drizzle the flesh side of the second fillet with the rest of the vodka and arrange it, skin-side up, on top of the first fillet—they should be touching on their flesh sides with their skin sides facing out. Rub the remaining spice mixture on the outside of the salmon and cover with the remaining dill. Pull the plastic wrap up and over to tightly secure the two fillets together. Wrap

Recipe continues on page 280

them in a second layer of plastic to secure the fillets and keep the juices inside. Place a second glass dish on top and weight it down with heavy cans. Refrigerate for 2 to 3 days. Every 12 hours, unwrap the salmon, baste it with any juices, and rewrap, then flip the salmon package over, weigh it down, and refrigerate. The gravlax should be ready after 2 days, but it will be more firm after 3 days.

Unwrap the gravlax and place it on a cutting board. Using a very sharp, thin-bladed knife, cut on the bias into very thin slices, leaving the skin behind. The gravlax can be tightly wrapped in plastic and refrigerated up to 3 days.

Make the blinis: In a large bowl, combine the yeast with the warm water and whisk thoroughly until the yeast is completely dissolved. Let proof for 10 to 15 minutes. The mixture should be foamy; if it's not, start over. Add the warm milk, along with the flour, egg yolks, and salt, and whisk to combine. Add the melted butter and whisk to combine. If there are any lumps in the batter, push it through a fine-mesh strainer into another large bowl. Cover and let the batter rest in a warm, dry place until puffed, foamy, and increased in size, 1½ to 2 hours.

In a large, very clean, preferably copper bowl, use a large balloon whisk to beat the egg whites until they hold stiff peaks (see page 335). Fold into the batter. Heat a crêpe pan or medium sauté pan over medium-high heat. Lightly brush the pan with butter. Using a small spoon, gently stir the batter, then pour it into the pan to make several small blinis, roughly 2 inches (5 cm) in diameter—be careful not to crowd the pan. Cook, flipping once, for 30 seconds to 1 minute per side. Keep warm while you make the rest of the blinis, stirring the batter, wiping out the pan, and adding more butter as needed.

To serve, arrange the blinis on a serving platter. Top with a slice of gravlax neatly arranged in the center of the blinis. Add a dollop of crème fraîche and garnish with caviar, chervil, and lemon zest. Serve immediately.

Citrus-Fennel Salad

SERVES 6 TO 8

With its bright array of colors and textures, this salad is both festive and satisfying during the winter months. We combine crunchy, crisp fennel with oranges, parsley leaves, and ruby red pomegranate seeds. Add the pomegranate seeds at the last minute so the color stays vibrant, and then serve the salad right away to ensure that the fennel remains bright and crisp.

2 oranges

3 fennel bulbs

2 watermelon radishes, peeled

½ cup (25 g) fresh flat-leaf parsley leaves

3 tablespoons extra-virgin olive oil, preferably French

Seeds of 1 pomegranate

Fleur de sel and freshly ground black pepper

Using a small, sharp knife, cut off the stem and blossom ends of the oranges to create flat surfaces on both ends. Stand one orange upright on one of its flat surfaces and, using your knife, follow the natural curved shape of the orange from top to bottom, removing the peel and all the white pith. Hold the orange in one hand over a bowl to catch the juice and begin to cut through each wedge alongside the white membrane, creating clean segments. Repeat with the second orange; set aside. Reserve the juices.

Trim the fennel bulbs, remove the tough outer layers, cut them in half, and remove the inner cores. Using a mandoline, thinly slice the fennel and radishes.

In a large bowl, drizzle the fennel with a little of the reserved orange juice to preserve its color. Add the radishes, orange segments, and parsley, drizzle with the olive oil, and toss to coat. Add the pomegranate seeds. Season with salt and pepper and toss again. Taste and season with additional salt, pepper, and orange juice, as needed. Serve immediately.

Côte de Bœuf with Braised Cabbage and Sauce Béarnaise

SERVES 6 TO 8

Côte de bœuf, or beef rib roast, is a very popular cut of meat in France. It's not only beautiful for presentation, but it's incredibly flavorful. Burgundy is a region known for its high-quality Charolais beef cows, though beef in France, generally speaking, is exceptional because of the way they raise their animals. The countryside is dotted with small herds of cattle from spring to early winter, grazing on grass. No matter where you live, seek out a local butcher who can provide high-quality (and ideally, local, grass-fed, hormone-free) beef for this rib roast. To complement this rich cut of beef, we serve a creamy béarnaise sauce and simple braised cabbage with crisp lardons.

1 (5½- to 6½-pound/2.5- to 3-kg) côte de bœuf (2- or 3-rib beef rib roast), Frenched (optional; see page 345)

Fleur de sel and freshly ground black pepper

4 tablespoons extra-virgin olive oil, preferably French

1 large bunch thyme

1 (¼- to ½-inch-/6- to 12-mm-thick) slice lard fumé, or 2 slices thick-cut bacon, cut into lardons

2 or 3 small or 1 medium head green cabbage, quartered

2 or 3 small or 1 medium head purple cabbage, quartered

1 quart (960 ml) Chicken Stock (page 357)

Small handful of fresh chervil leaves, for garnish

1 recipe Sauce Béarnaise (page 369), warm

Make the beef: Remove the beef from the refrigerator and let it come to room temperature before roasting.

Preheat the oven to 400°F (205°C).

Pat the beef dry and tie it (see page 345) if needed, then season with salt and pepper.

Heat a cast-iron pan large enough to hold the meat over medium-high heat. Add 2 tablespoons of the olive oil and heat until hot but not smoking. Add the beef and sear, turning, until browned and caramelized on all sides, 8 to 10 minutes. Add the thyme, place the pan in the oven, and roast until a meat thermometer inserted into the thickest part of the meat reaches 125° to 130°F (52° to 55°C) for medium-rare, 45 minutes to 1 hour, depending on the size. Let the beef rest on a warm cutting board for at least 15 minutes before carving.

Make the cabbage: Heat a large Dutch oven over medium heat. Add the remaining 2 tablespoons olive oil and heat until hot but not smoking. Add the lardons and sauté until crispy and cooked through, 5 to 8 minutes. Use a slotted spoon to transfer the lardons to a small bowl and set aside. Working in batches, add the cabbage wedges, cut-side down, to the pot and season with salt and pepper. Cook, turning, until lightly browned, about 2 minutes. Transfer the cabbage to a platter and continue until all the cabbage wedges are browned. Return all the cabbage to the Dutch oven, along with the chicken stock and lardons, then cover, reduce the heat to low, and braise until just tender, 15 to 20 minutes. Season with salt and pepper. Using a slotted spoon, remove the cabbage from the braising liquid and place on a warm platter. Garnish with the lardons and fresh chervil, and keep warm while you make the sauce béarnaise.

Arrange the beef on a board and serve with the warm béarnaise and cabbage.

Chocolate Truffles and Mendiants

MAKES ABOUT 30 TRUFFLES AND 30 MENDIANTS

Dark chocolate truffles are one of the simplest and most festive of holiday desserts.
Mendiants are a traditional French Christmas candy with chocolate, candied citrus, dried
fruit, and nuts. We like to serve them on Christmas Eve, as part of the Thirteen Desserts.
It's important to use best-quality ingredients for both recipes.

FOR THE TRUFFLES

1 pound (455 g) high-quality bittersweet chocolate (at least 70% cacao), finely chopped

1 cup (240 ml) heavy cream

Unsweetened cocoa powder, for dusting

FOR THE MENDIANTS

1 pound (455 g) high-quality bittersweet chocolate (at least 70% cacao), finely chopped

½ cup (70 g) hazelnuts, toasted and skins removed

¼ cup (30 g) pistachios

¼ cup (25 g) sliced almonds

¼ cup (35 g) dark or golden raisins

¼ cup (40 g) chopped Candied Citrus peels (page 305)

Fleur de sel, for garnish (optional)

Make the truffles: Place the chocolate in a large heatproof bowl.

In a small saucepan, heat the heavy cream over medium heat until just under a boil. Pour it over the chocolate, then gently stir with a rubber spatula, just until the chocolate is smooth and velvety. Let it stand at room temperature until firm, about 1 hour.

Sift the cocoa powder into a large, shallow bowl. Line a baking sheet with parchment paper.

Use a spoon to scoop out a small amount of the chocolate, then gently roll it between your palms to form a round. Repeat until all the chocolate has been rolled.

Roll the truffles in the cocoa powder until completely coated, then place them on the parchment-lined baking sheet. Refrigerate briefly to set, then transfer to an airtight container and refrigerate for up to 2 weeks.

Make the mendiants: Chill a marble slab or line two baking sheets with parchment paper. If your kitchen is warm, it's best to use the parchment-lined baking sheets to avoid the chocolate sticking to the marble.

Temper the chocolate (see page 387).

Using a small spoon, dollop some of the tempered chocolate into circles about 2½ inches (6 cm) in diameter onto the chilled marble slab or the parchment-lined baking sheets. Before the chocolate sets, sprinkle it with the hazelnuts, pistachios, almonds, raisins, candied citrus, and salt (if using). Let the chocolate stand at room temperature until set, about 30 minutes. If the kitchen is warm and the mendiants don't set, refrigerate them briefly.

Use an offset spatula or small knife to release the chocolate from the marble or the parchment-lined baking sheets. Enjoy immediately or store the mendiants in an airtight container for up to 2 weeks.

WINTER GATHERING

I n January and February, classes wind down and the market becomes sleepy. Our winter meals are very casual, and we often look to our French larder for inspiration. We try to keep our pantry well-stocked so we can easily prepare an impromptu meal.

One of our preferred winter dishes is *pot-au-feu*, a savory stew of beef shanks, chuck roast, and oxtails, slowly simmered in homemade beef stock with vegetables and a bouquet garni until the meat is fork tender.

After an early morning visit to the market, and while the pot-au-feu is simmering on the back of the stove, we take the time to set our table with some of our favorite treasures we've collected over the years—French creamware, mixed vintage flatware, well-worn linens, and Burgundy wine glasses.

The shop fills with wonderful aromas and friends stop by for a late lunch. We especially enjoy this leisurely type of cooking when the cold sets in.

Marrow Bones and Warmed Brioche

SERVES 6 TO 8

We serve the marrow bones on warm plates with brioche toast, and light, refreshing radish and parsley salad on the side. We are still searching for a set of vintage marrow spoons, but a simple butter knife will do for scooping out the delicate and flavorful marrow.

6 to 8 pounds (2.7 to 3.6 kg) beef or veal marrow bones, cut into 3-inch- (7.5-cm-) long pieces

Extra-virgin olive oil, preferably French

Fleur de sel and freshly ground black pepper

Brioche (page 371), warmed for serving

Rinse the marrow bones in cold water and dry thoroughly. Using a paring knife, carefully scrape off any meaty bits or sinew from the exteriors of the bones. Refrigerate until ready to cook.

Preheat the oven to 450°F (230°C).

Drizzle the marrow bones with olive oil and season with salt and pepper. Arrange them on a baking sheet and roast until the marrow is soft when pierced with a paring knife and the bones are caramelized, about 20 minutes. Be sure not to overcook the marrow, or it will melt out of the bones. Sprinkle with salt and serve immediately with the warm brioche.

Shaved Radish and Parsley Salad

SERVES 6 TO 8

This light, crisp salad is a perfect complement to a rich dish like Marrow
Bones and Warmed Brioche (page 294). We thinly shave a pretty trio of watermelon, white,
and breakfast radishes on a mandoline, and then toss them with sliced shallots,
parsley leaves, and a bright lemon vinaigrette.

4 watermelon radishes, peeled

4 white radishes, peeled

1 bunch breakfast radishes

2 shallots, thinly sliced into rings

Handful of fresh flat-leaf parsley leaves

1 recipe Vinaigrette (page 354), using the lemon juice variation

Fleur de sel and freshly ground black pepper

Fill a bowl with ice and water.

Using a mandoline, thinly slice the watermelon and white radishes. Place them in the bowl of ice water to crisp while you prepare the remaining ingredients. Wash and scrub the breakfast radishes. Using a stainless-steel vegetable peeler, carefully slice the breakfast radishes lengthwise into thin shavings. Add them to the bowl of ice water.

Drain the radishes and set them on a clean kitchen towel to absorb excess moisture.

Add the radishes, shallots, and parsley to a large serving bowl. Add the vinaigrette and toss to combine. Season with salt and pepper and serve immediately.

Pot-au-Feu

SERVES 6 TO 8

A comforting, classic French stew, pot-au-feu is a traditional dish recognized throughout France and can vary depending on the region. This savory one-pot meal is a two-day process, but well worth the effort, as it fills the kitchen with the most wonderful aromas.

FOR THE POT-AU-FEU

2 pounds (910 g) beef shank, tied (see page 345)

1¾ pounds (800 g) chuck roast

1 small whole oxtail, cut into pieces and tied into a bundle

Fleur de sel and freshly ground black pepper

4 quarts (3.8 L) Brown Veal Stock (page 359)

4 leeks, white and light green parts only

2 yellow onions, cut into wedges

1 bouquet garni (see page 61)

2 large carrots

8 marrow bones

3 sprigs thyme

FOR THE FINISHING VEGETABLES

10 white pearl onions

Boiling water

Fleur de sel

10 small white radishes, peeled

10 breakfast radishes

10 small carrots, peeled

10 small turnips, peeled

10 small Brussels sprouts, outer leaves removed, halved lengthwise

Handful of fresh chervil leaves

Make the pot-au-feu: Rinse and thoroughly dry the beef shank, chuck roast, and oxtail. Using a sharp knife, score the chuck roast in a crosshatch pattern on both sides. Season the beef shank, chuck roast, and oxtail with salt and pepper, then arrange them on a baking sheet or in a large dish; cover and refrigerate overnight.

Place the beef shank, chuck roast, and oxtail in an 8- to 10-quart (7.5- to 9.5-L) Dutch oven. Add the stock and enough cold water to cover the meat. Bring to a simmer, skimming any foam that comes to the surface.

Halve each leek lengthwise. Thoroughly wash the leeks, then tie the halves together.

Once the stock is simmering, add the leeks, onions, and bouquet garni and gently simmer, adjusting the heat, as needed, until the meat is tender, about 3 hours.

Fill a large bowl with ice and water.

Remove the meat from the stock and set aside to cool, then cover and refrigerate overnight.

Using a ladle, strain the stock through a cheesecloth-lined chinois into a large container. Discard the vegetables and bouquet garni. Place the container inside the bowl of ice water and let it cool, stirring occasionally, until it reaches room temperature. Cover and refrigerate overnight, so the fat will congeal at the top and be easier to remove.

The next morning, skim the fat from the top of the stock. Discard the fat. Return the stock to the Dutch oven over medium heat. Once the stock is warm, add the beef shank, chuck roast, and oxtail.

Cut the carrots lengthwise into thin strips that roughly equal the diameter of the marrow bones. Place the carrot strips over the open ends of the marrow bones and tie them in place to secure the marrow inside.

Recipe continues on page 301

Add the marrow bones and thyme to the Dutch oven, season with salt and pepper, and bring to a gentle simmer. Gently simmer, adjusting the heat and skimming any foam as needed, until the meat is very tender, about 2 hours.

Make the finishing vegetables: Using a small paring knife, make an X on the root end of each pearl onion. Place them in a large heatproof bowl and add just enough boiling water to cover. Let them stand until the skins soften, 10 to 15 minutes. Drain the onions and let them stand until cool enough to handle. Using a small, sharp knife, trim the nonroot ends, then peel back and remove the skins; discard the skins.

Bring a large pot of salted water to a boil and fill a bowl with ice and water. Add the peeled pearl onions to the boiling water and blanch until tender, about 7 minutes. Immediately plunge the pearl onions into the ice water to stop the cooking. Once the onions are cool, set them on a clean kitchen towel to drain.

Fill the pot with fresh water, add salt, and bring to a boil. Fill the bowl with fresh ice and water. Leaving some of the green stems attached, halve the radishes, carrots, and turnips lengthwise. Add the white radishes to the boiling water and blanch until tender, 2 to 3 minutes, depending on the size. Shock them in the ice water until cool, then set them on a clean kitchen towel to drain.

Return the salted water to a boil and add more ice to the ice water. Add the breakfast radishes to the boiling water and blanch until tender, 2 to 3 minutes, depending on the size. Shock them in the ice water until cool, then set them on a clean kitchen towel to drain. Repeat the blanching and shocking method for the carrots, turnips, and Brussels sprouts.

Add the blanched vegetables to the pot-au-feu and simmer for 10 to 15 minutes so the flavors meld. Season with salt and pepper. Remove the beef shank and chuck roast from the Dutch oven and cut them into individual servings. Cut the string holding the oxtail together. Cut the string around the marrow bones, discarding the carrot slices. Divide the beef shank, chuck roast, oxtail, and marrow bones among warm bowls, ladle the vegetables and stock over the meat, garnish with fresh chervil, and serve.

Orange Cake with Candied Citrus

SERVES 8 TO 10

During the winter months, the market is full of beautiful citrus fruits from Italy
and Corsica, and we enjoy using fresh oranges in everything from salads to desserts.
This elegant, orange-infused cake is topped with a drizzle of candied orange simple syrup,
fresh whipped cream, candied orange slices, and a sprinkling of orange sugar.

1 cup (200 g) sugar

2 tablespoons orange zest

10 tablespoons (1¼ sticks/140 g)
unsalted butter, at room
temperature, plus more for
the pan

4 large eggs, separated

¾ cup (180 ml) whole milk

¼ cup (60 ml) fresh orange juice

2 cups (250 g) unbleached all-
purpose flour, plus more for
the pan

1½ teaspoons baking powder

¼ teaspoon fleur de sel

¼ cup (60 ml) Simple Syrup
from Candied Citrus Slices
(page 305)

1 cup (240 ml) heavy cream,
whipped

10 to 12 Candied Orange Slices
(page 305)

Preheat the oven to 350°F (175°C).

Place a piece of parchment paper on a cutting board
and set a 9-inch (23-cm) round cake pan on top. Holding
the pan securely with one hand, use a paring knife to
trace around the pan, cutting a parchment circle to fit in
the bottom of the pan. Butter the cake pan, then place
the parchment circle in the bottom. Butter the parchment.
Dust the cake pan with flour, tapping out any excess.

In the bowl of a stand mixer fitted with the paddle
attachment, beat together the sugar and orange zest
to perfume the sugar. Reserve 1 tablespoon for garnish
and set aside. Add the butter to the mixer bowl with the
orange sugar and beat on medium-high speed until light
and fluffy, 2 to 3 minutes. Add the egg yolks and beat on
medium-high speed, scraping down the sides of the bowl
with a rubber spatula as needed, until pale and thick,
4 to 5 minutes. Add the milk and orange juice and stir
until combined, about 30 seconds. Sift the flour, baking
powder, and salt over the batter, then fold with a large
rubber spatula until just combined.

In a large, very clean, preferably copper bowl, use a
large balloon whisk to beat the egg whites until they hold
stiff peaks (see page 335). Using a large rubber spatula,
carefully fold the egg whites into the batter, being careful
not to deflate the batter.

Pour the batter into the prepared pan and use an
offset spatula to spread it evenly. Bake until a paring knife
inserted into the center of the cake comes out clean, 40
to 45 minutes. Set the pan on a wire rack and let it cool
completely. Once cool, remove it from the pan.

Place the cake on a cake plate or pedestal. Using a
small spoon, drizzle some of the candied citrus simple
syrup on top of the cake. Dollop the whipped cream in the
center, then arrange the candied orange slices around it.
Sprinkle with the reserved orange-scented sugar and serve.

Candied Citrus

MAKES ABOUT 1¼ POUNDS (570 G)

We use finely chopped candied citrus peels in our chocolate Mendiants (page 287) and candied citrus slices as a garnish for our Orange Cake (page 302). The candied citrus simple syrup, which is used to cook the citrus in this recipe, can be reserved and drizzled on cakes and other pastries.

4 cups (800 g) sugar, plus more for dusting

4 oranges

4 lemons

In a large saucepan, combine the sugar and 4 cups (960 ml) water over medium-high heat and heat until the sugar is dissolved. Turn off the heat.

Use a citrus stripper to cut long thin strips of peel from two oranges and two lemons. Reserve the oranges and lemons for another use. Place the strips in a small saucepan, cover with cold water, and bring them to a boil over medium-high heat. Strain the peels and repeat—this process will remove all the bitter white pith from the citrus.

Bring the sugar water to a boil and add the orange and lemon peels. Simmer until translucent, about 1 hour. Turn off the heat and let the peels cool in the syrup.

Line two baking sheets with parchment paper and top with cooling racks. Once the orange and lemon strips are cool, use a slotted spoon to place them on one of the cooling racks to drain. Reserve the simple syrup.

In a large bowl, gently toss the orange and lemon strips with sugar. Tap off any excess sugar and return the strips to the cooling rack. Let them stand at room temperature until set, 6 to 8 hours, or overnight.

To make the candied citrus slices: Cut a circular piece of parchment paper slightly larger than the saucepan holding the simple syrup. Bring the simple syrup back to a boil.

Cut two oranges and two lemons into thin round slices, remove any seeds, and add them to the simple syrup. Arrange the parchment round on top of the pan, then gently push it into the pan, so that it touches the citrus rounds and the edges go up the sides of the pan. Reduce the heat and simmer until translucent, about 1 hour. Turn off the heat and let the citrus rounds cool in the syrup.

Use a slotted spoon to place the citrus rounds on the other cooling rack. Let them stand at room temperature until set, 6 to 8 hours, or overnight. The orange and lemon rounds can be sugared like the peels, if desired.

Once sugared and dried, candied citrus will keep for several days in an airtight container at room temperature.

FIRESIDE COOKING

Winter months in Burgundy can be cold and damp, so we often have a fire going all day to keep the chill out of the air. Traditional houses in Beaune are made of stone, and many still have the original fireplaces and stone hearths. We gather bushels of firewood and place them in zinc buckets near the hearth, and our fireplaces at home become welcome extensions of our kitchens. We often bake and cook in the original wood-fired bread oven at Kendall and Laurent's house, and through trial and error, we have experimented with fire-roasting *à la ficelle* in the large fireplace at my home in Beaune. This ancient cooking method involves roasting birds or meat from a string in front of a roaring fire, and creates a crisp, golden skin and tender meat. A precursor to oven-roasting, cooking in front of a fireplace is still popular in many regions of France today.

We enjoy fire-roasting everything from wild pheasants to whole Bresse chickens. We'll light the fire a good hour in advance, to make sure it's had time to burn down a bit. We truss the birds and then hang them by their feet from long pieces of butcher's twine around old, iron butcher's hooks. While they roast in front of the fire, we prepare the rest of the meal, basting the birds regularly in duck fat, and turning them so they cook evenly. We catch the drippings in a pan below, and, once the cooking is done, we turn that into a delicious pan sauce.

As cooks, it's been very satisfying to go back to this traditional method of fire-roasting, and to learn as we go.

Roasted Beet Salad with Petite Cress and Orange Vinaigrette

SERVES 4 TO 6

This is a beautiful composed salad of *petite cress* (delicate micro watercress),
tiny roasted red and golden beets, and orange segments, drizzled with a tart orange vinaigrette.
We like how the earthiness of the roasted beets complements the sweetness of the oranges.
When they're available, we use blood oranges in the salad, as well as in the vinaigrette.

1½ pounds (680 g) small ruby red and golden beets, with greens attached

3 tablespoons extra-virgin olive oil, preferably French

Fleur de sel and freshly ground black pepper

6 sprigs thyme

2 oranges

2 shallots, thinly sliced into rings

1 cup (35 g) small or micro watercress

¼ cup (7.5 g) fresh flat-leaf parsley leaves

1 recipe Vinaigrette (page 354), using the orange juice variation

Preheat the oven to 400°F (205°C).

Trim the beet greens and reserve any small leaves to use in the salad. Set the leaves in a bowl of ice water to freshen and crisp. Reserve the large leaves for another use.

Wash and scrub the beets to remove any dirt. Dry thoroughly. Place the ruby red beets on a sheet of foil and the golden beets on a second sheet of foil. Drizzle the beets with the olive oil and season with salt and pepper. Place 3 thyme sprigs on top of each beet variety, then wrap the foil around the beets to form packets, and seal tightly by pinching the foil ends together. Place them on a baking sheet and roast until tender, about 40 minutes—the beets are ready when you can easily pierce the center with a paring knife. Let them stand until cool enough to handle.

Using your hands, carefully remove the beet skins. Cut the beets into halves or quarters, depending on the size. Set aside, keeping the colors separate.

Using a small, sharp knife, cut off the stem and blossom ends of both oranges to create flat surfaces on both ends. Stand one orange upright and, using your knife, follow the natural curved shape of the orange, from top to bottom, removing the peel and all the white pith. Hold the orange in one hand over a bowl to catch the juice and begin to cut along the membranes to release clean segments and let them fall into the bowl. Repeat with the second orange. Use the juice to make the orange vinaigrette.

Divide both the ruby red and golden beets among salad plates, arranging them in the center. Place the orange segments, shallots, watercress, parsley, and any reserved small beet greens around the beets in a decorative fashion. Drizzle with the orange vinaigrette, season with salt and pepper, and serve.

Braised Endive Gratin

SERVES 6

We often cook and serve endive in the autumn and winter months, as they are readily available at the market. We enjoy this chicory in salads with other greens, roasting it with just a drizzle of olive oil, salt, and pepper, or braising it in flavorful vegetable or chicken stock. When shopping, look for fresh endive that are compact and crisp, bright in color, and unblemished.

2 cloves garlic, smashed

2 tablespoons butter, plus more for the gratin dishes

3 or 4 slices day-old bread or lightly toasted fresh bread

9 small heads Belgian endive

1 quart (960 ml) Chicken Stock (page 357)

Fleur de sel and freshly ground black pepper

18 slices jambon cru (dry-cured ham) or prosciutto

½ cup (120 ml) heavy cream

2 cups (220 g) finely grated Comté or Gruyère cheese

Preheat the oven to 350°F (175°C). Rub the bottom and sides of six individual gratin dishes with the smashed garlic. Butter the gratin dishes.

Tear the bread into pieces and place them in a blender. Pulse until coarsely ground. Set aside.

Cut the endive lengthwise in half, remove any rough outer leaves, and trim the root ends. Place the endive, cut-side down, in one layer in a large, deep sauté pan. Add the chicken stock and bring to a boil over medium-high heat. Reduce the heat and braise, adjusting the heat, as needed, to maintain a simmer, just until tender, 3 to 5 minutes. Transfer the endive to a plate and let cool; reserve the stock.

Once the endive is cool enough to handle, use a paring knife to remove the tough root ends, being careful not to separate the layered leaves. Season with salt and pepper. Wrap each endive half with a slice of jambon cru.

Spoon 1 tablespoon of the heavy cream into the bottom of each gratin dish. Place three endive halves, cut-side down, in each gratin dish. Drizzle 1 tablespoon of the reserved chicken stock over each gratin dish. Reserve the remaining stock for another use, such as making soup. Cut the butter into small pieces and sprinkle over the gratin dishes, then drizzle with the remaining 2 tablespoons of heavy cream. Divide the cheese among the gratin dishes.

Place the gratin dishes on a baking sheet and bake for 25 minutes. Sprinkle the bread crumbs over the gratin dishes and bake until the gratins are bubbling and the bread crumbs are nicely browned, about 5 minutes more. Serve immediately.

Roasted Pheasant with Lemon and Caper Cauliflower

SERVES 4 TO 6

Autumn and winter are hunting seasons in Burgundy. We buy wild pheasant from our butcher friend in Pommard, when possible, who works directly with a local hunter to source fresh game. We often opt for fire-roasting à la ficelle, but you can achieve the same result by oven-roasting. We like to serve this pheasant with a side of lemon-caper cauliflower and Braised Endive Gratin (page 312). If pheasant is not available, you can adapt this recipe by using a small pasture-raised farm chicken, pintade, or quail.

FOR THE PHEASANT

2 small (2- to 3-pound/910-g to 1.4-kg) pheasants

Fleur de sel and freshly ground black pepper

¼ cup (50 g) duck fat (optional)

FOR THE CAULIFLOWER

2 small heads cauliflower, rough root stems removed, cut into florets

¼ cup (60 ml) extra-virgin olive oil, preferably French

Fleur de sel and freshly ground black pepper

2 lemons, cut into wedges

6 sprigs thyme

2 tablespoons salt-packed capers, rinsed

Small handful of fresh chervil leaves, for garnish

FOR THE PAN SAUCE

1 shallot, finely chopped

3 sprigs thyme

1 fresh bay leaf

1 cup (240 ml) dry white wine, such as Burgundy Chardonnay

1 cup (240 ml) Chicken Stock (page 357)

1 teaspoon unsalted butter

Fleur de sel and freshly ground black pepper

Make the pheasant: Preheat the oven to 350°F (175°C). Place a roasting pan large enough to hold both pheasants in the oven to warm.

Remove the pheasants from the refrigerator and let them come to room temperature before roasting. Rinse and thoroughly dry the pheasants inside and out. Use kitchen tweezers to remove any pin feathers or quills, as needed. Season the inside of both pheasants with salt and pepper, then truss (see page 348). Using your hands, rub the duck fat all over the outside of both pheasants. Season with salt and pepper.

Carefully remove the roasting pan from the oven and place both pheasants, breast-side up, inside. Roast, basting with the pan juices every 15 minutes, until the skin is golden brown and a meat thermometer inserted into the thickest part of the breast reaches 160°F (70°C), 45 minutes to 1 hour. The internal temperature of the pheasants will rise to 165°F (75°C) upon standing.

Make the cauliflower: Arrange the florets on one or two baking sheets and drizzle with the olive oil. Season with salt and pepper and toss to coat. Add the lemon wedges and thyme. Add the cauliflower to the oven while the pheasants are roasting and roast until tender and nicely caramelized, 30 to 40 minutes. Add the capers and roast for 5 minutes more. Season with salt and pepper.

Remove the pheasants from the oven and transfer them to a warm cutting board, letting them rest for 10 to 15 minutes while you make the pan sauce.

Make the pan sauce (see page 334) with the ingredients, as listed.

Carve the pheasants into pieces and arrange on a warm platter. Serve with the pan sauce and the cauliflower, garnished with the chervil.

Crêpes Suzette

SERVES 4 TO 6

Though the ingredients and method are simple, the secret to making great crêpes is practice.
Ideally, you want the batter to be nice and thin, so the finished version turns out light and airy.

FOR THE CRÊPES

3 tablespoons unsalted butter,
plus more melted butter for
cooking

2 cups (250 g) unbleached all-
purpose flour

1 tablespoon sugar, plus more
for sprinkling

½ teaspoon fleur de sel

3 large eggs

4 cups (960 ml) whole milk

FOR SERVING

½ cup (1 stick/115 g) unsalted
butter, at room temperature

1 tablespoon orange zest

1 tablespoon fresh orange juice

½ cup (120 ml) Grand Marnier

Preheat the oven to 300°F (150°C). Line a plate with parchment paper.

In a saucepan, melt 3 tablespoons of the butter. Set it aside to cool.

In a large bowl, whisk together the flour, sugar, and salt. Add the eggs and milk and whisk until well combined. Add the cooled butter and whisk until well combined. Cover and refrigerate for 1 to 2 hours.

Once the batter has rested, check to see if it has any lumps and strain it through a fine-mesh strainer, if needed.

Heat a crêpe pan over medium-high heat and lightly brush it with butter. Using a ladle, pour about ¼ cup (60 ml) of the batter into the pan. Immediately pick up the pan and swirl the batter so it covers the bottom of the pan in a uniform round. Return the pan to the heat and cook until the edges turn golden, 45 to 60 seconds. Using a small spatula, release the edges of the crêpe, then use your fingertips to carefully flip it over. Cook until the other side is golden brown, 30 to 45 seconds. Transfer the crêpe to the parchment-lined plate and sprinkle it with sugar. Continue with the remaining crêpe batter, layering the crêpes and sprinkling with sugar as you go. When finished, clean the crêpe pan and set aside.

In a small bowl, combine the remaining ½ cup of butter, the orange zest, and orange juice and stir until well combined. Add a small spoonful of the orange butter to the center of a sugared crêpe. Fold the crêpe in half and then in half again to form a triangle. Continue buttering and folding the remaining crêpes, then place them in the oven on a parchment-lined baking sheet until warmed through, about 5 minutes.

Arrange the crêpes in the crêpe pan or on a large heatproof platter. In a small sauté pan, warm the Grand Marnier over medium heat. Very carefully tip the pan to ignite the Grand Marnier, then carefully pour the flaming liquid over the warm crêpes. Use a long-handled spoon to baste the crêpes until the flame naturally burns out. Serve immediately.

THE NEW YEAR

The arrival of the New Year is a time to make plans for the year ahead. As cooks, we are continuously learning, trying new things, and striving to become better at what we do. One of our goals at The Cook's Atelier is to show guests that learning to cook is an approachable process, and one to be enjoyed. It takes time and practice, but the rewards are endless. We enjoy sharing our cooking knowledge, as well as learning from other cooks.

The first meal of the year feels bright and joyful. Typically, the French celebrate the New Year with *fruits de mer* and plenty of fresh, briny oysters. We appreciate this tradition, and sometimes think we could live solely on oysters and a good bottle of Raveneau Chablis.

When the New Year arrives, we are already thinking ahead to the vibrant flavors of spring, anticipating the lightness of a new season. We enjoy the last few restful weeks of winter before the hustle and bustle of our new season begins, and we take time to reflect on how fortunate we are to be cooks in Burgundy and to call this region home.

Oysters on the Half Shell with Champagne Mignonette

SERVES 6 TO 8

It's a French tradition to serve fresh oysters over the holidays—typically, on Christmas Eve and New Year's Day. We buy oysters from our favorite fishmonger, Virginie, which she sources from Brittany and Normandy. We carefully shuck them just before serving with a sturdy oyster knife. Once the oysters are shucked, we place them on a bed of ice and serve them immediately, with lemon wedges and Champagne mignonette, a Champagne vinegar and shallot sauce.

2 shallots, minced

1 cup (240 ml) Champagne vinegar

Freshly ground black pepper

36 to 48 chilled oysters

Lemon wedges, for serving (optional)

In a small bowl, whisk together the shallots and Champagne vinegar. Season with pepper and set aside.

Using a firm-bristled brush, rinse and scrub the exteriors of the oyster shells under cold running water to remove any sand or grit.

Using a towel, secure an oyster, flat-side up, in one hand. With the other hand, put the tip of an oyster knife into the joint area where the shells meet. Rock the knife in a back-and-forth motion until the shells separate. Carefully slide the oyster knife horizontally and close to the top shell to separate the oyster from the top shell. Once the top is removed, slide the oyster knife underneath the oyster on the cup side to free it from the shell. Be careful to reserve the juices when shucking.

Neatly arrange the shucked oysters on a bed of ice. Serve with the Champagne mignonette and lemon wedges (if using).

Coquilles St. Jacques with Herbs and Lemon

SERVES 6 TO 8

There are a few tricks to making perfectly seared scallops. First, it's important to thoroughly dry the scallops before cooking them. Then season them well on both sides. We season with our homemade Fishmonger's Fleur de Sel, a mixture of fleur de sel, lemon zest, and dried herbs. Make sure the sauté pan is hot and the butter bubbling before adding the scallops—if the pan isn't hot enough, the scallops won't get a nice crust. Additionally, it's important not to add too many scallops to the pan—if it's too crowded, the scallops will steam instead of sear. We serve *Coquilles St. Jacques* with a bright lemon-parsley garnish and a little drizzle of beurre noisette.

2 lemons

½ cup (25 g) coarsely chopped fresh flat-leaf parsley leaves, plus more for garnish

18 to 24 fresh sea scallops, side muscles removed

Fishmonger's Fleur de Sel (page 67), plus more for serving

Freshly ground black pepper

8 to 10 tablespoons (1 to 1¼ sticks/115 to 140 g) unsalted butter

Zest the lemons into a small bowl and set aside.

Using a small, sharp knife, cut off the stem and blossom ends of both lemons to create flat surfaces on both ends. Stand one lemon upright and, using your knife, follow the natural curved shape of the lemon from top to bottom, removing the remaining peel and all the white pith. Hold the lemon in one hand over a bowl to catch the juice and begin to cut along the membranes to release clean segments and let them fall into the bowl. Repeat with the second lemon. Add the parsley to the bowl with the lemon segments and juice, gently toss to combine, and set aside.

Rinse and thoroughly dry the scallops. Season with the fishmonger's salt and pepper.

In a large sauté pan, melt 2 tablespoons of the butter over medium-high heat. When the foam subsides, add about six scallops, being careful not to crowd the pan. Sear, basting continuously with the butter, until a golden crust develops on the bottom, 1 to 2 minutes. Flip the scallops and sear, basting continuously with the butter, until the other side has a golden crust, 1 to 2 minutes more. Transfer the scallops to a plate and keep warm. Repeat with the remaining scallops, wiping out the pan with a paper towel and adding more butter each time.

In a small saucepan, melt the remaining 2 tablespoons butter over medium heat. Heat the butter until it just starts to turn golden brown, about 1 minute—be careful not to let it burn. Remove from heat.

Divide the scallops among six to eight warm salad plates and drizzle with the browned butter. Add a bit of the lemon and parsley mixture. Sprinkle with the lemon zest and more parsley. Serve immediately.

Sole Meunière with Beurre Blanc and Parsleyed Potatoes

SERVES 6 TO 8

Sole meunière is a classic French dish that requires soaking whole Dover sole, a delicate white-fleshed fish, in milk, dredging it in flour, and sautéing it in clarified butter until browned and crisp. Sautéing fish can be a bit tricky, as it can have a tendency to stick to the pan. Make sure to first preheat the pan until hot before adding the clarified butter. Try not to move the fish while it's cooking, so you get a nice, brown crust—the pan will release the fish when it's ready.

FOR THE SOLE

1 to 2 cups (240 to 480 ml) whole milk

6 to 8 small whole Dover sole, cleaned and prepared by your fishmonger

Unbleached all-purpose flour, for dredging

Fleur de sel and freshly ground black pepper

1¼ to 1½ cups (300 to 360 ml) Clarified Butter (page 352)

½ cup (25 g) finely chopped fresh flat-leaf parsley leaves

1 to 2 lemons, for garnish

1 recipe Sauce Beurre Blanc (page 367), warm

FOR THE POTATOES

18 to 24 small new potatoes, such as Yukon Golds, peeled and boiled until tender

¼ cup (60 ml) Clarified Butter (page 352)

Fleur de sel and freshly ground black pepper

½ cup (25 g) coarsely chopped fresh flat-leaf parsley leaves

Make the sole: Preheat the oven to 350°F (175°C).

Put the milk in one or two gratin dishes large enough to hold the sole, depending on the number and size. Add the sole and flip to coat them in the milk. Let them stand, flipping occasionally, for 10 minutes.

Put the flour on a platter that's large enough for dredging the sole. Remove the sole from the milk, shaking it gently to remove any excess milk. Season both sides with salt and pepper, then dredge in the flour, turning several times, until fully coated. Shake the sole to remove any excess flour, then arrange them in a single layer on a large platter or baking sheet. Let them stand for 10 minutes.

In a heavy-bottomed sauté pan large enough to fit the sole, heat 3 tablespoons of the clarified butter over medium-high heat. When the butter is hot, add one sole, skin-side down, and sauté until golden brown, 3 to 4 minutes. Slide a fish spatula underneath the sole. Using your other hand to guide it, carefully flip the sole and sauté the other side until golden brown, 2 to 3 minutes more. Transfer the sole to a baking sheet and set aside. Repeat with the remaining sole, wiping out the pan with a paper towel and adding more clarified butter each time. Place the sole in the oven just to warm through.

Finish the potatoes: In a large sauté pan, warm the clarified butter over medium-high heat. Add the potatoes and sauté until browned on all sides, 5 to 7 minutes. Season with salt and pepper, sprinkle with the parsley, and keep warm while you make the beurre blanc.

Serve the sole immediately along with the potatoes, a few wedges of lemon, and the beurre blanc.

Lemon Soufflés

SERVES 6 TO 8

When we make soufflés, we can't help but think of Julia Child.
Inspired by her classic recipe, we begin with a sauce *bouilli*, a thickened mixture of
milk, sugar, and flour, which makes them especially delicate. Light and airy with
just a hint of lemon, they can be adapted using orange juice and zest or vanilla.

7 tablespoons (90 g) granulated sugar

1¼ cups (300 ml) whole milk

¼ cup (30 g) unbleached all-purpose flour

4 large egg yolks

3 tablespoons unsalted butter, plus more for the molds

1 tablespoon lemon zest

1 tablespoon fresh lemon juice

6 large egg whites

⅛ teaspoon fleur de sel

Confectioners' sugar, for dusting

Set a rack in the middle of the oven and preheat the oven to 400°F (205°C).

Butter the insides of eight individual 1-cup (240-ml) ramekins or one large 6-cup (1.4-L) soufflé mold. Using 2 tablespoons of the granulated sugar, sprinkle the inside of the mold(s), tapping to remove any excess. Set aside.

In a medium saucepan, whisk together the milk, ¼ cup (50 g) of the granulated sugar, and the flour until well-combined. Place over medium-high heat and cook, whisking continuously, until the mixture thickens and comes to a boil, about 3 minutes. Transfer to a large bowl and let it cool for 2 to 3 minutes.

Add the egg yolks, one at a time, whisking until fully incorporated before adding the next yolk. While the mixture is still warm, add the butter, lemon zest, and lemon juice and whisk until fully combined.

In a large, very clean, preferably copper bowl, use a large balloon whisk to beat the egg whites with the remaining 1 tablespoon granulated sugar and the salt until firm peaks form. Stir a large spoonful of the whipped egg whites into the soufflé base to begin lightening it. Using a rubber spatula, gently fold in the remaining egg whites, leaving some white streaks in the mixture and working quickly to keep the base light and airy.

Pour the finished mixture into the prepared mold(s), filling them just below the top rim. Run your thumb along the inside edge of the molds to remove any excess and ensure a proper lift. Bake until the tops of the soufflés are golden brown and lifted about 2 inches (5 cm) over the tops of the ramekins, 15 to 18 minutes (25 to 30 minutes for the soufflé mold). Do not be tempted to open the oven during baking or the soufflés will fall. Dust with confectioners' sugar and serve immediately.

COOKING METHODS AND KITCHEN RITUALS

There are certain basic kitchen skills—from properly using a knife to whipping egg whites and making a pan sauce—that every cook needs to know. Before mastering more advanced cooking techniques, we feel these basic cooking methods are the building blocks to becoming a confident cook.

Blind Baking

This is baking a tart crust partially or completely before adding the filling. Chilled tarts, such as our Summer Berry Tart with pastry cream filling (page 168), should be fully baked before filling. Baked fruit tarts or savory tarts, such as our Rustic Apricot Tart (page 116) or our Savory Tart with Spinach and Mushrooms (page 86), need to be partially baked before adding the fruit, or filling, and then returned to the oven to finish baking.

To **fully blind bake a tart or tartlets**, take the chilled, unbaked crust, shaped in a tart pan, and place it on a baking sheet. Cut a parchment paper circle slightly larger than the circumference of the tart or tartlets (leaving a 1-inch/2.5-cm overhang) and place it on top. Fill the parchment-lined tart shell with pie weights or dried beans to the top of the tart pan. Cook the tart crust at 375°F (190°C) for 15 to 20 minutes (8 to 10 minutes for tartlets), or until the edges are set and beginning to turn golden. Remove the parchment and beans or pie weights. In a small bowl, prepare an egg wash (1 large egg yolk whisked with 3 tablespoons heavy cream). Use a pastry brush to lightly brush the egg wash on the bottom of the tart shell. For a sweet tart or tartlets, sprinkle with a little sugar. Bake until the bottom of the tart shell is completely baked through and golden, 15 to 20 minutes more (10 minutes for tartlets). Set the tart shell on a wire rack to cool completely before filling.

If making a tart or tartlets that require **partial blind baking,** follow the directions above for blind baking. After you've added the egg wash, return the tart shell or tartlet shells to the oven and bake just until the egg wash is set, about 5 minutes total for tarts (2 to 3 minutes for tartlets) before adding the filling and returning it to the oven.

Deglazing and Pan Sauces

Deglazing is the process of pouring wine, stock, or water into a hot pan to remove and dissolve the flavorful brown bits of food (called the *fond*) stuck on the bottom of the pan after searing or roasting meat. These brown bits are full of flavor and help to create a pan sauce. Many of our recipes in the book call for making such a sauce, which may be created using slightly different ingredients for each recipe, but always following the method below.

To make a pan sauce, sear your meat in a hot pan on all sides until a dark crust forms and finish it in the oven until cooked to your liking. Transfer the meat to a cutting board to rest. Pour most of the fat out of the pan and return the pan to medium heat, leaving all the brown bits on the bottom of the pan. Add any aromatics, such as shallot, thyme, or bay leaves, and sauté. Add some wine (red or white, depending on what the recipe calls for) and bring the mixture to a simmer. Using a wooden spoon, scrape the bottom of the pan to loosen all the brown bits. Add a little stock or demi-glace, if you like, and keep stirring until the sauce has reduced by half. Once it has reduced to the desired consistency, remove the pan from the heat. Strain the sauce, if you like (though it isn't necessary), return the sauce to the pan, and then add a knob of butter off the heat. Gently swirl the pan to incorporate the butter into the sauce, adding silkiness. Season with salt and pepper. Slice the meat and serve with the pan sauce.

Knife Skills (Chopping, Dicing, Mirepoix)

It's important to start with a good, sharp chef's knife, a flat work surface, and a sturdy wooden cutting board.

Hold your knife by gripping the blade just above the handle with your thumb on one side and your index finger curled around the other side of the blade. Your remaining fingers will grip around the handle. Holding your knife this way will ensure that you maintain a firm grip on the knife and will allow you to chop quickly, using a rocking motion.

Use your other hand to hold the food steady on your board, making sure to curl your fingers away from the knife. Place the pointed end of the knife down on your board and slice downward in a slow rocking motion. Gradually, as you practice, you will be able to go faster.

Dicing indicates a small, uniform cut. Chopping is rougher and less precise. *Mirepoix* is the trio of diced onion, carrot, and celery that is the aromatic base of many soups, stews, and sauces in France.

To dice a shallot or onion, for example, cut off the top of the bulb with a paring knife or chef's knife. Place it with the cut-side down and slice it in half through the root. Remove the skin and place the two halves, cut-side down, on the board, leaving the root ends intact. Starting with one half, make two or three horizontal cuts, taking care not to slice it all the way through the root end. Turn it and make about six vertical cuts, again taking care not to slice it all the way through the root end. Finally, slice it across about six times, and you'll end up with an even dice.

To cut bacon into lardons (diced bacon), slice a piece of lard fumé or 2 slices thick-cut bacon (¼- to ½-inch-/6- to 12-mm-thick) into 1-inch strips.

Mise en Place

In a classic French kitchen, *mise en place* means "put in place," or refers to ingredients being measured out and ready to be used in the recipe. Everything is kept neat and organized, and all the prep work is done before meal service, so the cooking can be executed in a calm, precise manner. At The Cook's Atelier, we operate with this same mentality, cleaning as we go and keeping everything in its place. During our classes, ingredients are cleaned and chopped and placed in bowls, ready for cooking, and scraps go into stone crocks for composting.

Preparing Mushrooms

It's important to know how to properly clean your mushrooms before sautéing them, as they won't cook properly if they are too damp. Start by selecting mushrooms that are plump and firm, free of bruises or blemishes, and that aren't too wet or too dry. For cèpes, turn them over and make sure the spongy under layer looks fresh. Gently clean each mushroom with a small horsehair mushroom brush or a damp kitchen towel. It's important not to soak or rinse them, as they will absorb the extra water and won't brown properly when cooked. (The one exception is black trumpet mushrooms: They tend to be very sandy, so you can quickly rinse them and dry them well afterward.) Use a paring knife to gently scrape off any tough spots on the stem and to trim the woody ends. For cèpes, use your knife to scrape off the dark gills underneath. For Paris button mushrooms, we peel off the outer layer by using a paring knife, starting at an edge just under the cap, peeling toward the center, to remove the thin layer.

Toasting Nuts and Spices

We often toast nuts to deepen their flavor before adding them to recipes. Place a handful of nuts (such as walnuts, pecans, pine nuts, or almonds) on a baking sheet and toast at 350°F (175°C) for 5 to 10 minutes, until golden brown. Cool completely and chop them, if desired.

To toast spices, place a small handful of the whole spice in a small, dry sauté pan. Cook over medium heat, shaking the pan often, until the spices begin to smell fragrant, taking care not to let them burn. Remove from the heat and transfer them to a mortar to cool. Grind the spices with your pestle to use in your recipe.

Weighing

Although we've noted measuring cups and spoons in many of our recipes, we generally prefer to weigh our ingredients, especially when it comes to baking. Weighing provides a more accurate and consistent result.

Whisking Egg Whites

We prefer to beat egg whites by hand in a copper egg bowl using a whisk. The copper reacts with the egg whites to create nice, firm peaks—no cream of tartar necessary. Make sure to use fresh farm eggs, and, if refrigerated, bring them to room temperature before whisking.

Before starting, make sure that your bowl and whisk are completely clean. Wash the bowl with hot, soapy water, add a little bit of salt, and then run the cut side of a lemon all over the inside of the bowl to remove any oxidation and to make sure the bowl is perfectly clean. Rinse well with hot water and dry thoroughly.

Add the egg whites. Hold the bowl toward your side and whisk vigorously in a clockwise motion. Continue whisking briskly until the egg whites turn foamy and gradually form soft peaks. Whisk rapidly until the whites are glossy and firm peaks form. You'll know you've reached this stage when you lift your whisk out of the egg whites and hold it in the air—you'll be able to see a peak standing up.

By beating your egg whites by hand, you can better control the process and prevent overbeating. See our Green Garlic Soufflé (page 110) or Lemon Soufflé (page 329) recipes.

CLASSIC FRENCH TECHNIQUES AND RECIPES

At The Cook's Atelier, we believe that having a strong grasp of basic French cooking techniques is the key to becoming a better cook. The following techniques and recipes are the building blocks of everything we do. They represent the most basic tenets of French cuisine and provide the serious home cook with a firm foundation on which to build. Once mastered, your confidence as a cook will soar, and then you will have the freedom to innovate.

BASIC COOKING TECHNIQUES

Blanching

Blanching is a cooking technique in which vegetables are quickly boiled in salted water until tender, but still crisp, and then plunged into an ice-water bath to stop the cooking and set the color. We often blanch vegetables during class, and find it especially useful with delicate varieties such as fava beans, asparagus, carrots, turnips, and parsnips. When preparing vegetables, we always leave a little bit of delicate green on (cut on a diagonal) for a nice presentation. Blanching is a great way to work ahead; you can prep and blanch your vegetables several hours in advance, and then sauté them in butter or olive oil just before

serving. If you are blanching several vegetables, ideally you should blanch each one in its own pot of salted boiling water and bowl of ice water, so it doesn't take on the color or flavor of the other vegetables.

If by chance, you want to blanch everything in the same pot for convenience, start with the more delicate, light-colored vegetables first, and end with the larger, strong-flavored and brightly colored vegetables. A good example of this technique is the way we prepare finishing vegetables for our Pot-au-Feu (page 298). We first blanch pearl onions in their own pot of water (due to the strong flavor) and then, in a new pot of water, continue blanching white radishes, breakfast radishes, carrots, turnips, and Brussels sprouts, cooking each variety individually. Keep in mind that you'll need to add additional ice to the ice-water bath each time you add in a new vegetable, as the hot vegetables will melt the ice.

To blanch vegetables, bring a large pot of salted water to boil. Fill a bowl with ice and water and set it near the stovetop, along with a slotted spoon.

Plunge the vegetables into the boiling water and cook until bright in color and tender, but still crisp. Using a slotted spoon, transfer the vegetable to the ice water to stop the cooking, and let them sit for 2 to 3 minutes, until completely cool but still crisp.

Remove the vegetable from the ice water and place on a dry kitchen towel to rest and soak up any moisture. Blanched vegetables can sit at room temperature until ready to sauté.

Braising

Braising is slowly cooking meat or vegetables in liquid—often a combination of wine and stock—over low heat, until fork-tender. Braising is the ultimate one-pot cooking method, as you end up preparing the food and creating a sauce at the same time. We generally braise in a Dutch oven or a copper braising pot with a tight-fitting lid.

When braising, it's important to keep the heat low. If you try to braise meat with the temperature too high, you will end up with tough, dry meat.

When braising meat, it's common first to sear the meat on the stovetop to create a caramelized surface, and then to add liquid to the pot and finish braising it over low heat in the oven. For example, when making Coq au Vin (page 232) or bœuf bourguignon (page 235), we sear the pieces of meat in a Dutch oven first, then add wine, stock, and aromatics and cook slowly over low heat in the oven until the meat is extremely tender.

It's possible to braise vegetables as well, only the process is much quicker. When braising vegetables, simmer them in vegetable or chicken stock for several minutes, or just until tender. Remove with a slotted spoon. See our recipe for Braised Endive Gratin (page 312).

Frying

There are two types of frying: pan-frying and deep-frying. Pan-frying, like sautéing, is a technique that involves cooking vegetables, meat, poultry, fish, or eggs in a small amount of hot oil or butter over medium-high heat. Unlike sautéing, pan-frying doesn't involve moving the pan or stirring the food, and there is usually more oil or butter, so you can baste the food with the additional fat while you cook.

To pan-fry vegetables, meat, poultry, fish, or eggs, heat a small amount of oil or butter over medium-high heat. Add the food and let cook, without moving, for several minutes until golden brown, basting with spoonfuls of fat. Flip the food and cook the other side until golden brown and cooked through to desired doneness. See page 175 for our recipe for fried quail eggs for our Croques Madames.

Deep-frying is a technique that involves cooking vegetables, herbs, poultry, or fish in a large pot of hot oil to create a crisp exterior on food. We often fry garnishes for dishes, like crispy shallot rings for soup, or fried basil (see page 167) or lemon slices as a pretty accent on a plate.

To deep-fry, fill a large pot halfway full of neutral-flavored oil, such as organic canola oil. Heat the oil to 350°F (175°C), using a deep-fat thermometer to monitor your temperature. When frying small items, like herbs, keep the oil very hot so it will crisp properly. With larger items, such as a piece of chicken, lower the oil temperature so that it is between 300° and 325°F (150° to 165°C) so the meat will cook through without burning. Remove smaller fried items,

such as herbs or vegetables, carefully to a paper towel–lined baking sheet to absorb extra oil. If frying chicken, remove it to a wire cooling rack so it will stay crisp.

Grilling

Grilling is a form of outdoor cooking that involves cooking meat, fish, poultry, or vegetables over an open flame, on top of a grill grate. We embrace grilling in the summertime—it's such a simple and enjoyable way to prepare an outdoor meal. Many cuts of meat are best grilled over high heat so they get a nice brown crust on the outside and stay rare inside, while more delicate foods, such as fish or chicken, are grilled at a lower temperature so they don't dry out. We often grill vegetables, such as leeks or asparagus, directly on the grate so they get char marks, while we grill tiny cherry tomatoes in a cast-iron skillet so they don't fall through. It's important to regulate your grill, so that you can create a hot side and a cooler one, to ensure proper cooking.

Grilling is so versatile: You can use natural charcoal briquettes or wood or even grape vines to create the flame, and each one imparts a different flavor onto the food. Though you can marinate meats or vegetables before grilling, just a simple drizzle of olive oil and some salt and pepper usually suffices.

Poaching

Poaching involves slowly cooking food in simmering liquid over low heat until just cooked through, as in the egg for our Warm Frisée Salad (page 257). Poaching liquid can be stock, water, wine (or some combination), often with aromatics such as herbs, spices, or citrus added. Because poaching cooks food very gently at a low temperature, it's ideal for cooking delicate items such as fish, eggs, or fruit.

To poach, bring your poaching liquid to a gentle simmer in a large, deep-sided pot over low heat. Add the food, and continue gently simmering until just cooked through. Keep the temperature very low and do not let it boil, as this could toughen the food, or cause it to fall apart, depending on what you are poaching. Using a slotted spoon, remove the food to a warm platter.

Roasting

Classic roasting is a method of cooking vegetables or meat in a very hot oven using dry heat. We especially love roasting in the autumn and winter, when the weather is cold and the extra warmth from the oven is welcome.

Roasting is one of the easiest—and most flavorful—ways to prepare vegetables, as they cook quickly and evenly, and the edges get deliciously crisp and caramelized. To roast vegetables, simply chop whichever variety you are using, such as carrots, potatoes, Brussels sprouts, parsnips, or turnips, and arrange them in individual gratin dishes or on a baking sheet, being careful not to overcrowd the pan. Drizzle the vegetables with olive oil, season with salt and pepper, and roast at 350° to 375°F (175° to 190°C) until tender and golden. For a more complex flavor, we like to roast vegetables, such as pumpkin or squash, before pureeing them into a soup.

When roasting meat or poultry, season the outside with salt and pepper. Place in a roasting pan along with any aromatics (such as herbs, citrus, garlic, shallots, or onions) that you are using, and roast until golden brown on the outside and cooked to the desired internal temperature. It's helpful to use a meat thermometer when roasting, to test for doneness. When roasting meat, we often sear it in a sauté pan until crisp and brown, such as in our veal chop (page 164) or côte de bœuf (page 284), and then finish it in the oven at a lower temperature.

This combines two techniques, and is called pan-roasting.

Fire-roasting à la ficelle is an ancient cooking method that involves roasting a piece of poultry or meat that is suspended from a string (*ficelle*) in front of a roaring fire. This style of cooking, similar to rotisserie cooking, was a precursor to oven roasting, and made use of the large kitchen hearths historically found in French kitchens. Today, many restaurants in France still cook using these ancient stone hearths, and you can order fire-roasted chicken, pheasants, or lamb roasted à la ficelle or on a spit. Fire-roasting creates a crisp, golden skin—thanks to regular basting with duck fat—and tender meat, as well as a wonderfully smoky flavor.

Sautéing

The verb *sauter*, in French, means "to jump," and in the culinary sense, sautéing accurately describes what happens when small pieces of meat or vegetables cook in a hot pan with a little bit of butter or oil. When you sauté, it's important to keep moving the pan, so that everything cooks quickly and uniformly. Sautéing is a quick-cooking technique, and a building block of many French recipes. Many stocks, soups, and sauces begin by sautéing a mirepoix, the classic triumvirate of onions, celery, and carrots, which adds a depth of flavor to the final dish.

Sautéing mushrooms is a specific version of the technique to master to ensure they caramelize instead of steam in the pan. In a large sauté pan, melt butter over medium-high heat. Once the foam subsides, add the cleaned and prepared mushrooms, being careful not to crowd the pan, and sauté, without stirring, until the mushrooms start to caramelize, 1 to 2 minutes. Gently shake the pan to release the mushrooms and flip them to the other side. Cook until the mushrooms are tender and nicely caramelized, 2 to 3 minutes more. Season with salt and pepper. See our recipe for Sautéed Cèpes on Toasts (page 210) for an example.

Searing

Searing results from browning meat in a hot pan, usually as a first step before braising or roasting. The high heat quickly caramelizes the outside, creating a dark crust, without cooking the meat all the way through, as in our Coq au Vin (page 232). Searing is the first step towards a flavorful sauce: The brown bits left in the pan are scraped up and deglazed with wine or stock, adding rich flavor to the final dish.

To sear a piece of meat, pat the meat dry with paper towels—this will ensure that it forms a proper crust—and season with salt and pepper. Heat some olive oil in a heavy, oven-proof sauté pan over medium-high heat. Carefully add the meat to the pan and let sit without moving for several minutes until a dark, golden crust forms. Turn the meat to the other side and let it cook for several more minutes, until golden. If it's a large piece of meat, continue to turn it, so that all sides of the meat get a nice crust on them. Continue cooking the meat according to the recipe, either adding liquid to the pan and braising it, or placing the pan in the oven to roast.

Classic Butcher's Tie

The butcher's tie is a classic way to prepare a piece of meat for roasting, by looping one long piece of cotton butcher's twine around the meat to create an even shape. This method can be used for a variety of meats, such as Roasted Leg of Lamb (page 113), or a beef tenderloin. Not only does the tie give the meat a tidy appearance, it helps the meat roast consistently, by holding in stray pieces and creating an even thickness throughout.

Start with your piece of meat, a sharp knife, and a roll of cotton butcher's twine. Carefully trim the gray membrane (silver skin) from the meat, taking care not to remove too much fat.

Cut one long piece of twine (3 to 4 feet/ 90 cm to 1.2 m) and bring it under the meat, about 1 inch (2.5 cm) from the end. Tie a regular knot on top of the meat, so there's one short piece and one very long piece. Make a loop and slide the loop underneath the meat, pulling the long end of the string on top to keep the meat taut. Continue making loops and passing them underneath the meat, pulling gently to tighten as you go. This will create a series of loops with one straight line of twine down the center. If you're using this technique on beef tenderloin, tuck the narrow end underneath and loop the twine around to create an even width.

Turn the meat over and thread the long piece of twine under the first loop and over then under again, pulling gently until taut. Repeat the process—threading over, under, and through—until you reach the other end of the meat. Flip the meat back over and tie the end of the long piece of twine with the original short piece from the first knot. Cut any remaining twine so it looks nice and even.

Frenching and Tying a Rib Roast

Frenching is a butchery technique that removes the meat, fat, and connective tissues from part of the rib bones on a piece of meat, to create a beautiful presentation. You can use this technique on a pork roast, rack of lamb, côte de bœuf (beef rib roast; see page 284), or côte de veau (veal chop; see page 164).

Start off with a sharp slicing or boning knife. First, cut away the flap of meat covering the bones. Then, cut between the bones, removing the meat and fat, and scraping along the bones to remove any membranes. Make sure the bones are completely clean, or they will burn when roasting. Save the extra pieces of meat—you can throw them in the roasting pan with the vegetables to create a delicious fond (see page 334).

Once the rib bones are clean, use butcher's twine to tie up the roast. Depending on the cut of meat and how many bones there are, cut individual pieces of twine, each three times the width of the roast. Tie in-between each bone, pulling up on the string to keep the meat taut.

How to Break Down Poultry

Breaking down poultry is a skill that every cook should master. Whether we are making Chicken Stock (page 357), Coq au Vin (page 232), or roasting a *pintade* (guinea hen; see page 98), we prefer to buy a whole bird and break it down ourselves, rather than buying pieces. That way, we can use all of the extra bits, like the neck and wing tips, to add to a stock. We always buy our poultry from a source that we trust, like our local butcher or a duck or chicken farmer, but, in general, buying a whole bird helps ensure that the meat is fresh.

To start, you'll need a sharp chef's knife or a boning knife, kitchen tweezers, and a pair of heavy-duty kitchen shears. Hone your knife on a steel a few times before beginning, to make sure it is extra-sharp.

Place a piece of parchment paper down on your cutting board and lay the bird on top, breast-side up. Rinse and pat the bird down with paper towels to make sure it is completely dry. Run your hands along the skin to feel for any quills, and remove them with kitchen tweezers.

Take the bird by one leg and carefully cut the skin between the breast and the leg until you reach the meat. As you are cutting around the leg, gently push the leg to the side so you can easily find the joint. Cut along the breast, toward yourself, and through the joint to remove the leg. If necessary, use your hand to pop the hip joint to make it easier to separate the legs from the body. Repeat the process on the other side. Separate the thighs from the legs, cutting through the joints. As you are cutting, take care not to rip the skin. The goal is to create neat pieces of meat with the skin still intact.

Next, cut the wings off at the joint, cutting as close to the breast as possible. Use your knife to find the joint and cut around the socket. Sometimes, we lift the bird up slightly to make it easier to find the joint to remove the wing.

Use kitchen shears to cut the breastbone from the back. Once the breasts are removed, cut each breast in half, so there are four pieces of breast meat. At this point, you should have ten pieces of chicken: four breast pieces, two thighs, two wings, and two legs.

Discard the parchment and wash the board, knives, and shears with hot, soapy water. Use white vinegar to disinfect the board, tools, and the sink (see pages 55–56).

Trussing Poultry

Trussing poultry is a simple technique that every cook should know. Essentially, it's tying up a whole bird with kitchen twine so the legs and wings stay close to the body, creating a neat little package that will roast evenly. Trussing also helps protect the breast meat from drying out, making for a juicier, more flavorful bird.

To start, carefully rinse and thoroughly dry the bird with paper towels. Place the bird on a piece of parchment paper, breast-side up, with its legs away from you. Lay out bowls of salt and pepper, along with a 3-foot (90-cm) piece of kitchen twine. Season the inside of the bird with salt and pepper. Place the center of the twine beneath the tailbone of the bird with the ends extending to the left and right. Make a figure-eight: Lift the twine, loop each end around the legs, and then reverse the twine to make a cross. Tie the legs tightly together.

Pull the twine toward you, looping it around the front of the bird and over the wings, securing it tight to plump up the breast. Flip the bird upside down so that the neck is now facing away from you, keeping the twine pulled tight. Tie a knot so that the twine stays secure underneath the neck bone. Trim any excess twine and flip the bird on its back again. Season the outside with salt and pepper.

Use white vinegar to disinfect the work surface, tools, and the sink (see pages 55–56).

We adore Julia Child for so many reasons, but we especially appreciate her love of butter. She once famously said, "With enough butter, anything is good." And we couldn't agree more. We go through vast quantities of butter at The Cook's Atelier. High-quality, European-style butter is essential in French cuisine. Its rich flavor and high fat content make for tender tart doughs and flaky pastries, and the decadent sauces that French haute cuisine is known for.

Additionally, there are three forms of butter that we find particularly useful in cooking: clarified butter, beurre noisette, and compound butters.

Clarified butter has been melted so that the water evaporates and the milk solids separate from the butterfat. The milk solids are strained out so you are left with pure butterfat. Clarified butter has a higher smoking point than regular butter, so you can use it to sauté at high heat without worrying about it burning.

Beurre noisette literally means "hazelnut butter," though it's referring to the color, rather than the nut. Commonly referred to as brown butter, it is made by cooking butter in a pan until it has a deep golden hue, with a pleasantly nutty aroma. This simple sauce is delicious served with sautéed fish, meat, or vegetables. Sometimes, we make it on its own to use as a finishing sauce for soups and vegetables, or to put in cakes and other desserts. When making beurre noisette, it is important to keep an eye on it as it is cooking to make sure the milk solids don't burn. For additional flavor, add chopped parsley or chervil.

Compound butter is a type of flavored butter made by adding chopped fresh herbs, citrus zest, shallots, garlic, and even sometimes truffles and foie gras to softened butter. Compound butters are often served on grilled or roasted fish, meat, or vegetables to create a simple sauce. A garlicky herb compound butter is essential when making Burgundian Escargots (page 231). The classic maître d'hôtel butter incorporates fresh thyme and lemon juice, but you can swap out the lemon for lime, and use cilantro or basil in lieu of thyme. The butter is best used within three days. For longer storage, place the butter mixture in the center of a piece of parchment paper and shape it into a rough log. Fold the parchment paper toward you, enclosing the butter. While holding the edge of the paper, use a pastry cutter on top of the paper to gently push the paper underneath the butter to shape it into a uniform log. Roll the rest of the parchment around the butter and secure the ends by twisting them tight. Wrap this log in a sheet of plastic wrap and store in the freezer for up to two months.

Clarified Butter

MAKES ABOUT 1½ CUPS (360 ML)

1 pound (450 g) unsalted butter, cut into pieces

In a small saucepan, melt the butter over low heat. Remove from the heat and let it stand for 3 to 4 minutes to settle. Using a small spoon, remove the white foam from the surface. Gently pour off the clear, yellow butter into a glass jar, leaving the white solids in the bottom of the saucepan. Let cool, then store in an airtight container in the refrigerator; the clarified butter will keep for at least 1 month.

Beurre Noisette

MAKES ½ CUP (120 ML)

½ cup (1 stick/115 g) unsalted butter
1 to 1½ tablespoons fresh lemon juice
Fleur de sel and freshly ground black pepper

In a small saucepan, melt the butter over medium-high heat, swirling the butter as it melts. Continue cooking and swirling the pan until the butter smells nutty and begins to brown. Remove from the heat and let it cool slightly. Add 1 tablespoon of the lemon juice, or more as needed to brighten the sauce. Season with salt and pepper and use immediately.

Truffle Butter

MAKES 1¼ CUPS (275 G)

1 cup (2 sticks/225 g) unsalted butter, softened
50 g fresh black truffle, finely chopped
Fleur de sel and freshly ground black pepper

Place the butter in a medium bowl. Using the back of a wooden spoon, smear and smash the butter until it becomes workable. Add the truffle, season with salt and pepper, and stir until thoroughly combined. Store the butter in an airtight container in the refrigerator; for the best flavor, use within 3 days.

Herb Butter

MAKES 2 CUPS (450 G)

6 cloves garlic
3 shallots
¾ cup (40 g) fresh flat-leaf parsley leaves
1½ cups (3 sticks/340 g) unsalted butter, softened
½ teaspoon freshly grated nutmeg
Fleur de sel and freshly ground black pepper

Using a mezzaluna or sharp knife, finely chop the garlic, shallots, and parsley and combine them in a small bowl. Set aside.

Place the butter in a medium bowl. Using the back of a wooden spoon, smear and smash the butter until it becomes workable. Add the garlic mixture and nutmeg, season with salt and pepper, and stir until thoroughly combined. Store the butter in an airtight container in the refrigerator. For the best flavor, use within 3 days.

Every cook should know how to make vinaigrette from scratch. It's so basic, and yet a well-made vinaigrette has the power to completely transform a bowl of lettuce leaves into a memorable salad or enhance cold vegetables, meat, and fish dishes. To make a vinaigrette, we whisk together 1 part acid (such as good-quality vinegar or freshly squeezed citrus juice) and 3 parts organic first cold-pressed extra-virgin olive oil in a bowl, and season with salt and pepper. If you keep the simple principle of 1:3 acid-to-oil ratio in mind, the variations are endless. For example, depending on the season and what we are using the vinaigrette for, we might add shallots or garlic, Dijon mustard, or freshly chopped herbs, or change the type of vinegar or variety of oil entirely. When using shallots, we place the shallots in the bowl and cover them with the vinegar and salt and let stand for 10 to 30 minutes to soften the flavor of the shallot.

A classic red-wine or balsamic vinegar stands up well to hearty greens, tomatoes, and meat while we often use a champagne or white wine vinegar for more delicate greens or for fish and shellfish. Lemon juice pairs well with a variety of greens, and other vegetables like cucumbers, fennel, and fish dishes, while orange juice complements the sweet, earthy flavor of roasted beets.

A variation of oils is also possible—in the autumn and winter months, we use a variety of high-quality nut oils, such as walnut and hazelnut oil, in place of extra-virgin olive oil to make more nuanced vinaigrettes for our hearty chicory salads using endive, radicchio, or escarole. Most vinaigrettes are whisked together to emulsify the oil and vinegar; however, this is not always necessary. We also enjoy making a "broken" vinaigrette, where we purposefully do not emulsify, so the vinegar stays separate from the oil, and we use it as a finishing touch when plating our Charentais Melon Salad (page 189).

When making vinaigrette for a big, leafy green salad, for example, we prepare it in the bottom of a big salad bowl and simply add the lettuce to the bowl (about one generous handful of greens per person), tossing gently to lightly coat the greens right before serving. To check for seasoning, we dip a piece of lettuce in the vinaigrette to taste it before adding the greens. If it's too acidic, we add a bit more oil; if it's too bland, we add a bit more acidity. It's important not to overdress the greens, or they will become limp, so we always err on the side of underdressing the salad. A 1:3 acid-to-oil ratio generally makes enough vinaigrette for four to six people. If making a salad for two, it's best to make the vinaigrette separately in a small bowl and only use what you need. We prefer to make our vinaigrettes fresh every time we make a salad, but if you like, you can make a larger batch in a glass jar and keep it in the refrigerator for a day or two. Let it come to room temperature before serving, and shake well.

For delicate salad greens, we often adjust the acid to oil ratio to 1:4 so the vinaigrette does not overpower the salad. For composed salads, or when making a "broken" vinaigrette, we make our vinaigrette in a small bowl or glass jar, and simply drizzle it over the salad with a spoon.

Vinaigrette

MAKES ABOUT ¼ CUP (60 ML)

1 shallot, minced (optional)
1 tablespoon red wine vinegar
Fleur de sel
3 tablespoons extra-virgin olive oil, preferably French
Freshly ground black pepper

Place the shallot (if using) and vinegar in a large bowl. Add a pinch of salt and let it stand for 10 to 30 minutes. This softens the shallot a bit, and infuses it with the flavor of the vinegar. Slowly add the oil in a steady stream, whisking continuously to emulsify the oil and vinegar. Season with pepper.

Variations: Add a teaspoon of Dijon mustard or substitute the red wine vinegar (the acid) with white wine, champagne, or apple cider vinegar, or lemon, orange, or lime juice before adding the oil. You can also use two types of vinegar as we do in the Balsamic and Sherry Vinaigrette that we use for our Charentais Melon Salad (see page 189). For this vinaigrette, we combine 1½ teaspoons of each of the vinegars and 3 tablespoons extra-virgin olive oil. Depending on the greens, you can also vary the type of oil that you use by substituting the olive oil with a walnut or hazelnut oil. Fresh herbs can always be tossed in at the end, if you like. When making any kind of variation, it's important to taste as you go and make adjustments, as needed, depending on how it will be used for the final dish.

Anchovy Vinaigrette

MAKES ABOUT ½ CUP (120 ML)

4 salted anchovy fillets, soaked in water for 20 minutes to remove salt and soften
6 tablespoons (90 ml) fruity extra-virgin olive oil, preferably French
2 tablespoons fresh lemon juice
Freshly ground black pepper

Drain the anchovy fillets, then use a heavy mortar and pestle to mash them into a paste. Add the olive oil and lemon juice and whisk to create a dressing. Season with pepper.

Homemade stock is the backbone of classic French cuisine, and each week, we'll have a pot of vegetable or chicken stock simmering on the back of the stove. A well-made stock—whether vegetable, chicken, veal, or beef—provides a flavorful foundation for soups, sauces, or an accompanying *jus*, and there is simply no substitute. Stocks are a bit time-consuming to make, but they are well worth the effort. And fortunately, they freeze well, so we always make a big batch and save some for later. Make sure you have a tall, narrow stockpot, and always use the best-quality ingredients.

It's important to understand the difference between white and brown stocks. **White stocks**, such as vegetable, chicken, and white veal, are light-colored stocks that don't involve roasting the vegetables or bones. They are typically used for light-colored soups, stews, or white sauces. **Brown stocks**, such as brown veal and beef, start by roasting the meat and vegetables until deeply caramelized to draw out extra flavor and deepen the color. Classic French cooks also add a charred onion to brown stocks to create a darker stock with added depth of flavor. They are more intensely flavored than white stocks and are used for making demi-glace, sauces, or consommé.

As with all stocks, the goal is to remove impurities while extracting as much flavor and gelatin as possible from the bones, vegetables, and herbs. Always start your stock with cold water and pay attention to the coverage—the bones and vegetables should be completely submerged. Bring the stock slowly up to a gentle simmer and cook over low heat for several hours, skimming regularly to remove any impurities. Never let your stock boil, as this will make it cloudy. Once the stock is done, use a ladle to strain it through a chinois over a container large enough to hold the stock, then chill it in an ice-water bath. The stock is best used immediately, but can be refrigerated for up to three days or frozen for one month. With meat stocks, once it has come to room temperature, refrigerate the stock overnight, then carefully spoon off the layer of fat that has formed on top and discard.

Vegetable Stock

MAKES ABOUT 4 QUARTS (3.8 L)

8 large leeks, white and light green parts only
Extra-virgin olive oil, preferably French
8 large carrots, coarsely chopped
2 large yellow onions, quartered
1 bouquet garni (see page 61)

Halve each leek lengthwise, then cut them crosswise into 1-inch (2.5-cm) pieces. Rinse the leeks in a large bowl of cold water, swishing to remove any sand. Using your hands, transfer the leeks to a colander to drain, leaving the sand in the bottom of the bowl.

Coat the bottom of a large stockpot with olive oil and place it over medium heat. Add the leeks, carrots, and onions, reduce the heat to low, and cook, stirring occasionally, until the onions are turning translucent, about 10 minutes. Add the bouquet garni and just enough cold water

to completely cover the vegetables. Raise the heat and bring it to a gentle simmer. Be careful not to let the stock boil. Simmer for about 1 hour, skimming the foam and adjusting the heat, as needed, then remove from the heat and let the stock rest for 10 to 15 minutes to settle and cool.

Fill a bowl large enough to accommodate a 4-quart (3.8-L) container with ice and water.

Strain the stock through a chinois into a 4-quart (3.8-L) container. Do not press on the vegetables, as this will make your stock cloudy; discard the solids. Place the container inside the bowl of ice water and let it cool, stirring occasionally, until it reaches room temperature. For vegetable stock, it's best to use it immediately as it loses its delicate flavor nuances quickly. Or, for longer storage, cool the stock and then immediately divide it into smaller containers and freeze for up to 1 month.

Chicken Stock

MAKES ABOUT 4 QUARTS (3.8 L)

1 (5-pound/2.3-kg) whole chicken, preferably farm-and-pasture raised

3 large leeks, white and light green parts only

2 large carrots, coarsely chopped

2 large yellow onions, quartered

1 bouquet garni (see page 61)

Cut the chicken into pieces (see page 348). Rinse the chicken pieces thoroughly, making sure you remove any traces of blood or organs attached to the carcass to prevent the stock from becoming cloudy. Use white vinegar to disinfect the work surface, tools, and sink (see pages 55–56).

Place the chicken pieces in a large stockpot and add just enough cold water to completely cover the chicken. Bring it to a simmer over medium heat, skimming the foam until all the impurities are removed. Be careful not to stir, which will make the stock cloudy, and don't let the water boil.

While the water is simmering, halve each leek lengthwise, then cut them crosswise into 1-inch (2.5-cm) pieces. Rinse the leeks in a large bowl of cold water, swishing to remove any sand.

Using your hands, transfer the leeks to a colander to drain, leaving the sand in the bottom of the bowl.

Add the leeks, carrots, onions, and bouquet garni to the chicken, and bring it to a gentle simmer. Be careful not to let the stock boil. Simmer for 4 hours, adjusting the heat, as needed, then remove from the heat and let the stock rest for 10 to 15 minutes to settle and cool.

Fill a bowl large enough to accommodate a 4-quart (3.8-L) container with ice and water.

Ladle the finished stock through a chinois into a 4-quart (3.8-L) container, avoiding the last little bit of stock in the bottom of the pot, as this holds all the impurities. It's important to ladle rather than pour the stock, as this ensures the stock will remain clear rather than cloudy. Do not press on the meat and vegetables, as this will make your stock cloudy. Discard the solids.

Place the container inside the bowl of ice water and let it cool, stirring occasionally, until it reaches room temperature. Once the stock is completely cool, cover and refrigerate it overnight, so that the fat will congeal at the top and be easier to remove. Skim the fat from the top of the stock and discard. Use the stock immediately or divide into smaller containers and refrigerate it for up to 3 days or freeze for up to 1 month.

Veal Stock

MAKES ABOUT 4 QUARTS (3.8 L)

6 pounds (2.7 kg) veal bones
1 calf's foot (optional)

FOR WHITE VEAL STOCK
2 large leeks, white and light green parts only
1 large yellow onion, quartered
1 bouquet garni (see page 61)

FOR BROWN VEAL STOCK
3 large leeks, white and light green parts only
2 tablespoons extra-virgin olive oil, preferably French
3 large yellow onions
5 large carrots, chopped
6 sprigs flat-leaf parsley
10 sprigs thyme
5 fresh bay leaves
1 bouquet garni (see page 61)
½ teaspoon whole black peppercorns

Rinse the veal bones and calf's foot (if using) under cold running water, then place them in a large stockpot. Add just enough cold water to completely cover the bones and bring it to a simmer, skimming the foam, as needed. It is necessary to blanch the bones first to draw out any impurities. Once the water comes to a simmer, remove the pot from the heat.

While the water is coming to a simmer, halve each leek lengthwise, then cut them crosswise into 1-inch (2.5-cm) pieces. Rinse the leeks in a large bowl of cold water, swishing to remove any sand. Using your hands, transfer the leeks to a colander to drain, leaving the sand in the bottom of the bowl.

Drain the bones in a separate colander. While the bones are still hot, rinse them well to remove any impurities that may be attached to the bones.

To make white veal stock: Place the blanched bones and calf's foot (if using) in a large clean stockpot. Add just enough cold water to completely cover the bones and bring it to a simmer over medium heat, skimming the foam until all the impurities are removed. Be careful not to stir, which will make the stock cloudy, and don't let the water boil.

Add the onion, leeks, and bouquet garni and bring it to a gentle simmer. Simmer for 4 hours, adjusting the heat, as needed, then remove from the heat and let the stock rest for 10 to 15 minutes to settle and cool.

To make brown veal stock: Preheat the oven to 450°F (230°C).

Heat a large flameproof roasting pan over medium-high heat. Add the olive oil and heat until hot but not smoking. Add the blanched veal bones and calf's foot (if using) in a single layer, then turn off the heat and place the roasting pan in the oven. Roast, stirring occasionally, until the bones are dark brown and nicely caramelized on all sides, 45 minutes to 1 hour. Depending on how large your roasting pan is, this first step may have to be done in batches. It's very important that the bones are thoroughly roasted to ensure a flavorful stock.

Without peeling, cut one of the onions horizontally in half. Place the onion halves, cut-side down, in a small, dry cast-iron or steel skillet over medium-low heat and cook until charred and beginning to turn black, 20 to 30 minutes. Peel and quarter the remaining onions.

Add the quartered onions, leeks, carrots, parsley, thyme, and bay leaves to the bones. Roast, stirring occasionally, until the vegetables are caramelized, 45 minutes to 1 hour more.

Remove the cooked vegetables from the roasting pan and set aside. Place the meat in a large colander over a baking sheet to drain off some of the excess fat. Discard any remaining fat and liquid in the roasting pan and place the pan over medium-high heat. Add 1 cup (240 ml) water and use a wooden spoon to scrape up any little bits from the bottom of the pan. Pour this fond into a large stockpot. Place the roasted veal bones in the stockpot and add just enough cold water to completely cover the bones. Bring it to a simmer over medium heat, skimming the foam until all the impurities are removed. Be careful not to stir, which will make the stock cloudy, and don't let the water boil.

Add the caramelized vegetables, charred onion halves, bouquet garni, and peppercorns and bring it to a gentle simmer. Be careful not to let the stock boil. Simmer for 4 to 5 hours, adjusting the heat, as needed, then remove from the heat and let the stock rest for 10 to 15 minutes to settle and cool.

While the stock is resting, fill a bowl large enough to accommodate a 4-quart (3.8-L) container with ice and water.

Ladle the finished stock through a chinois into a 4-quart (3.8-L) container, avoiding the last little bit of stock in the bottom of the pot, as this holds all the impurities. It's important to ladle rather than pour the stock, as this ensures the stock will remain clear rather than cloudy. Do not press on the meat and vegetables, as this will make your stock cloudy. Discard the solids.

Place the container inside the bowl of ice water and let it cool, stirring occasionally, until it reaches room temperature. Cover and refrigerate it overnight, so that the fat will congeal at the top and be easier

to remove. Skim the fat from the top of the stock and discard. Use the stock immediately or divide it into smaller containers. Refrigerate for up to 3 days or freeze for up to 1 month.

Beef Stock

MAKES ABOUT 4 QUARTS (3.8 L)

2 tablespoons extra-virgin olive oil, preferably French

6 pounds (2.7 kg) meaty beef bones, such as shank, neck, and marrow bones, cut into pieces

3 large yellow onions

3 large leeks, white and light green parts only

5 large carrots, coarsely chopped

1 head garlic, cut in half horizontally

6 sprigs flat-leaf parsley

6 sprigs thyme

3 fresh bay leaves

1 bouquet garni (see page 61)

½ teaspoon whole black peppercorns

Preheat the oven to 450°F (230°C).

Heat a large flameproof roasting pan over medium-high heat. Add the olive oil and heat until hot but not smoking. Add the beef bones in a single layer, then turn off the heat and place the roasting pan in the oven. Roast, stirring occasionally, until the bones are dark brown and nicely caramelized on all sides, 45 minutes to 1 hour. Depending on how large your roasting pan is, this first step may have to be done in batches. It's very important that the bones are thoroughly roasted to ensure a flavorful stock.

Without peeling, cut one of the onions horizontally in half. Place the onion halves, cut-side down, in a small, dry cast-iron or steel skillet over medium-low heat and cook until charred and beginning to turn black, 20 to 30 minutes. Peel and quarter the remaining onions.

Halve each leek lengthwise, then cut them crosswise into 1-inch (2.5-cm) pieces. Rinse the leeks in a large bowl of cold water, swishing to remove any sand. Using your hands, transfer the leeks to a colander to drain, leaving the sand in the bottom of the bowl.

Add the quartered onions, leeks, carrots, garlic, parsley, thyme, and bay leaves to the bones. Roast, stirring occasionally, until the vegetables are caramelized, 45 minutes to 1 hour more.

Remove the cooked vegetables from the roasting pan and set aside. Place the meat in a large colander over a baking sheet to drain off some of the excess fat. Discard any remaining fat and liquid in the roasting pan and place the pan over medium-high heat. Add 1 cup (240 ml) water and use a wooden spoon to scrape up any little bits from the bottom of the pan. Pour this fond into a large stockpot. Place the roasted beef bones in the stockpot and add just enough cold water to completely cover the bones. Bring it to a simmer over medium heat, skimming the foam until all the impurities are removed. Be careful not to stir, which will make the stock cloudy, and don't let the water boil.

Add the caramelized vegetables, charred onion halves, bouquet garni, and peppercorns and bring it to a gentle simmer. Be careful not to let the stock boil. Simmer for 4 to 5 hours, adjusting the heat, as needed, then remove from the heat and let the stock rest for 10 to 15 minutes to settle and cool.

Fill a bowl large enough to accommodate a 4-quart (3.8-L) container with ice and water.

Ladle the finished stock through a chinois into a 4-quart (3.8-L) container, avoiding the last little bit of stock in the bottom of the pot, as this holds all the impurities. It's important to ladle rather than pour the stock, as this ensures the stock will remain clear and translucent rather than cloudy. Do not press on the meat and vegetables as this will make your stock cloudy. Discard the solids.

Place the container inside the bowl of ice water and let it cool, stirring occasionally, until it reaches room temperature. Cover and refrigerate it overnight, so that the fat will congeal at the top and be easier to remove. Skim the fat from the top of the stock and discard. Use the stock immediately or divide it into smaller containers. Refrigerate for up to 3 days or freeze for up to 1 month.

Just a spoonful of **demi-glace** adds great nuance and depth to soups, stews, and sauces. Traditionally, a classic demi-glace combines equal parts *espagnole* (Spanish) sauce and brown stock reduced by half. We prefer, instead, to reduce a well-made beef or veal stock for many hours until it is very concentrated. We simmer it without adding a roux (equal parts flour and butter cooked together), which is often used as a thickening agent. The flavor of the stock naturally intensifies as it reduces slowly.

Aspic, or *gelée* in French, is a savory jelly made from a meat consommé. Typically, aspic is made by heating up consommé and adding sheet gelatin, also called leaf gelatin, to create a jellylike consistency. Because we add a calf's foot, which already contains high levels of natural gelatin, to our veal stock, we find that we don't need to add any additional gelatin to set our veal aspic. In France, sheet gelatin is readily available, whereas in other countries, powdered or granulated is more common. We prefer to use sheet gelatin when necessary, because it makes a clearer gelée with a much better flavor. Traditionally, aspic creates a clear layer of gelée on top of terrines. In Duck Pâté en Croûte (page 244), warmed aspic fills the space between the meat and the dough. As the meat naturally shrinks as it cooks, the aspic fills the negative space and gels as it cools, thereby creating a nice presentation when sliced.

A **red wine reduction** is red wine that has been simmered with aromatics until reduced and thickened. We use it in the same fashion as a demi-glace and add it to pan jus, sauces, and stews to enrich the flavor and enhance the velvety texture. We make ours by combining a bottle of good-quality red wine (one you would enjoy drinking) with vegetables and a bouquet garni and simmering it until it has reduced down to a thick consistency. The reduction is then strained and added, one spoonful at a time.

Consommé is a clear broth or clarified stock made by refining beef, veal, chicken, or fish stock into an intensely flavored clear liquid that can be used in soup or for making aspic for terrines or pâtés. It is a two-day process, but once you have mastered the basics, you will find this to be a very rewarding technique.

When making a consommé, we take an extra step by making a double stock. This potent stock results from simmering a batch of beef, veal, chicken, or fish stock with aromatic fresh vegetables, garlic, and herbs to intensify the flavor. The stock is then strained, cooled, and chilled overnight. The next day (after skimming off the additional layer of fat), we clarify it with the addition of egg whites, ground beef or chicken, and additional mirepoix. This creates a "raft" that collects all the impurities on the surface, leaving crystal-clear broth below.

Demi-Glace

MAKES ABOUT 1 CUP (240 ML)

4 quarts (3.8 L) Brown Veal Stock (page 359) or Beef Stock (page 360)

In a large saucepan, heat the stock over medium-high heat until it is about to boil. Reduce the heat and simmer, skimming any fat or particles that float to the top every 15 minutes or so. Be careful not to let the stock boil, which will make the demi-glace cloudy. Continue simmering and skimming until the stock is reduced by two-thirds, about 2 hours. Keep a watchful eye on the stock: As it reduces, it will become darker and the flavors will intensify. Once the stock has reduced by two-thirds, transfer it to a smaller saucepan so it won't reduce too quickly. Simmer, adjusting the heat and skimming, as needed, until reduced to 1 cup (240 ml). Let the demi-glace cool to room temperature. The final result will be thick, velvety, and shiny. It can be used immediately, refrigerated in a jar with a tight-fitting lid for about 1 week, or frozen for a few months.

Aspic

MAKES ABOUT 2 CUPS (480 ML)

3 sheets gelatin (250 bloom, 1.7-g each) or 1 (¼-ounce/7-g) packet unflavored powdered gelatin
2 cups (480 ml) Consommé (opposite)

If using sheet gelatin, soak it in a bowl of cold water for about 10 minutes to soften; drain. In a medium saucepan, warm the consommé over medium heat, then add the softened gelatin. Reduce the heat to low and stir until the gelatin has completely dissolved, about 1 minute.

If using powdered gelatin, combine the gelatin and ¼ cup (60 ml) of the consommé and whisk to combine; let stand for 5 to 10 minutes. Heat the remaining 1¾ cups (420 ml) consommé over medium heat. Add the gelatin mixture, reduce the heat to low, and stir until the gelatin has completely dissolved, about 1 minute.

To test the aspic, pour a small amount on a plate and refrigerate it for 10 minutes. After 10 minutes, the aspic will be firm like jelly.

Let the aspic cool to room temperature, then add it to pâtés or terrines. Aspic can be stored in an airtight container in the refrigerator for up to 3 days and should be rewarmed and melted before using.

Red Wine Reduction

MAKES ABOUT 1 CUP (240 ML)

3 large leeks, white and light green parts only
3 white button mushrooms
2 medium yellow onions, chopped
5 medium carrots, chopped
3 shallots, chopped
4 cloves garlic, smashed
1 bouquet garni (see page 61)
½ teaspoon whole black peppercorns
1 (750-ml) bottle red wine, such as Burgundy Pinot Noir

Halve each leek lengthwise, then cut them crosswise into 1-inch (2.5-cm) pieces. Rinse the leeks in a large bowl of cold water, swishing to remove any sand. Using your hands, transfer the leeks to a colander to drain, leaving the sand in the bottom of the bowl.

Using a paring knife, gently peel back the top layer of each mushroom by holding it upside down, gently catching the edge of the cap, and carefully peeling it back to remove the clean mushroom cap. Thinly slice the mushrooms.

In a large saucepan, combine the leeks, mushrooms, onions, carrots, shallots, garlic, bouquet garni, peppercorns, and red wine and bring them to a boil. Reduce the heat and simmer until the wine has thickened and reduced to about 1 cup (240 ml), about 45 minutes. Strain through a fine-mesh strainer into a small bowl; discard the solids. The reduction can be used right away or refrigerated in a jar with a tight-fitting lid for up to 3 days.

Consommé

MAKES ABOUT 2 QUARTS (2 L)

FOR THE DOUBLE STOCK

1 small yellow onion

3 quarts (2.8 L) Beef Stock (page 360), Brown Veal Stock (page 359), or Chicken Stock (page 357)

2 large carrots, chopped

6 white button mushrooms, quartered

2 cloves garlic, smashed

6 sprigs flat-leaf parsley

6 sprigs thyme

2 fresh bay leaves

1 teaspoon whole black peppercorns

FOR THE CONSOMMÉ

6 large egg whites

1 pound (455 g) finely chopped or ground lean beef, veal, or chicken

½ cup (25 g) finely chopped celery

½ cup (65 g) finely chopped yellow onion

½ cup (70 g) finely chopped carrot

½ cup (30 g) finely chopped white button mushrooms

Leaves from 2 sprigs thyme, finely chopped

½ tablespoon finely chopped fresh flat-leaf parsley

Make the double stock: Without peeling, halve the onion horizontally. Put the onion halves, cut-side down, in a small dry cast-iron or steel skillet over medium-low heat and cook until charred and beginning to turn black, 20 to 30 minutes.

Place the charred onion, stock, carrots, mushrooms, garlic, parsley, thyme, bay leaves, peppercorns, and 2 cups (480 ml) water in a stockpot and bring to a simmer over medium-high heat. Simmer, adjusting the heat, as needed, for 45 minutes to infuse the stock.

Fill a bowl large enough to accommodate a 3-quart (2.8-L) container with ice and water.

Strain the stock through a cheesecloth-lined chinois into the container. Discard the solids. Place the container inside the bowl of ice water and let it cool, stirring occasionally, until it reaches room temperature. Refrigerate the stock overnight. The next day, or when ready to finish the consommé, skim the fat from the top of the stock and discard. The double stock will keep, refrigerated, for up to 3 days.

Make the consommé: In a large bowl, whisk the egg whites until frothy. Add the meat, celery, onion, carrots, mushrooms, thyme, and parsley and mix well to combine. Transfer the mixture to a stockpot and add the warm double stock. Cook over very low heat, stirring gently, just until the egg whites start to congeal, 5 to 10 minutes. Bring to a simmer and cook over very low heat until all the ingredients start to adhere to the egg whites, forming a large mass floating on top of the stock—this is the "raft," and it draws up any impurities from the stock, making it crystal clear. The raft can take up to 45 minutes to form, so be patient. Once the raft has formed, simmer over very low heat until the raft is firm and the stock is clear. It is important not to rush this process, as it can easily take up to 1 hour to completely clarify the stock. It's also important not to let the liquid get too hot, as this will damage the raft and make the consommé cloudy. After 45 minutes to 1 hour, turn off the heat and let the stock stand for a few minutes.

Using a ladle, gently poke a hole, just large enough for the ladle to pass through, in the middle of the raft. Being careful not to disturb the raft, gently ladle the clear broth into a cheesecloth-lined chinois set over a medium saucepan. Discard the raft. The consommé should be clear. The consommé can be used immediately or stored in a container and refrigerated for up to 3 days.

Sauces are essential to classic French cuisine. In the early nineteenth century, chef Marie-Antoine Carême declared in his gastronomic work *L'Art de la Cuisine Française* that béchamel, *velouté*, espagnole, and *allemande* were the four essential sauces of French cooking. Later, chef Auguste Escoffier reestablished the list in his 1903 culinary tome *Le Guide Culinaire*. He decided that allemande was just a derivative of velouté, and added two more sauces to the list: *sauce tomate* and hollandaise. Escoffier's five "mother" sauces are still taught in culinary school, and form the basis for hundreds of sauce variations.

Sauces are broken down into two basic categories: white and brown. White sauces, including béchamel and velouté, are made from a liquid (milk and white stock, respectively) thickened with a white or pale roux. Brown sauces, such as espagnole, are made from brown stock and thickened by reduction and a brown roux.

With any sauce, flavor and texture are of the utmost importance. A sauce must be thick enough to coat or cling to food. The texture results from one of three techniques: a roux, a reduction, or an emulsion.

A **roux**, used in four of the five sauces, is equal parts butter and flour, cooked over medium heat to remove any raw flour taste. Some type of liquid is then added, and the mixture is whisked and simmered until thickened to the desired consistency.

It's also possible to thicken sauces with a *beurre manié*, equal parts softened butter and flour. This is a traditional French technique where the butter and flour are blended together by hand to form a paste. While the sauce is simmering, small pieces of the beurre manié are dropped into the sauce, while whisking constantly to prevent lumps. The sauce is simmered until it reaches the desired consistency.

There are three colors of roux: white, pale, and brown. White roux is the palest in color, and is used as a base for béchamel and white sauces. Pale roux is cooked slightly longer, and is used to thicken veloutés and cream sauces. Brown roux is cooked until dark brown in color with a nutty smell, and it is often used in brown sauces such as espagnole.

A **reduction** is a sauce created by slowly cooking down liquid (like stock or wine) over low heat until thickened, creating a flavorful, concentrated, and clean-tasting sauce. Reduction is a great way to thicken stock-based or tomato sauces, as the desired consistency is reached without having to add a roux, which would result in a less-refined sauce.

Finally, an **emulsion** uses a binding agent (like egg yolks) to bring together two elements that don't normally combine (water and butter) into a cohesive mixture (such as a hollandaise sauce). Hollandaise is the only mother sauce that does not use a roux.

Béchamel is a creamy white sauce that results when white roux and milk cook over low heat until thickened. Seasoned with a dash of nutmeg, béchamel is used as a base in many dishes, from soufflés to gratins. It is also the base for other classic French sauces to accompany eggs, vegetables, fish, meat, and poultry. The addition of cheese turns béchamel into a *sauce mornay*.

Velouté is a velvety sauce that combines pale roux whisked over low heat with white stock, such as chicken, white veal, or fish stock, until slightly thickened and glossy. With the addition of cream, velouté becomes a *sauce suprême*.

The classic form of **espagnole**, a rich brown sauce, is made by combining mirepoix, a dark brown roux, beef or veal stock, and tomato puree or fresh tomatoes. The mixture simmers for several hours, skimmed regularly, until reduced by half. The addition of shallots creates a *bordelaise* sauce.

The original version of **tomate** was thickened homemade tomato sauce, made from fresh tomatoes, pork, and aromatic vegetables, with a roux. Today, this classic tomato sauce is seldom used, replaced instead by a slow-simmering marinara sauce, made from fresh or canned tomatoes, garlic, and olive oil.

Hollandaise is not like the other mother sauces, which are thickened by roux; it is a fluffy yellow sauce created by an emulsion of egg yolks, butter, and lemon juice.

Once you've mastered the five mother sauces, many variations and derivatives are possible, such as *sauce moutarde*, *sauce vin blanc*, madeira, and *chasseur*, among others. Two of our favorite variations include the following:

Béarnaise is a rich sauce that pairs perfectly with côte de bœuf or any sort of steak. Béarnaise is a derivative of hollandaise, seasoned with a reduction of tarragon, black peppercorns, white wine vinegar, white wine, and shallots.

Hollandaise and béarnaise can be tricky to work with, as they are delicate emulsions and can easily break. You can fix a broken hollandaise or béarnaise by adding it, drop by drop, to an egg yolk, and continuously whisking until the sauce comes together again.

Beurre blanc is the perfect companion for a piece of sole or other white fish, this delicate sauce is both an emulsion and a reduction. Minced shallots, white wine, and white wine vinegar are reduced and then strained. Cold butter is whisked in over low heat, piece by piece, to form a flavorful sauce. As with all emulsions, it's important to keep whisking continuously, as the force of the whisk will help the sauce come together.

At The Cook's Atelier, we commonly teach, and often make, the following four sauces to accompany varying menus: béchamel, hollandaise, béarnaise, and beurre blanc.

Sauce Béchamel

MAKES ABOUT 2 CUPS (480 ML)

1½ cups (360 ml) whole milk
5 whole white peppercorns
1 fresh bay leaf
3 tablespoons unsalted butter
3 tablespoons unbleached all-purpose flour
Pinch of freshly grated nutmeg
Fleur de sel and freshly ground black pepper

In a small saucepan, heat the milk, peppercorns, and bay leaf over medium heat and bring to just under a boil. Remove from the heat and let the aromatics steep for about 10 minutes.

In a medium saucepan, melt the butter over medium heat. Add the flour and cook, whisking vigorously and being careful not to let the mixture brown, until the roux thickens and bubbles, 1 to 2 minutes.

Strain the warm infused milk through a fine-mesh strainer, then gradually add it to the roux, whisking continuously. Place the saucepan over medium-high heat and cook, whisking continuously, until the sauce thickens, 3 to 5 minutes. Season with the nutmeg, salt, and pepper. Keep warm.

Sauce Hollandaise

MAKES ABOUT 1¼ CUPS (300 ML)

3 large egg yolks
¼ cup (½ stick/55 g) cold unsalted butter, cut into small pieces
¾ cup (180 ml) Clarified Butter (page 352), warm
1 tablespoon fresh lemon juice
Fleur de sel and freshly ground white pepper
Pinch of piment d'Espelette (optional)

In a small heavy saucepan, combine the egg yolks with 3 tablespoons water and whisk until light in color and foamy. Add half the cold butter, place the saucepan over low heat, and cook, whisking continuously, until the mixture thickens, 2 to 3 minutes. Remove from the heat, add the remaining cold butter, and whisk until fully incorporated. Add the clarified butter in a slow, steady stream, whisking continuously, until the sauce is velvety. Be careful not to add the butter too quickly or the sauce will separate. Add the lemon juice and whisk to incorporate, then season with salt and white pepper and sprinkle with the *piment d'Espelette* (chili pepper; if using). Serve immediately. Hollandaise can be kept warm for a few minutes by keeping it over a pot of hot water. If it looks like it's getting too hot, remove it from the heat and whisk in a tablespoon of cold butter.

Sauce Béarnaise

MAKES ABOUT 1¼ CUPS (300 ML)

½ cup (120 ml) white wine vinegar

½ cup (120 ml) dry white wine, such as Burgundy Chardonnay

1 large shallot, finely chopped

8 whole black peppercorns

2 tablespoons coarsely chopped fresh tarragon

3 large egg yolks

¼ cup (½ stick/55 g) cold unsalted butter, cut into small pieces

¾ cup (180 ml) Clarified Butter (page 352), warm

1 tablespoon fresh lemon juice

½ teaspoon fleur de sel

In a small saucepan, combine the vinegar, wine, shallot, peppercorns, and 1 tablespoon of the tarragon. Place over medium heat and bring to just under a boil. Reduce the heat and simmer until there are only 2 tablespoons of the mixture left in the pan. Strain through a fine-mesh strainer into a small bowl and set aside to cool.

Fill another small saucepan with 1 to 2 inches (2.5 to 5 cm) water, set over medium heat, and bring to a simmer.

In a large heatproof bowl, combine the egg yolks with 3 tablespoons water and whisk until light in color and foamy. Add the strained vinegar mixture and whisk to combine. Add half the cold butter and place the bowl over the pan of simmering water, making sure the bottom of the bowl doesn't touch the water. Reduce the heat to low and cook, whisking continuously, until the mixture thickens, 5 to 6 minutes. Slowly add the remaining cold butter and whisk until fully incorporated. Add the clarified butter in a slow, steady stream, whisking continuously, until the sauce is velvety. Be careful not to add the butter too quickly or the sauce will separate. Add the lemon juice and the remaining 1 tablespoon tarragon, then add the salt and serve immediately.

Sauce Beurre Blanc

MAKES ABOUT 2 CUPS (480 ML)

½ cup (120 ml) dry white wine, such as Burgundy Chardonnay

½ cup (120 ml) white wine vinegar

2 shallots, finely chopped

2 cups (4 sticks/455 g) cold unsalted butter, cut into small pieces

1½ tablespoons fresh lemon juice

Fleur de sel and freshly ground white pepper

In a small saucepan, combine the wine, vinegar, and shallots. Place over medium heat and bring to just under a boil. Reduce the heat and simmer until the liquid has reduced to about 2 tablespoons. Strain the sauce through a fine-mesh strainer, then return it to the saucepan and place over low heat. While whisking continuously, gradually add the butter, 1 piece at a time, until it has all been incorporated and the sauce is thick and velvety. Remove from the heat, add the lemon juice, season with salt and pepper, and serve immediately.

Bread, like wine, is a staple at the French table. One wouldn't dare invite a Frenchman over for dinner without plenty of fresh bread to serve throughout the meal. It accompanies every course and the French think nothing of using a piece of bread to wipe up every last bit of sauce from their plates.

Artisan boulangeries that still practice traditional baking techniques abound in France, and there are so many breads to choose from. Everything from big, simple boules, to buttery brioche, grainy loaves, rustic *vigneron* (winemaker) varieties with nuts and raisins, and classic baguettes adorn the shelves of every bakery. Each morning, people line up outside of their favorite boulangerie to buy their daily loaf, often visiting twice in one day to buy fresh bread in the morning for breakfast, then more for their evening meal.

Although we have access to wonderful bread, on occasion we enjoy the ritual of making our own from scratch. We buy organic, locally milled flour from our local baker, and make brioche whenever we can.

Brioche is a lightly sweet yeasted bread that can be baked in a loaf pan or in little vintage brioche tins, into buns called *têtes parisiennes*. We like to toast it and serve it alongside foie gras or roasted marrow bones (see page 294). It's also delicious for breakfast with homemade jam. When baking, we feel it is important to weigh the dry ingredients using a scale. This ensures the measurements will be accurate and the end result will be successful, no matter what is being baked.

Brioche

MAKES ABOUT 20 SMALL BRIOCHE

FOR THE BRIOCHE DOUGH

4 cups (500 g) unbleached all-purpose flour, plus more as needed

5 large eggs

1 tablespoon active dry yeast

½ cup (120 ml) whole milk, warm (about 110°F/43°C)

¼ cup (50 g) sugar

2 teaspoons fleur de sel

1½ cups (3 sticks/340 g) unsalted butter, at room temperature, plus more for the bowl

FOR THE TÊTES PARISIENNES

Unsalted butter, for the brioche tins

1 large egg yolk

3 tablespoons heavy cream

Make the brioche dough: On a cool work surface, preferably marble, place 1 cup (125 g) of the flour. Make a well in the center. Add 1 egg, the yeast, and the warm milk. Using a bench scraper and your hands, gently work the mixture into a rough dough—it will be fairly wet. Place the dough in a bowl and cover with another ½ cup (65 g) of the flour. Let it stand for about 30 minutes; it's ready when the flour on top cracks. Add the remaining 4 eggs, the sugar, salt, and 2 cups (250 g) of the remaining flour to the dough and mix to combine.

Using the remaining ½ cup (65 g) flour, lightly dust your work surface. Scrape the dough out of the bowl and onto the lightly floured work surface. Knead until elastic and workable. Continue kneading, adding more flour, as needed, until the dough is smooth, soft, and shiny, about 15 minutes total. To test the dough, make an

indentation with your finger; the dough will bounce back up when sufficiently kneaded.

Lightly butter a large bowl.

Using a bench scraper, cut the butter into small pieces. Using the palm of your hand, smear the pieces of butter across the cool work surface until smooth but not melted; the butter should be the same temperature as the dough. Use your bench scraper to move the softened butter to the side of your work surface, removing any trace of butter.

Lightly flour the work surface. Gradually start incorporating the butter into the dough, kneading after each addition and adding more flour as needed. Once all the butter has been added, continue kneading, adding more flour, as needed, until the dough is smooth and shiny, about 5 minutes.

Shape the dough into a ball and place it in the buttered bowl, turning to coat the dough. Cover with plastic wrap and let it rest in a warm dry place until doubled in size, about 2 hours.

Deflate the dough completely by turning it over several times, then return it to the bowl, cover with plastic wrap, and refrigerate overnight.

Make the têtes parisiennes: Preheat the oven to 400°F (205°C).

Generously butter twenty 3-inch (7.5-cm) brioche tins and place them on a baking sheet. Take out the cold dough and cut off one-third. Divide the larger portion of dough into twenty small rounds about two-thirds the size of the brioche tins—each round should measure about 1¾ inches (4.5 cm). Roll the remaining dough into twenty smaller rounds, each measuring about ¾ inch (2 cm). Squeeze one end of each of the smaller rounds so the ends resemble a cone shape. Place the larger rounds of dough into the buttered brioche tins, then use a finger to make an indentation in the center of each. Placing the cone-shaped ends inside the indentations, set the smaller balls of dough on top of the larger ones. Cover with buttered plastic wrap and let the broiche rest in a warm, dry place until almost doubled in size, 1 to 1½ hours.

In a small bowl, whisk together the egg yolk and heavy cream.

Lightly brush the tops of the têtes parisiennes with the egg wash, then bake until just golden brown, about 20 minutes. Remove from the oven and serve immediately.

Pastry doughs are truly an art form in France, and they are the foundation not only for many desserts, but savory dishes as well. At The Cook's Atelier, we make all our pastry doughs from scratch, using organic flour and sugar, fresh farm eggs, fleur de sel, and unsalted European-style butter. It's important to use high-quality ingredients when making pastry doughs in order to achieve a rich, buttery flavor and tender texture. Fortunately, pastry doughs freeze well, so we always make extra, and keep a few rounds of pâte sucrée or *pâte brisée* (short dough), and sheets of pâte feuilletée in the freezer, for a last-minute tart or apéritif.

Learn to make these pastry doughs by hand first, rather than using a stand mixer or food processor, so you really get the feel for how the dough comes together.

We prepare pastry doughs directly on our marble work surface to keep the dough cool and manageable. Even if you don't have marble countertops, it's a good idea to have a small piece of smooth marble to use for rolling your doughs and making pastry. The following are the pastry doughs we recommend mastering.

Pâte à choux is a light and airy pastry dough that is the base for profiteroles, éclairs, and savory gougères. Our savory Gougères recipe (page 228) was mastered at La Varenne and is adapted from Anne Willan's classic recipe.

Pâte sablée is a sweet, crumbly dough that tastes like a buttery shortbread cookie, and we use it as a base for our Summer Berry Tart (page 168) and other fresh fruit tarts. Our pâte sablée contains confectioners' sugar instead of granulated, softened butter instead of cold, and a bit of cream to create an especially rich, tender crust.

A *galette* is a simple, free-form tart that can be sweet or savory, depending on the filling. Our sweet **galette dough** (page 378) is very straightforward and forgiving, and incorporates almond flour, which gives the dough a pleasant, nutty flavor, making it an ideal pairing for seasonal fruit fillings.

Pâte sucrée is a classic French pastry dough that we use all the time at The Cook's Atelier for dessert tarts and tartlets. We love it because it's light, buttery, and ever-so-slightly sweet. It's always better to make the dough the day before and let it rest in the refrigerator, as it will be easier to roll out. We often vary it by adding lemon or orange zest or a handful of ground nuts.

Pâte brisée is a classic French savory tart dough. When making pâte brisée, it is very important not to overwork the dough, or it will make your pastry tough. We use only butter for the fat, plus a tiny bit of white vinegar, which makes for a tender, flaky dough.

To make a tart shell from pâte sablée, pâte sucrée, or pâte brisée: Remove the dough from the refrigerator 10 to 15 minutes before rolling to ensure it is slightly soft and ready to roll.

Each disk of dough will make 1 (9-inch/23-cm) tart or 8 (4-inch/10-cm) tartlets. For one large tart, place the dough on a lightly floured surface. Lightly flour a rolling pin. Begin rolling the dough, turning the dough as you roll to make an even circle. Be sure to check that you have enough flour under the dough so it doesn't stick. Roll the dough into a ¼-inch- (6-mm-) thick, 10- to 11-inch (25- to 28-cm) diameter round.

If making tartlets, use a bench scraper to divide each disk of dough into 8 triangular pieces. Using your hands, gently shape each triangular piece into a small ball, then flatten the balls into small disks and roll them into ⅛-inch- (3-mm-) thick, 5- to 6-inch (12- to 15-cm) diameter rounds.

Once the dough is slightly larger than your tart pan (or tartlet pans), gently roll it around the rolling pin, brushing off any excess flour

with a pastry brush as you go. Unroll it over the tart pan (or tartlet pans), being careful not to stretch it as you ease it into the bottom and up the sides. Begin trimming the edges by pushing your thumb against the side edges of the pan. Use your other thumb to peel away the extra dough at the edge. Be careful to make the dough the same thickness all the way around to create a uniform edge.

Freeze for 15 to 20 minutes before baking. If you want to freeze the tart shell for longer, wrap it in a double layer of plastic wrap and freeze for up to 2 months. The frozen tart shell can be baked straight from the freezer without thawing.

Pâte feuilletée is a flaky French pastry dough that has hundreds of layers of paper-thin dough sandwiched between thin layers of butter that puff up beautifully in a hot oven. Pâte feuilletée anchors a variety of desserts, such as napoleons and tarte tatins, and savory canapés like *vol-au-vents*. Making puff pastry can be a bit intimidating, even for the experienced cook. As cooks, when we strive to continue to expand our own culinary knowledge, we look to classic French chefs for guidance and inspiration. We adapted Jacques Pepin's pâte feuilletée recipe from *La Technique*, adding distilled white vinegar as we do in our Pâte Brisée (page 379). The process is time-consuming, but once you've mastered the technique, making puff pastry is really enjoyable. Best of all, it freezes well, so you can make a large batch and have some on hand for a future use.

Pâte à Choux

MAKES ABOUT 24 ÉCLAIRS OR PROFITEROLES

4 large eggs
⅓ cup (75 ml) whole milk
6 tablespoons (¾ stick/85 g) unsalted butter
2 teaspoons sugar
½ teaspoon fleur de sel
⅔ cup (80 g) unbleached all-purpose flour
1 recipe Crème Pâtissière (page 385)
1 recipe Chocolate Ganache (optional; page 127)

Make the pâte à choux: Preheat the oven to 350°F (175°C).

In a small bowl, whisk one of the eggs and set aside. Crack the remaining three eggs into a separate bowl or measuring cup with a spout. Do not mix; set aside.

In a small heavy-bottomed saucepan, combine ⅓ cup (75 ml) water, milk, butter, sugar, and salt over medium heat.

Cook until the butter has melted, then bring the mixture to a full boil. Immediately add the flour all at once and beat vigorously with a wooden spoon. Stir until the mixture forms a smooth ball that pulls away from the sides of the pan and a film forms on the bottom of the pan, at least 2 minutes. Reduce the heat to low and beat the mixture to remove any excess moisture and dry out the dough, at least 1 minute.

Remove the pan from the heat and let it cool slightly. Add the remaining three eggs, one at a time, beating thoroughly with a wooden spoon after each addition. The dough should be shiny and smooth. To test the consistency, use a wooden spoon to scoop out as much of the dough as possible. Hold the wooden spoon over the pot and turn it on its side. If the dough is ready, it will fall from the spoon in a thick plop or dollop. If the dough is too thick, it will just stick to the side of the spoon. If the dough is too thick, add a small amount of the reserved beaten egg to achieve the right consistency. Be careful not to add too much of the beaten egg, or the dough will become too thin. If the dough falls from the spoon like a sheet, it's too thin and you'll need to start over. When in doubt, it's better to have a slightly dry dough to ensure the éclairs or profiteroles puff properly when baking.

Transfer the choux paste to a pastry bag fitted with a large round tip. Pipe a very small amount of dough in the corners of a baking sheet to hold down the paper, then line the baking sheet with parchment paper.

If making profiteroles, pipe roughly 1½-inch (4-cm) rounds onto the parchment-lined baking sheet, allowing enough room for them to double in size. **If making éclairs**, pipe roughly 2½-inch (6-cm) lines onto the parchment-lined baking sheet, allowing enough room for them to double in size.

Use your fingertips to gently brush the tops of the éclairs or profiteroles with a small amount of the reserved beaten egg, being careful not to smash them or let any excess egg fall on the parchment.

Bake until the éclairs or profiteroles are puffed, nicely golden, and feel light for their size, 20 to 22 minutes. Let cool slightly. Once cooled, use a pastry bag fitted with a medium round tip to fill them with crème pâtissière, then dip the tops in chocolate ganache, if desired. Serve immediately. Éclairs and profiteroles are best eaten the day they are made.

Pâte Sablée

MAKES ENOUGH FOR 2 (9-INCH/23-CM) TARTS OR 16 (4-INCH/10-CM) TARTLETS

3½ cups (440 g) unbleached all-purpose flour, plus extra for kneading

1 cup (125 g) sifted confectioners' sugar

1 teaspoon fleur de sel

2 cups (4 sticks/450 g) unsalted butter, cut into small pieces and softened slightly

3 large egg yolks

3 tablespoons heavy cream

In a large bowl, whisk together the flour, sugar, and salt. Add the butter. Using your hands, gently toss to coat the butter in the flour mixture. Scoop the mixture in your hands and gently press the flour mixture and butter between your fingertips until the mixture looks grainy, with some small pieces of butter still visible. Work quickly to ensure the butter stays cold.

In a small bowl, lightly beat the egg yolks and cream. Drizzle over the dough and use a fork to gently toss until incorporated. Continue working the dough, gently squeezing it between your fingertips until it comes together and there is no dry flour visible. Be careful not to overwork the dough. It's ready as soon as you can squish the dough in one hand and it stays together.

On a lightly floured and cool work surface, preferably marble, knead the dough just until it is completely smooth.

Divide the dough in half and shape each half into a disk. Wrap them in plastic wrap and refrigerate for at least 1 hour, or preferably overnight. Pâte sablée can be wrapped in a double layer of plastic wrap and refrigerated for up to 2 days or frozen for up to 2 months.

Galette Dough

MAKES ENOUGH FOR 2 (9-INCH/23-CM)
GALETTES OR 16 (4-INCH/10-CM)
GALETTES

2½ cups (315 g) unbleached all-purpose flour

½ cup (60 g) almond flour

2 tablespoons sugar

1 teaspoon fleur de sel

1 cup (2 sticks/225 g) cold unsalted butter, cut
into small pieces

½ cup (120 ml) ice water, strained

¼ cup (60 ml) crème fraîche

In a large bowl, whisk together the all-purpose flour, almond flour, sugar, and salt. Add the butter. Using your hands, gently toss to coat the butter in the flour mixture. Scoop the mixture in your hands and gently press the flour and butter between your fingertips until the mixture looks grainy, with some small pieces of butter still visible. Work quickly to ensure the butter stays cold.

In a small bowl, whisk together the cold water and crème fraîche. Drizzle over the dough and use a fork to gently toss until incorporated. Continue working the dough, gently squeezing it between your fingertips until it comes together and there is no dry flour visible. Be careful not to overwork the dough. It's ready as soon as you can squish the dough in one hand and it stays together.

Divide the dough in half and shape each half into a disk. Wrap them in plastic wrap and refrigerate for at least 1 hour, or preferably overnight. The galette dough can be wrapped in a double layer of plastic wrap and refrigerated for up to 2 days or frozen for up to 2 months.

Pâte Sucrée

MAKES ENOUGH FOR 2 (9-INCH/23-CM)
TARTS OR 16 (4-INCH/10-CM) TARTLETS

3 cups (375 g) unbleached all-purpose flour

½ cup (100 g) sugar

½ teaspoon fleur de sel

1 cup (2 sticks/225 g) cold unsalted butter, cut
into small pieces

2 large egg yolks

⅓ cup (80 ml) heavy cream

In a large bowl, whisk together the flour, sugar, and salt. Add the butter. Using your hands, gently toss to coat the butter in the flour mixture. Scoop the mixture in your hands and gently press the flour mixture and butter between your fingertips until the mixture looks grainy, with some small pieces of butter still visible. Work quickly to ensure the butter stays cold.

In a small bowl, lightly beat the egg yolks and cream. Drizzle over the dough and use a fork to gently toss until incorporated. Continue working the dough, gently squeezing it between your fingertips until it comes together and there is no dry flour visible. Be careful not to overwork the dough. It's ready as soon as you can squish the dough in one hand and it stays together.

Divide the dough in half and shape each half into a disk. Wrap them in plastic wrap and refrigerate for at least 1 hour, or preferably overnight. Pâte sucrée can be wrapped in a double layer of plastic wrap and refrigerated for up to 2 days or frozen for up to 2 months.

Variations: For a nut dough: Replace ½ cup (65 g) of the flour with ½ cup (55 g) finely chopped toasted skinned hazelnuts or almonds.

For a citrus dough: Add 2 to 3 teaspoons finely grated lemon or orange zest to the flour, sugar, and salt mixture.

Pâte Brisée

MAKES ENOUGH FOR 2 (9-INCH/23-CM)
TARTS OR 16 (4-INCH/10-CM) TARTLETS

3 cups (375 g) unbleached all-purpose flour

1 teaspoon fleur de sel

1½ cups (3 sticks/340 g) cold unsalted butter,
cut into small pieces

¼ cup (60 ml) ice water, strained

1 teaspoon distilled white vinegar

In a large bowl, whisk together the flour
and salt. Add the butter. Using your hands,
gently toss to coat the butter in the flour
mixture. Scoop the mixture in your hands
and gently press the flour and butter
between your fingertips until the mixture
looks grainy, with some small pieces of
butter still visible. Work quickly to ensure
the butter stays cold.

In a small bowl, whisk together the
cold water and vinegar. Drizzle over the
dough and use a fork to gently toss until
incorporated. Continue working the
dough, gently squeezing it between your
fingertips until it comes together and there
is no dry flour visible. Be careful not to
overwork the dough. It's ready as soon as
you can squish the dough in one hand and
it stays together.

Divide the dough in half and shape
each half into a disk. Wrap them in plastic
wrap and refrigerate for at least 1 hour,
or preferably overnight. Pâte brisée can be
wrapped in a double layer of plastic wrap
and refrigerated for up to 2 days or frozen
for up to 2 months.

Pâte Feuilletée

MAKES ABOUT 5 POUNDS (2.3 KG)
PUFF PASTRY

2 pounds (8 sticks/910 g) very cold unsalted
butter

2 pounds (910 g) unbleached all-purpose flour,
plus more for rolling

2 cups (480 ml) ice water, strained

1 tablespoon distilled white vinegar

2 teaspoons fleur de sel

Place the butter on a cool work surface,
preferably marble. Sprinkle it with ½ cup
(65 g) of the flour. Using a bench scraper,
chop the cold butter into large pieces.
Using your hands, mix the butter with the
flour until it comes together and is smooth.
Using your rolling pin, beat the butter and
flour mixture into an even ½-inch (12-mm)
thickness and use both hands to form it
into a square measuring about 7 inches
(17 cm) on each side. Wrap the butter in
plastic wrap and refrigerate while you
prepare the *détrempe* (dough).

Place the remaining flour on the
cool work surface. Make a well in the
center. Whisk together the ice water and
vinegar and gradually add them to the
center of the well. Sprinkle with the salt.
Using your hand and a bench scraper,
gradually incorporate the flour into the
water mixture to form a rough dough. Be
careful not to overwork the dough. Shape
the dough into a ball, then use the bench
scraper to make an X on top. Wrap the
dough in plastic wrap and refrigerate for
30 minutes.

Remove the butter and dough from the
refrigerator and let them rest until they're
manageable, about 10 minutes. When
making pâte feuilletée, it's important
that the butter and dough are the same
temperature when you combine them into
a single package. The butter should be

pliable and easy to work with—if it's too cold, it won't spread evenly and will be difficult to roll.

Lightly flour the cool work surface and use a lightly floured rolling pin to roll the dough from the center outward into a roughly ½-inch- (12-mm-) thick square measuring about 16 inches (40.5 cm) on each side. Using the rolling pin, beat the butter just until pliable, then place the butter block in the center of the rolled-out dough. Wrap the dough over and around the butter, overlapping it and pinching the seams together to completely seal the butter inside.

Roll the butter and dough package into a roughly ¾-inch- (2-cm-) thick rectangle measuring about 10 by 17½ inches (25 by 44.5 cm). If the butter and dough still feel cold and manageable, you can continue with the first turn. Otherwise, wrap them in plastic wrap and refrigerate for 30 minutes to allow them to come to the same temperature.

Remove the dough from the refrigerator and place it on the lightly floured cool work surface. Roll the dough from the center outward in both directions, not in a back-and-forth motion, creating a roughly ½-inch- (12-mm-) thick rectangle measuring about 11 by 22 inches (28 by 56 cm). Be careful not to roll too forcefully, or the butter may come through the dough. Using a pastry brush, dust off any excess flour. The dough should now be a smooth rectangle with the butter fully encased in the dough, so that there is no butter showing through.

Beginning with the short end of the dough nearest you, fold the bottom one-third of the rectangle up and away from you, placing it over the center of the rectangle. Use a pastry brush to dust off

any excess flour. Fold the top one-third of the rectangle up and toward you, placing it over the fold previously made and making sure the hinge of this fold meets the edge of the first fold. The complete fold should resemble the way you fold a business letter. This is one "turn."

Rotate the dough so the short side is near you. Roll the dough again, creating a roughly ½-inch- (12-mm-) thick rectangle measuring about 11 by 22 inches (28 by 56 cm). Repeat the folding process described above. That makes two turns. Use a pastry brush to dust off any excess flour. Use your fingers to make two indentations in the dough to mark the number of turns made. Wrap the dough in plastic wrap and refrigerate for 1 hour to let the dough chill and rest.

Each time you roll the dough into a rectangle and fold it like a business letter, that counts as one turn. You can do this two times, or two turns, before it's necessary to return the dough to the refrigerator to chill and rest for 1 hour. If the dough seems a little too cold to begin the process again, leave it on the cool work surface to soften for a few minutes until you're able to roll it easily.

Classic pâte feuilletée requires a total of six full turns. If you're going to use the dough right away, continue the rolling and folding process two more times (for a total of six turns), making indentations with your fingertips to remind you if you've done two, four, or six complete turns and using a pastry brush to dust off any excess flour. Once you complete the turns, wrap the dough in plastic wrap and refrigerate for at least 30 minutes before using. You want the dough to be cool enough to hold its shape but soft enough that you can roll it easily. If you need just a small piece of pâte feuilletée, use a very sharp, thin-bladed knife to cut off a piece; refrigerate or freeze the rest.

If you want to freeze the dough for a few days or up to a few weeks, cut the folded rectangle-shaped dough (after six complete turns) in half using a very sharp thin-bladed knife. Roll each half into a sheet that will fit in your freezer, trimming as necessary to make a nice, clean edge. Stack the sheets of puff pastry with a layer of parchment paper in between and wrap them in a double layer of plastic wrap. Freeze until ready to use, up to 2 months. This extra step allows you to pull one sheet, or half a recipe of puff pastry, from the freezer to use immediately, such as for a tarte tatin.

It's also possible to roll the dough into various shapes and freeze—be sure to wrap it in a double layer of plastic wrap.

In addition to mastering the art of pastry doughs, there are several classic French sweet fillings and sauces that should be a part of every home cook's dessert repertoire. We make all our dessert creams and sauces by hand, whisking the mixtures until thickened rather than using a stand mixer or food processor. It's important to understand the technique behind each recipe, and to really get a feel for the look and consistency of the cream or sauce by first making it by hand. Always use a fine-mesh strainer when making *crème pâtissière* (pastry cream) and *crème anglaise* (custard sauce), as they must be strained after cooking to remove any lumps.

Once again, as with all of our recipes, it's important to use best-quality ingredients, as this will impact the flavor and consistency of the final dish. For pastry creams and sauces, we always use organic whole milk and cream, farm eggs, organic flour and sugar, good-quality vanilla beans, and European-style butter. For *crème d'amande* (almond cream), we use almond flour, made from very finely ground almonds.

Crème pâtissière is a classic, vanilla-infused custard used in a variety of French desserts, such as fresh fruit tarts and an assortment of French pastry like éclairs, profiteroles, and other tarts and cakes. It is commonly known as pastry cream. When making fresh fruit tarts, we prefer a silkier pastry cream and often add a dollop or spoonful of whipped cream to it as in our Summer Berry Tart (page 168) to lighten it. When using pastry cream for other desserts such as éclairs or profiteroles (page 376), the extra dollop of cream is not needed.

Crème anglaise, or English cream, is a creamy, vanilla-scented, pourable custard sauce that is cooked on the stovetop until thick, and then chilled for several hours. It is very similar to crème pâtissière in flavor, just not as thick. It can be served warm or cold, and is a lovely accompaniment to tarts or dessert soufflés.

Strain the mixture through a fine-mesh strainer before serving or chilling, so it's extra smooth.

Crème d'amande is a simple almond cream filling used in fruit tarts and pastries, including almond croissants and *galette des rois*. We use it as a filling in our summertime Nectarine and Blueberry Tart (page 183) and other fresh fruit tarts. This simple almond cream contains almond flour—very finely ground almonds that have the consistency of flour—and takes just minutes to make. Unlike crème pâtissière and crème anglaise, crème d'amande is not cooked on the stovetop. Instead it is whisked together and chilled, then baked in the tart shell (or pastry) before serving. Keep in mind that it must chill for several hours to firm up before it is baked.

Crème Pâtissière

MAKES ABOUT 1¼ CUPS (300 ML)

2 cups (480 ml) whole milk
½ cup (100 g) sugar
1 vanilla bean pod, seeds removed (see page 64)
5 large egg yolks
3 tablespoons unbleached all-purpose flour
1 tablespoon unsalted butter

In a medium saucepan, heat the milk, all but 1 tablespoon of the sugar, and the vanilla seeds and pod over medium heat until the sugar has dissolved and the milk is just about to boil.

In a medium bowl, combine the egg yolks and the remaining 1 tablespoon sugar and whisk until thick and pale yellow. Sift the flour over the lightened egg yolks and whisk to combine.

Very slowly add the warm milk mixture to the egg mixture, whisking continuously. Pour the mixture back into the saucepan over medium heat. Cook, whisking continuously, until the mixture thickens and just comes to a boil, about 2 minutes. Push the pastry cream through a fine-mesh strainer into a large bowl; discard the vanilla bean. Whisk in the butter. Press plastic wrap directly against the surface of the pastry cream to prevent a skin from forming. Let it cool slightly, then refrigerate until chilled and set, about 2 hours. Pastry cream can be used once chilled or can be stored in the refrigerator for up to 3 days.

Crème Anglaise

MAKES 2½ CUPS (600 ML)

1 cup (240 ml) whole milk
1 cup (240 ml) heavy cream
1 vanilla bean pod, seeds removed (see page 64)
½ cup (100 g) sugar
4 large egg yolks

Fill a bowl large enough to accommodate a 1-quart (960-ml) container with ice and water.

In a small saucepan, combine the milk, cream, and vanilla seeds and pod. Place over medium heat and bring to just under a boil.

In a large bowl, whisk together the sugar and egg yolks until thick and pale yellow. Very slowly add the warm milk mixture to the egg mixture, whisking continuously. Pour the mixture back into

the saucepan over low heat. Cook, stirring continuously with a wooden spoon, just until the mixture thickens and coats the back of the spoon—if you draw a finger across the back of the spoon, it should leave a mark in the sauce—3 to 5 minutes. Pour the crème anglaise through a fine-mesh strainer into a 1-quart (960-ml) container; discard the vanilla bean. For a chilled dessert sauce, place the container inside the bowl of ice water and, stirring occasionally, allow it to completely chill. Serve immediately or store in the refrigerator for up to 3 days.

Crème d'Amande

MAKES ABOUT 1 CUP (240 ML)

⅔ cup (75 g) almond flour
6 tablespoons (75 g) sugar
1 tablespoon unbleached all-purpose flour
6 tablespoons (¾ stick/85 g) unsalted butter, at room temperature
1 large egg

In a medium bowl, whisk together the almond flour, sugar, and all-purpose flour. Add the butter and egg and beat until smooth and fully combined. Cover and refrigerate until firm, about 3 hours, before using. Almond cream can be stored in the refrigerator for up to 3 days.

Before using the cream, let it sit at room temperature to soften slightly to a spreadable consistency.

Tempering Chocolate and Chocolate Ganache

When working with chocolate, there are two important things to keep in mind. One, use the best-quality chocolate you can find. This has everything to do with the result of the finished product. And two, take care not to overheat it, or the texture will become grainy. This is why we don't recommend heating chocolate directly in a saucepan—the chocolate can easily scorch and you'll have to start all over again.

Tempering is the process of slowly heating and cooling chocolate, while stirring continuously, to give it a shiny appearance and smooth texture. This technique is used for unbaked chocolate confections, such as chocolate candies, chocolate bars, and mendiants (page 287), which are chocolate discs topped with dried fruit or nuts. Chocolate that has not been tempered will look dull and streaky. Tempering not only creates more visually appealing chocolate, but it also allows you to store it for an extended period of time.

To temper chocolate, fill a medium saucepan with an inch or two of water. Place on the stove and bring it to a boil. Place the chocolate in a large heatproof bowl—several inches larger than the pot so the steam does not absorb into the chocolate—over the simmering water, making sure that the bottom of the bowl is not touching the water. Reduce the heat to a simmer and slowly melt the chocolate, stirring continuously with a spatula. Check the temperature with a candy thermometer: Dark chocolate should reach a temperature of 88° to 90°F (31° to 32°C). Once it reaches the proper temperature (i.e. "in temper"), remove it from the heat. Tempered chocolate solidifies quickly, so it is important to keep stirring as you go. The chocolate will continue to cool as you work, so continue to check the temperature. If you notice that the chocolate is no longer glossy, and is beginning to set on the sides—or simply becoming too thick to stir—this means that the chocolate is "out of temper" and you will need to reheat it. If so, simply set the bowl of chocolate back over the pot of hot water, stirring continuously for several seconds, until it reaches the proper temperature again. Then, remove from the heat, and continue working.

Alternatively, if you have a marble work surface in your kitchen (or a marble slab for pastry), simply pour the melted chocolate directly on the cool marble surface as we do at The Cook's Atelier and use a long-handled spatula to work the chocolate back and forth, consistently moving it until it reaches the desired consistency and temperature.

When making a **ganache**, a decadent glaze, frosting, or filling for cakes, you only need two ingredients: dark chocolate and heavy cream. The ratio is often half chocolate and half cream, but it can vary depending on whether you are making a glaze, truffles, or filling. Cut the chocolate into very small pieces—this will help it melt more easily—and place in a large bowl. Heat the heavy cream in a small heavy-bottomed saucepan until steaming—just under a boil. Remove from the heat and pour the warm cream over the chocolate. Use a spatula to gently stir the chocolate into the cream until smooth. We always use a spatula instead of a whisk, as a whisk will add too much air to the mixture.

Let the ganache sit at room temperature until it reaches the desired consistency. If you're pouring the ganache over a cake, it should be more of a liquid, but if it's a frosting, it will need to rest longer in order to thicken.

Summertime is a season of abundance in Burgundy. During these warm months, our garden and the Beaune market are absolutely overflowing with fruits and vegetables at their peak. After eating our fill of just-picked berries and rosy apricots, vine-ripened tomatoes, crisp cucumbers, green beans, and artichokes, we set to work preserving summer's bounty through pickling, jam-making, and canning. All you need for preserving are some sterile canning jars, a funnel, and a large pot.

Pickling is the process of preserving food by placing it in a brine or vinegar solution. The brining process not only extends the lifetime of the food, but it completely changes its flavor and texture, giving it a pleasant crunchiness and bright splash of acidity. We make pickles in the summertime with tiny cucumbers from our garden. They are perfect to serve with charcuterie, as the tartness of the pickle pairs well with fatty meats. You can pickle most any vegetable and many fruits as well—green beans, beets, pearl onions, artichokes, peaches, cherries, and strawberries are all delicious.

To pickle vegetables, you'll need sterilized canning jars, a brine, and whatever seasonings you intend to use. We use coriander seeds, white and black peppercorns, and spicy little dried red peppers. We also like to place lemon slices on top as a pretty way to hold the mixture down.

We enjoy making **confiture** from the beautiful fruits at the market and giving it as gifts to friends and guests. We especially look forward to making jam from the tiny and flavorful Gariguette strawberries that flood the market every spring, and the rosy Bergeron apricots that arrive in early summer—it's a great way to preserve the flavor of the season to enjoy later in the year.

When making jam, there are two important principles to keep in mind: One, use really fresh—rather than bruised or old—fruit, and two, cook it over high heat, very quickly. These two things will ensure that the fresh fruit flavor really shines through. We don't like our jam overly sweet, so we use less sugar than typical French jam. This means it doesn't keep as long, so we just make it in smaller, more frequent batches.

If you plan on making jam often, it's definitely worth investing in a big, copper confiture pot. We bought our first one at a market in Auxerre more than ten years ago, and we use it every season. The copper conducts heat so well that you can cook the fruit quickly, so the flavor and color stays nice and bright. A jam pot is wider than it is tall—this way the fruit can spread out evenly to cook more quickly. Before using your pot, make sure to scrub the inside with coarse salt and half a lemon, and then rinse and dry it well.

It's important to understand that when making jam, every batch is different, depending on the fruit used, the moisture in that batch of fruit, and the amount of jam you are processing.

To sterilize jars: Wash and dry the jars thoroughly. Place the jars and jar lids in a large stockpot filled with water. Bring it to a boil and boil for 5 minutes. Keep the jars and jar lids in the hot water until ready to use. If using Weck or Le Parfait jars, place the rubber rings from the jars in a separate small saucepan filled with water. Bring it to just under a boil and turn off the heat. Leave the rings in the hot water until ready to use.

To process filled sterilized jars: Carefully lift the filled and sealed jars and place them back in the original pot of hot water, making sure there is at least a couple of inches of water covering the jars. Depending on the number of jars, you may need to tuck kitchen towels in and around them to prevent them from rattling. Bring them to a boil and boil for 10 minutes, or as directed in the recipe.

Carefully remove the hot jars from the stockpot and place them on a clean, dry kitchen towel. Let them sit overnight at room temperature. It's best not to move the jars at this point, to ensure a proper seal.

The next morning, check the seals. Ball jars are sealed when the little "button" on the top is indented. If using Le Parfait jars, check the seal by opening the clamp. If sealed properly, the glass lid will not lift up and the tip on the rubber ring gasket will be pointing down. If using Weck jars, you should be able to remove the stainless-steel canning clamps and the lid should remain tightly in place when lightly trying to lift it. The pull tab of the rubber ring should also face down on properly sealed jars. Once the jars are sealed and cooled, the clamps should be removed. If one jar is not sealed properly, refrigerate that one and enjoy it first, within the time specified in the recipe.

Pickled Cucumbers

MAKES 2 (1-QUART/960-ML) JARS

2½ pounds (1.2 kg) small cucumbers

4 tablespoons (55 g) coarse sea salt

1 cup (240 ml) white wine vinegar

1 teaspoon whole coriander seeds

1 teaspoon mixed whole black and white peppercorns

6 small fresh or dried spicy red peppers

1 lemon, cut into 4 slices

Sterilize two 1-quart (960-ml) jars as directed on page 389.

Place the cucumbers in a large colander, sprinkle with 1 tablespoon of the salt, and set them in the sink (or over a large bowl) for about 30 minutes to remove excess moisture.

In a large saucepan, combine 4 cups (960 ml) water with the vinegar and the remaining 3 tablespoons of salt and bring to a boil to make the brine.

Using a damp cloth, rub the cucumbers to remove any dirt and salt. Cut the cucumbers in half or quarters, depending on their size, then place them in the sterilized jars—they should fit quite tightly. Divide the coriander, peppercorns, and red peppers between the jars, then add enough brine to cover the cucumbers and top each jar with two overlapping lemon slices—there may be leftover brine. Seal and date the jars, let them cool to room temperature, then refrigerate them overnight. The pickles can be enjoyed immediately and will keep in the refrigerator for up to 2 weeks.

Gariguette Strawberry Confiture

MAKES 3 TO 4 CUPS (720 TO 960 ML)

2 pounds (910 g) Gariguette strawberries, or other small ripe organic strawberries, hulled and halved

3 cups (600 g) sugar

3 tablespoons fresh lemon juice

Seeds of 1 vanilla bean (optional; see page 64)

Sterilize 3 or 4 half-pint (240-ml) jars as directed on page 389.

In a large confiture pot, combine the strawberries, sugar, lemon juice, and vanilla seeds (if using). Place over high heat and cook, stirring continuously with a wooden spoon as the sugar dissolves and the fruit begins to break down. As soon as the mixture comes to a boil, foam will begin to appear on the surface. Using a large stainless-steel spoon, remove and discard the foam. Continue this process until the foam subsides. It is important to remove the foam, as it ensures a clear and transparent jam. As you're stirring, periodically pick up the wooden spoon, hold it horizontally, and watch the liquid drip off—the jam is almost ready when two drips come together to form a thick syrup. If you have a candy thermometer, the jam will set at 221°F (105°C). The jam should be bright in color; some of the halved berries will keep their shape. It's important not to overcook the jam, as it will continue to thicken once it's jarred and sealed.

Remove the sterilized jars from the hot water and place them on a clean, dry kitchen towel. Reserve the pot of hot water. If using Weck or Le Parfait jars, attach the rings to the lids of the jars. Sterilize a ladle and jam funnel by submerging them in the hot water for a few seconds. Carefully ladle the hot jam into the warm sterilized jars and fill them up to ¼ inch (6 mm) below the rim. Wipe the lip of the jars with a clean, damp kitchen towel to ensure a proper seal. Seal and date the jars and let them cool overnight.

For short-term storage, refrigerate and use within 1 week.

For longer storage, process the filled jam jars immediately for 10 minutes, as directed on page 389. If one jar did not seal properly, refrigerate that jar and enjoy it first, within 1 week.

Apricot Confiture

MAKES 3 TO 4 CUPS (720 TO 960 ML)

2¼ pounds (1 kg) Bergeron apricots, or other small ripe organic apricots, halved and pitted

3 cups (600 grams) vanilla sugar (see page 64)

3 tablespoons fresh lemon juice

Sterilize 3 or 4 half-pint (240-ml) jars as directed on page 389.

In a large glass bowl, combine the apricot halves, vanilla sugar, and lemon juice and gently toss to combine. Cover with plastic wrap and refrigerate for 6 to 8 hours to macerate the apricots.

Place the apricots, along with the sugar mixture and any juices from the bowl, in a large confiture pot and bring them to a simmer over medium-high heat, skimming off any foam, as necessary. Transfer the mixture to a large bowl and let it cool. Cover and refrigerate overnight.

The next day, use your fingers to slip the skins off the apricots. Return the

apricots, along with the sugar mixture and any juices from the bowl, to a large clean confiture pot. Place it over high heat, and cook, stirring continuously with a wooden spoon as the sugar dissolves and the fruit begins to break down. As soon as the mixture comes to a boil, foam will begin to appear on the surface. Using a large stainless-steel spoon, remove and discard the foam. Continue this process until the foam subsides. It is important to remove the foam as it ensures a clear and transparent jam. As you're stirring, periodically pick up the wooden spoon, hold it horizontally, and watch the liquid drip off—the jam is almost ready when two drips come together to form a thick syrup. If you have a candy thermometer, the jam will set at 221°F (105°C). The jam should be bright in color; some of the apricot halves will keep their shape. It's important not to overcook the jam as it will continue to thicken once it's put in the jars and sealed.

Remove the sterilized jars from the hot water and place them on a clean, dry kitchen towel. Reserve the pot of hot water. If using Weck or Le Parfait jars, attach the rings to the lids of the jars. Sterilize a ladle and jam funnel by submerging them in the hot water for a few seconds. Carefully ladle the hot jam into the warm sterilized jars and fill them up to ¼ inch (6 mm) below the rim. Wipe the lip of the jars with a clean, damp kitchen towel to ensure a proper seal. Seal and date the jars and let them cool overnight.

For short-term storage, refrigerate and use within 1 week.

For longer storage, process the filled jam jars immediately for 10 minutes, as directed on page 389. If one jar did not seal properly, refrigerate that jar and enjoy it first, within 1 week.

RESOURCES

As you prepare the recipes in this book, we hope that you will source your ingredients as locally as possible. Your local farmers' markets, butchers, cheese makers, bakers, and wine merchants are the best resources for fresh, high-quality products. We believe it is important to build relationships with your local food and wine purveyors; not only will you enjoy better-tasting food, but you'll find that they possess a wealth of culinary knowledge.

When selecting seeds for your own kitchen potager or herb garden, we recommend that you seek out seed companies that specialize in heirloom varieties and are free of GMOs (seedsavers.org, rareseeds.com, and reneesgarden.com)

If you're not able to find certain specialty ingredients, like wild game, meats, or French cheese and charcuterie locally, we recommend ordering online from specialty food shops, such as Dean and Deluca (deananddeluca.com), Murray's Cheese (murrayscheese.com), D'Artagnan (dartagnan.com), Chef Shop (chefshop.com), Hudson Valley Foie Gras (hudsonvalleyfoiegras.com), and Heritage Foods USA (heritagefoodsusa.com).

For meticulously sourced French cook's tools, pantry provisions, copper, vintage finds, and wine, we hope that you will visit us at The Cook's Atelier (thecooksatelier.com).

INDEX

ACKNOWLEDGMENTS

This book stems from the heart and represents the power behind following a dream. It is the culmination of the last ten years we've spent creating The Cook's Atelier. We are grateful and humbled to have been given the opportunity to share our story with others.

We would like to extend our sincere heartfelt thanks to the many people who have helped us along the way, making this book a reality.

Special thanks to our agent and friend, Judy Linden, who believed in our book project from the very beginning and who remained extremely patient with us as we found our voice.

To the team at Abrams for your enthusiasm about this book, and to Deb Wood, our designer, for letting us be part of the design process. A special thanks in particular, to our editor, Laura Dozier, for your unwavering support and guidance, for your ability to see our vision for this book, and for making it all possible.

To Anson Smart, our friend and talented photographer, for capturing the magic in such beautiful detail and for being so passionate about this project. Thank you for always making time in your busy schedule and for visiting us each season so we can share the true beauty of Burgundy with others.

To Anna Watson Carl, for always being such a good friend and for helping us get our words on paper. We've known you since the early days, when we were first dreaming up the concept for The Cook's Atelier. Thank you for helping us tell our story.

To Lauren Salkeld, our recipe tester, for your extraordinary precision and attention to detail in testing each and every recipe. Thank you for your willingness to try the *pâté en croûte* and for trekking all over Brooklyn to find the oxtail.

To Julie Devarenne, for your endless creativity and willingness to wear many hats throughout the project. We couldn't have done it without you.

To our artisan food producers, thank you for preserving the art of small farming and the food culture of France. You are all truly part of the spirit behind The Cook's Atelier, merci.

To Chrissy Lufkin and our "band of boys," Benjamin Michaud, Louis Jonard, Marius Remoissenet, and Alan Guillemin—thank you all for your help with our little ones, Luc and Manon, and for being the "big sister" and "big brothers." Thank you for helping to keep them entertained throughout the project and ultimately becoming part of the family.

To petit Luc and Manon, for your sweet dispositions (most of the time) and patience throughout the whirlwind.

Thank you to Laurent, for your sense of humor and your ability to see the bigger picture, for your patience, and the love that you bring to the family.

And to Bill, for encouraging us to dream even bigger.

Thank you to our guests, past, present, and future, for making The Cook's Atelier possible, and for visiting us from all over the world to share in a love of food and wine with others around our table.

Editor: Laura Dozier
Designer: Deb Wood with Liam Flanagan
Production Manager: Denise LaCongo

Library of Congress Control Number: 2017945113

ISBN: 978-1-4197-2895-2
eISBN: 978-1-68335-223-5

Printed and bound in China
10 9 8 7 6 5 4 3 2 1

ABRAMS The Art of Books
195 Broadway, New York, NY 10007
abramsbooks.com